SCOBBIE

D1809611

Language Change and Sociolinguistics

Palgrave Macmillan Studies in Language Variation

The study of language variation in social context, and the study of specific language communities in detail, are central to the linguistic enterprise. In this series we look for impressive first-hand fieldwork from speech communities of various kinds, analysed within a range of frameworks, quantitative and qualitative. All work reported in the series will raise important arguments about methodologies for researching language in social context, with analysis that challenges or extends current theory building.

Titles include:

JonathanMarshall
LANGUAGE CHANGE AND SOCIOLINGUISTICS
Rethinking Social Networks

Daniel Scherier
ISOLATION AND LANGUAGE CHANGE
Contemporary and Sociohistorical Evidence from Tristan da Cunha English

Language Change and Sociolinguistics

Rethinking Social Networks

Jonathan Marshall
The University of Edinburgh

First published 2004 by
PALGRAVE MACMILLAN
Houndmills, Basingstoke, Hampshire RG21 6XS and
175 Fifth Avenue, New York, N.Y. 10010
Companies and representatives throughout the world

PALGRAVE MACMILLAN is the global academic imprint of the Palgrave
Macmillan division of St. Martin's Press, LLC and of Palgrave Macmillan Ltd.
Macmillan® is a registered trademark in the United States, United Kingdom
and other countries. Palgrave is a registered trademark in the European
Union and other countries.

ISBN 1–4039–1487–7

This book is printed on paper suitable for recycling and made from fully
managed and sustained forest sources.

A catalogue record for this book is available from the British Library.

Library of Congress Cataloging-in-Publication Data

Marshall, Jonathan, 1963–
   Language change and sociolinguistics : rethinking social networks /
Jonathan Marshall
      p.   cm.— (Palgrave studies in language variation)
   Includes bibliographical references and index.
   ISBN 1–4039–1487–7 (cloth)
   1. Linguistic change—Social aspects.   2. Sociolinguistics.
   I. Title.   II. Series.

   P40.5.L54M37 2003
   306.44—dc21

                                                            2003054872

10   9   8   7   6   5   4   3   2
13   12   11   10   09   08   07   06   05   04

Printed and bound in Great Britain by
Antony Rowe Ltd, Chippenham and Eastbourne

To my daughter, Megan

Contents

Preface

This book presents a sociolinguistic study based on modern recorded dialect data. The purpose of the study was to develop a theoretical sociolinguistic framework which can aid our understanding of the diffusion of language change within a community. The study was conducted in order to establish what social factors might be involved in the process of language change, though the particular emphasis was on *resistance* to change. Some speakers of the variety studied, known in Scotland as 'the Doric', seem to have resisted change quite strongly, and this has drawn attention to the area. Sociolinguistic theory attempts, among other things, to explain the factors and motivations involved in the process of language change, and the social network framework has in the past been influential in our understanding of the process of vernacular maintenance. This study replicates the methodology used in most network studies, but also incorporates other sociological, including various attitudinal, factors. This was done by building up sociological and linguistic indices for each individual, and testing for correlations between the various indices. The results will indicate a cautious view of the ability of the supposed norm-enforcement effect of social networks to adequately account for vernacular maintenance. A more complex, inclusive model is offered, incorporating attitudinal factors, such as orientation to the local community. Social factors have been considered to operate simultaneously but variably on the individual. As such, the methodology developed here has the ability to consider the effects of the various sociological variables simultaneously.

List of Figures

List of Tables

Abbreviations

ATTDIA	Attitude to the Dialect
f60, m60	females, males over 60
f2540, m2540	females, males between 25 and 40
f1417, m1417	females, males between 14 and 17
f812, m812	females, males between 8 and 12
GRC	Grampian Regional Council
IPA	International Phonetic Alphabet
LEXREC	Lexical Recognition Index
MENURB	Mental Urbanisation Index
NATPRI	National Pride Index
NORM	Non-Mobile, Older, Rural Male
PHOVAR	Phonetic Variable Index
SEML	South-East Midlands
SOCLAS	Social Class Index
SOCNET	Social Network Index
SOED	Scottish Office Education Department
SSSCOR	Spontaneous Speech Index
SSE	Scottish Standard English

1
Historical and Demographic Details

In this chapter I introduce the subject of language change, and review some of the views expressed in the literature, before going on to discuss the topic selection, and the choice of sampling area. There follows a discussion of the socio-political history of Scotland, as well as the geographical and linguistic details of the area studied.

1.1 Language change

The subject of language change, and the possible factors involved in such a process, has for many years prompted interest. Investigators have shown renewed interest in the loss of non-standard varieties and the process of standardisation. This has given important insights into the types of geographical area, social network, and social group in which language changes originate and the mechanisms involved in the process of diffusion. Some studies of attitudes have tested for correlations between attitudes and social (including linguistic) behaviour, but the relationship between the two has not always been clear-cut.[1] Dialect *maintenance* has not received the same amount of attention, perhaps as a result of early dialectological methods and focus. Dialectologists went to great lengths to record (usually lexical or phonological) dialect forms before they vanished. However, the critics of (earlier) geographical dialectology, mostly variationist sociolinguists of the Labovian school, point to a focus on:

> a *geographical* account of linguistic differences, with the end-product being a map or maps showing the broad areal limits of the linguistic features (usually lexical or phonological) chosen for the study. In general, any reference in the dialectological literature to the social significance of variability is anecdotal (Milroy 1980: 4).

McMahon (1994: 231) points out that most early dialect surveys were carried out in the same way, with interviews and/or questionnaires, followed by the publication of an atlas with the areas of dialect use shown. The problem is that there is mostly no attempt at explanation, and also, there is a concentration on the 'purest' form of the dialect, spoken by NORMS (Chambers and Trudgill 1980), or Non-Mobile, Older, Rural Males.

The methods used were not designed to deal with the fact that the same speaker may use a very wide range of different pronunciations, and *explanations* for the variation were not normally to be found. Traditional dialectology focused on regions having 'place', 'difference', and 'distinctiveness' as their most prominent features to be analysed: 'rather than focusing on spatial processes or structures, individual areas were analysed for individual unique characteristics, totally independently of their neighbours' (Britain 1991: 202, cited in Hernández-Campoy 1996: 1).

The main theoretical construct was the isogloss. Dialectologists operated with the intention of dissecting and displaying the discreteness of dialect areas (Chambers and Trudgill 1980: 21, Stoddart, Upton and Widdowson 1999: 82–83) and the dynamism of society was often ignored. A more recent sub-field, geolinguistics, (Chambers and Trudgill 1998, Hernández-Campoy 1996, Britain 1991, Hindley 1990) has arisen probably as a result of the need to explain the interaction between language and geography, in addition to social and cultural factors. Statistics from human geography are used in order to analyse linguistic facts, something largely ignored in Labovian sociolinguistics. This type of research has not, however, become part of the sociolinguistics mainstream.

Dialectology was not completely separate from sociolinguistics, however, and one cannot ignore its contribution to modern sociolinguistics. Butters (1997: 1) takes issue with Chambers' (1995) book *Sociolinguistic Theory*, as he feels that the book ignores variationism's structuralist dialectological roots and ongoing tradition. Butters offers some possible explanations for the divide which crept in between dialectologists and sociolinguists. The former had been interested in what was socially less exciting than what was going on in the city: old, rural men's speech, whereas the latter had as their object of study the glamorous, the young, the urban, the feminist, and the racial. He believes that geographical variation is not, however, greatly different from other sources of linguistic variation in a complex post-industrial society (Butters 1997: 9). According to Chambers, however, Labovian variationists are now redressing the dialect geographers' excessive focus on isolation by emphasising social mobility. Butters believes that Chambers' 1995 work reflects the prevailing attitude of variationist sociolinguistics, which ignores regional variation (1997: 3).[2] The tradition Chambers describes as 'sociolinguistics' began as a reaction to the area-linguistics studies of Kurath and others, and is seen as a paradigm-shift away from structuralist dialectology. Butters, however, proposes that the two myths in the Chambers book be abandoned, namely:

> there is no serious intellectual connection between dialectologists and sociolinguists, and geographical location is not one of the independent social variables worthy of inclusion in sociolinguistics.

It is also true that dialectologists have often taken into account social factors such as class, education, age, and sex, especially the more modern ones like Pedersen and McDaniel (Butters 1997: 4). Labov himself notes that

> The linguists who have contributed most to the study of language in its social context are primarily those who have worked in dialect geography (Labov 1966: 21).

Thus early Labovian linguistics began against the backdrop of dialect geography, not a blank slate. Variationism had as its antecedent the area dialectologists (Butters 1997: 5). Bloomfield did believe that the most striking differences in American speech were geographical, but he also had an interest in social and stylistic variables:

> ... the differences of speech within a speech community are local – due to mere geographic separation – and non-local, or as we usually say, social. [...] The most striking line of cleavage in our speech is one of social class (Bloomfield 1933: 47–48, cited from Butters 1997: 5).

Bloomfield wrote a chapter entitled 'Fluctuation in the Frequency of Forms' (392–403), but what he lacked was the technology to record casual speech and to determine the intricate quantificational patterns which we can now discern with the aid of compact, affordable cassette recorders. Labov, on the other hand, did have access to recording equipment, and realised that the patterned variability that he found was of enormous methodological and theoretical importance (Butters 1997: 6). Bloomfield was also aware that individuals vary in their use of language, and lamented the fact that there was no way to record and analyse the variation quantitatively:

...if we had a record of every utterance that was made in a speech community during whatever period of time we wanted to study [...] we could score a point on the tally sheet of every form in this utterance. In this way we should obtain tables or graphs which showed us the ups and downs in frequency of every form during the time covered by our records, [giving] us a picture of what is actually going on at all times in every speech community (Bloomfield 1933: 394, cited in Butters 1997: 8).

Butters claims that for thirty years sociolinguists have been operating under the myth that structuralists rejected the linguistic heterogeneity of speech-communities as being worthy of study, as he states that their problems were mostly technological. The present study has taken what has been learnt in both dialectological and sociolinguistic studies, and employed it in what is essentially a study of both regional and social dialectology using social dialectological methods.

McIntosh (1961) attempts to dispel some of the earlier dialectological myths. He says that dialects vary not only because of geographical separation or isolation, but because each is in a way a reflex of the culture pattern of the community which uses it (1961: 27). No dialect is 'pure' at all. According to him, trade, invasions, movements of population, intermarriage, the importation of new ways of doing things, the development of new crafts and industries and other factors have always been at work and no place has escaped all of them. As a result, the dialect of every place in the country has been undergoing constant modification ever since it first began to be used there (p. 39).

McIntosh writes that it is generally possible to say that in a given community there is an 'old-fashioned' type of speech. That is to say, one which, as far as our knowledge will permit us to judge, has been less affected than other types of speech spoken there by recent influences from outside. For convenience, those who use this kind of speech can be called 'resistant types': they will often, though not always, prove to have lived all or most of their lives in the area which is being investigated. McIntosh writes that these resistant types will generally be middle-aged or older, *but it will turn out that some young people are also resistant types* and that some older persons are not (p. 85, my emphasis).[3] He does not go on to say what it is about these speakers that causes them to be resistant, and this leaves a theoretical vacuum for us to take up. He emphasises that 'resistant' is a purely relative term, and that 'resistance' is often a factor of environment rather than disposition [...] (p. 87). In the present study, this notion of 'resistant types' has become very important.

The social and ethnographic data of such resistant individuals will show certain patterns under the quantitative analysis in chapters 5 and 6.

People's attitudes to changes and to the groups in which they originate are specific and measurable, and have an important effect on the success of the diffusion of linguistic change (Kerswill and Williams 1994: 9). This has been an important consideration in the present study, and attitudes have been measured as part of a questionnaire.[4] Providing attitudinal factors are favourable, speakers of mutually intelligible dialects seem to transfer items from one variety to the other, and this can lead to language change.

Seen in terms of Giles' model of interpersonal speech accommodation, we may accept that situational factors alone will not determine choice, but that interpersonal relations have an effect. Short-term accommodation normally takes place in first, or temporary contacts, and does not usually result in change. Long-term accommodation can be observed, as it mostly occurs when regionally mobile individuals or minority groups come to live among a non-mobile majority. The problem is then to determine how speakers accommodate, and why accommodation varies between situations and individuals.

The question of how a language community maintains vernacular norms in the face of relentless pressure from the standard is one which interests many sociolinguists (Aitken 1979b, Milroy 1980, Andersen 1989, Britain 1991, Chambers 1996, Ladegaard 2000, Lippi-Green 1989). It is very clear that vernacular norms are persistently maintained in many communities, and that they have important social functions. But when language change finally begins to occur in a hitherto conservative variety, it offers the researcher a good opportunity to study the social factors involved in language change. Most modern sociolinguists see language variation as inextricably tied with language change, and this study is based upon this notion.

Language variation provides an explanation of how transmission takes place, but the problem of actuation remains elusive. Weinreich, Labov and Herzog (1968: 100, cited from McMahon 1994: 225) take the view that language is a system containing 'orderly heterogeneity'. Historical linguists recognise this, too:

> language variation is not random, but rather strictly controlled, often by extra-linguistic factors, and the specification of these factors may help us account for change (McMahon 1994: 226).

The purpose of the present study is to discover more about these very extra-linguistic factors.

In this study, a variety of Scots[5] spoken in the valley between the towns of Insch and Huntly in the county of Aberdeenshire in Scotland has been focused upon. Until recently, the dialect was conservative, but now that change is taking place rather rapidly, a study of the social factors involved in language change can be undertaken. The study has drawn on the social network framework, as well as Højrup's (1983) theory of Life Modes, and Pedersen's (1994) extension of it. Age, sex, social class, attitude to dialect and national pride are the other independent variables, and a stratified sample based on age and sex has been used. The socio-political history of Scotland is surely an influential factor in the dialect maintenance found in this area, and although all the contributing factors cannot be analysed quantitatively, some of the synchronic social scores adopted for the study, such as national pride and attitude to the dialect must represent attitudes which have resulted from this complex past. But it is the subject of language change which is focused upon here. This study will examine the influence of the social factors involved in language change, in an attempt to test some of the main sociolinguistic models in a rural setting.

1.2.   Topic selection

The selection of the main topic came about as a reaction to the abundance of studies of linguistic change and the social mechanisms involved in the diffusion of change. The choice of sampling area was due to my period of residence there a decade ago, and to my interest in Scots. According to Aitken (1979b: 145), the fact that Scots has only recently begun to take a more prominent role in linguistic studies is surprising, as it is informative for the historical phonology of the English language, as well as in linguistic variation studies.

Macaulay (1997) also writes about the 'development and survival of linguistic differences' (1997: 3). He writes:

> Scottish English is on several counts one of the most conservative varieties of English, with some features which have remained unchanged since the days before English was a separate language but which were lost or altered in most varieties of English by the sixteenth century (1997: 3).

These features survive despite the fact that they are not used in education, government and the media. Macaulay lists some possible reasons for this conservatism:

the desire of a minority group to maintain its distinctiveness from the majority group; a relatively low level of prosperity, which limited social mobility and contributed more to emigration than immigration; a cultural tradition that takes many forms; the Scots' view of their own national character; and no doubt many others (1997: 3).

Macaulay's main question is why linguistic differences persist (1997: 4). The view that many social differences in language are the result of the failure to learn the form of language that is promulgated by the educational establishment is flawed. The answer in short is that all linguistic varieties are functional for their speakers. He cites Myers-Scotton as saying:

> [...] the particular linguistic variety used in an exchange carries social meaning. This model assumes that all linguistic code choices are indexical of a set of rights and obligations holding between participants in the conversational exchange. That is, any code choice points to a particular interpersonal balance, and it is partly because of their indexical qualities that different languages, dialects, and styles are maintained in a community (1988: 152, cited in Macaulay 1997: 5).

The dialect studied in the present project, known locally as 'the Doric', is spoken (with slight variation) throughout the north-east of Scotland in Aberdeenshire (see Map 1), and shows remarkable linguistic distance from Standard English and southern British dialects in general, as the following extract will show:

> Relatively few people speak unequivocal Scots on some occasions and unequivocal English on others (though this does occur, in areas such as the north-east, where the local form of Scots *is both well-preserved and highly differentiated* – I have found it, for example, in Aberdeen University students) (McClure 1979: 27, emphasis mine).

This is supported by the evidence from the Huntly data, at least as far as the middle age group is concerned. The members of the oldest group speak the dialect fluently and unselfconsciously, and some are able to style-shift to a certain extent. This is especially true of the more educated and widely travelled among them, though they account for a small percentage, and the choice of code is sociolinguistically determined.

Members of the middle age group are mostly able to code-switch. Speech events in which we were participants usually triggered a code-switch initially, until enough time was spent chatting informally to allow the speaker to relax. This was especially true once the speaker began to see that we were interested in the dialect, and not simply someone trying to find out who couldn't speak 'properly'.[6] Members of the two youngest age groups did not have a full and fluent command of the dialect, except for a few individuals. Here, people use something resembling the Aberdeen urban variety, which is basically Scottish Standard English with a few phonetic, prosodic and lexical features, such as a bilabial or denti-labial fricative at the beginning of 'wh-words', extensive use of diminutive forms of nouns, and a characteristic intonation pattern.[7] While there have been various studies conducted in north-east rural areas (Wölck 1965, Löw 1997, Smith 2000), lack of material on urban Aberdeen city language features prevents a more direct comparison. What is interesting is the question of which individuals are more resistant to change than others, ignoring age and sex grading. The Scots spoken in the Gordon and Buchan areas, where the Huntly study was conducted, has conserved many features of older states of the language, and it therefore provides clear, highly differentiated variables with which to test the influence of independent social variables on language use. With the ever-decreasing effect of social and geographical isolation, and increased language change, the effects of these social factors on language change can

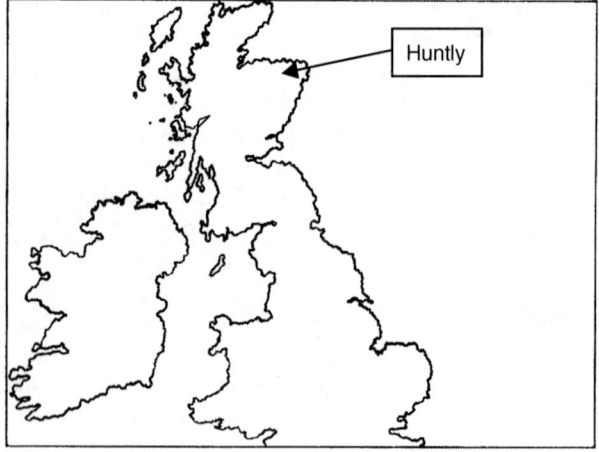

Map 1 Location of the sampling area

be tested in this area. This has become the central focus of the Huntly study: to explain which social mechanisms predict language change, at least in rural speech communities. Map 1 shows the location of the sampling area. The location may be regarded as a relic area for linguistic purposes, as will become clear from the data. Migration is usually outwards from the rural areas to Aberdeen and further afield (except for small numbers of people retiring to a quiet life, often from England).

1.3 Socio-political history

As mentioned, the picture is not simply one of a relic area in an ethnically and linguistically homogeneous community with one or more cities from which innovations diffuse, but rather one where history, ethnicity, and politics play an important role in linguistic realities. Not only is the constitution of Scottish identity place-based, but the articulation of separatist politics is embedded in the histories and geographies of particular regions in Scotland (Johnson 1995: 102). Until the seventeenth century Scotland was independent, and mainly Celtic (Gaelic) speaking. The area between the Forth and the Tweed was ceded to King Edward of England by Kenneth II in 973, bringing a large number of people under English rule. The varieties of English which displaced Gaelic were therefore *northern*, and from textual evidence the same as other northern English south of the border. There was also contact with southern English, for example Malcolm Canmore III lived in Wessex for three years, and married an English princess (Lass 1987: 251). After the Norman Conquest, large-scale contact with southern English and French began. English refugees streamed north, as well as Normans and their English allies. English began to become the 'establishment' language, and Gaelic 'was forced into the hinterlands' (Romaine 1982a: 57, cited from Lass 1987: 251).

Gaelic remained the language of the Highlands and Islands till the English military occupations after the Jacobite risings of 1715 and 1745, when southern English was brought in directly. Scots has therefore never been a Highlands language. Battles of the Middle Ages led to the development of two separate anglophone nations (with very different standards), separated by the Tweed. They had in common a French-type high literary culture, but for the rest they were essentially two different European nations that used dialects of English (Lass: 251). Consequently, a fully functional standard Scots developed, independent of the southern forms, but which looked increasingly to the south-east Midlands and

London for a norm. This did, however, meet with resistance, as the following extract shows:

> Giff king James the fyft war alyue quha hering ane of his subjectis knap suddrone, declarit him ane trateur: quhidder vald he declaire you triple traitoris, quha not onlie knappis suddrone in your negative confession bot also hes causit it to be imprentit at London in contempt of our naytive language?

> 'If King James the fifth, after hearing one of his subjects speak southern, declared him a traitor, why would he not declare you triple traitors, as you not only speak southern in your negative confession, but have also had it printed in London in contempt of our native language?' (Johne Hamilton 1563, cited in Buchan et al. 1924: 107, my translation).

Scots writers by the end of the fifteenth century were using the word *Scottis* for their language instead of *Inglis*, and it had the status of full literary standard (the only non-SEML[8] variety to have it then) (Lass 1987: 251). However, there was also extensive contact with southern English, as the two nations had diplomatic and cultural relations, and the linguistic fashions of London made their way to Edinburgh (p. 252). The Reformation brought the influence of English into Scotland in the form of the official translation of the Bible, and this became the basis for the Scottish liturgical language, and was used to teach children to read. If God himself spoke southern English, then the people presumed it to be in some way 'correct'. Printers also began to print largely in English, and even translated Scots manuscripts into Sudron.[9]

By the late sixteenth century, bi-dialectalism was becoming common, and literacy skills were learned in a foreign dialect. The register spectrum became polarised, with Scots at the 'familiar' end, and English at the elevated and public end. During the eighteenth century, the Augustan trend of 'ascertaining' and 'correcting' the language in England moved north, sapping Scots confidence in indigenous forms (p. 252). By the middle of the eighteenth century, Scots as a prose medium had practically vanished. Books were expensive, and Scotland was poor. If a book was to appeal to a wider audience in order to pay, it had to be written in English (Buchan et al. 1924: 116). The register polarisation still exists in most of Scotland today, with Scottish Standard English (SSE) being used in all formal exchanges and for education and in the media. This is very similar to Standard English, with the only differences being phonological and, and to a small extent, syntactic and lexical. The boundary between Scottish Standard English and Scots is not clear-cut, however, and in this study only clear markers of Scots have been used as dependent variables. As Aitken (1979b: 12) puts it: Scots speakers mostly have two different registers, and *dialect-switch* between the two.

According to McClure (1979: 39), a language spoken naturally in all domains by all sections of a culturally homogeneous society is self-renewing, as was the case in late-mediaeval Scotland. Nowadays the situation is that Scots is only spoken by a section of the community, and discouraged by the education system, meaning that it is surviving against all odds, even though:

> it has suffered a massive attrition of its active vocabulary and a progressive dilution of its distinctive grammatical and phonological features (McClure 1979: 40).

Since McClure wrote these words in 1979, there have been some educational measures in favour of Scots, though some would argue not enough. Hendry (1997) bemoans the fact that the education system has been designed to systematically eradicate dialect use in schools, as he shows in the following extract:

> [...] the first duty of the infant teacher and the continuing duty of all primary teachers, is to implant and cultivate fluent speech in standard English (*Primary Education* (1946), cited from Hendry 1997: 19).

As a schoolteacher in Banchory, Aberdeenshire, he acknowledges that learning and using Standard English in appropriate contexts is beneficial to the child, although he believes that a bilingual approach would have served the community well. One indication of an *official* change in attitudes towards the use of Scots in schools is the Scottish Office Education Department (SOED) document *English Language 5–14* (1991), which states:

> The speech of Scottish people is often distinctive. It may display features of pronunciation and intonation, which together constitute an accent. It may contain features of dialect, such as vocabulary, syntax, idiom and economies of expression. These reflect the histories of communities, and are part of the language children bring to school.

> The first tasks of schools are therefore to enable pupils to be confident and creative in this language, and to begin to develop the

notion of language diversity, within which pupils can appreciate the range of accents, dialects and teachers in valuing pupils' spoken language, and introducing them to stories, poems and other texts, which use dialect in a positive way (SOED 1991: 67, cited from Hendry 1997: 25).

Of course, this falls short of recognising Scots as a national language, but goes some way towards recommending the study of Scots in schools. The following year, a motion was passed in the Grampian Regional Council to draw up a report on how best to implement more support for Scots. *Scots Language and Heritage in Schools* (GRC 1993) made a number of recommendations, which included the secondment of experienced teachers to devise programmes of work for Scots language, culture and heritage. These programmes were included in pre-service teacher training (Hendry 1997: 27).

Despite these guidelines, little seems to have been done by many primary schools to provide structured programmes of Scots language work within their language curricula. There is also little indication of any procedures having been put in place to monitor the implementation of these recommendations. Political and educational will are not seen to be addressing Scots language provision in Scottish schools. The sum total of language planning for Scots is two pages in SOED 1991 (English Language 5–14), which in Hendry's opinion indicates a lack of serious commitment (Hendry 1997: 98).

1.4   Geographical and linguistic details of the sampling area

The Huntly farming community is located in the Strathbogie valley of the River Deveron, between Inverness and Aberdeen. It is bounded to the south by the Correen Hills, to the west by Tap o' Noth and Cransmill Hill, and to the east by Wichach Hill. The river flows northwards into the sea, with the towns of Banff and Macduff flanking the mouth on either side.

The main economic activity is farming. The town is situated on the A96, roughly midway between Aberdeen and Elgin, and on the railway line which links these two towns. Another road, the A97, links Huntly with Rhynie in the south, and with Banff in the north, allowing swift movement between these towns and the smaller villages in between. Local people speak of strangers coming to live in the town, and of folk not even knowing their neighbours any more, something which was uncommon before. The community spirit does not seem to be as strong as it was, and fewer community events, such as ceilidhs, are organised. The in-migrants are from other parts of Scotland, Britain, and even as far as North America. Although the town is by no means as cosmopolitan as a city like Aberdeen, the effect of the increase in the number of outsiders is being noticed by locals, who report having to accommodate linguistically.

Improved transport links and increased geographical mobility have also meant that local townsfolk have become more exposed to the influences of supra-local norms, including the possibility of becoming 'mentally urbanised'.[10] Whereas, before, many villagers would have seldom, if ever, journeyed into Aberdeen, many do nowadays, reducing the friction of distance.[11] Their earlier conceptions of cities and their inhabitants may change as a result of this mobility, and this may have implications for their social behaviour. The rise of the oil industry off the north-east coast has brought with it immense changes in wealth for those who have been able to become involved in it, and they are associated with ambition and modernity.

As will be seen in chapter 3, rural north-east Scots has some particular features not found in General Scots. For example, the word 'book' is pronounced [bjuk], and 'good' is pronounced [gwid]. Words like 'bull', 'pull' and 'full' are pronounced with [ʌ], as in the words 'but', 'putt' and 'fuss'. Words with 'wh-onsets' are pronounced with a denti-labial [f]. A velar fricative, in words such as 'daughter' and 'bought', is still pronounced in a restricted lexical set. Lexical items, such as 'loun' (boy), 'blad' (to damage) and 'puddock' (frog) are still used. In Aberdeen city, these features are not found, at least in middle class speech.[12] Some of them may occasionally be heard in the speech of working class speakers, but this speech is probably not the target for rural people.

In sum then, the presence of dialect features is sparser in Aberdeen city, and is societally, rather than regionally, distributed. It is the adoption of regional standard features over local vernacular features, or rather the resistance to such adoption, which has become the focus of this study. The presence of societal influences on individuals will be examined, as will the reactions of those individuals to such influences. These influences may be seen as the stimuli, but will the individuals all respond in the same way as those in their sex and age groups? What of the intermediary factors, such as attitudes, between the stimulus and response? Sociolinguistic explanations for the patterns found in the data will be sought in chapter 7. In this chapter, after giving an overview of the subject of language change, and an explanation for the topic selection,

I covered the socio-political history, geographical and linguistic details of the sampling area. The next chapter will review the literature, covering the main social mechanisms thought to operate in the process of language change.

Notes

1. For a more detailed discussion, see section 2.5.
2. Earlier, this was the only source of synchronic variation studied, and Chambers himself has published important works in the field.
3. It is this very fact which has become the focus of the present study: if age is not the only factor causing 'resistance' to change, it is important to find out which other social factors are correlated.
4. See section 2.6 for a discussion of Ladegaard's (2000) work on attitudes and linguistic behaviour.
5. The term is used to describe the language of the lowlands of Scotland, a descendant of Old Northumbrian, not the same as Scottish Standard English (SSE).
6. A research assistant, a retired local lady who had observed the first few interviews, conducted the rest herself.
7. Robert Millar, University of Aberdeen, personal communication. The paucity of studies on Aberdeen City speech makes a closer comparison impossible.
8. South-east Midlands.
9. Southern.
10. This concept will be discussed in depth in chapters 2 and 7.
11. A term used in geolinguistics, discussed below.
12. Robert Millar, personal communication, though there are no quantitative studies with which to compare.

2
Theoretical Background and Previous Research

In this chapter I examine the theoretical background to sociolinguistic studies of language change, covering some of the major studies in this area. First, I examine the more general theoretical issues surrounding the phenomenon of language change, after which I review the social network framework, looking specifically at Milroy's Belfast study. Next I review Højrup's (1983b) notion of Life Modes, the concept of exocentric versus endocentric change, Cognitive Dissonance, attitudes and language change, language choices and their results, age and language change, dialects in contact and geolinguistics. The intention is to review each model or factor thought to be involved in the process of language change, and to see whether the Huntly data supports such models or not.

2.1 Variation and change

Theory in sociolinguistics is mainly concerned with integrated models to account for the links between linguistic variation, linguistic change and social structures. While variation can lead to change, it is important to note that this is not automatic. As Weinreich, Labov and Herzog (1968: 188) point out: 'Not all variability and heterogeneity in language structure involves change; but all change involves variability and heterogeneity'. Labov's (1966) New York City study started a process of development of quantitative methods for sociolinguistic work. Though Labov has focused on the status-based approach, others have also examined non status-based factors, for example Le Page (1978). In the introduction to her 1982a collection, Romaine writes:

> The papers here focus special attention on a number of aspects of sociolinguistic methodology and theory, e.g. the role of the individual,

15

problems of quantifying and analysing variables and the integration of social factors into linguistic description. Taken as a whole, they reflect a movement away from the prevailing theoretical assumption that the patterning of sociolinguistic behaviour is to be explained by reference to social class or status (Romaine 1982a: 2).

Figueroa's (1994) book *Sociolinguistic Metatheory* reviews the major contributions to sociolinguistic theory. She points out that linguists have for many years considered the social factors involved in language use.

Practical questions of how language is an integral part of society and, above all, how social or rather extralinguistic factors have shaped and are shaping language...were in fact the concern of linguistic research long before the term sociolinguistics was coined, so that linguistics has always had a social aspect (Neubert 1976: 152, cited from Figueroa 1994: 1).

Language is an integral part of social life, and sociolinguistics attempts to deal realistically with the facts of language. Hymes (1997, cited from Coupland and Jaworski 1997: 7) argues for a socially constituted linguistics, an approach in which whatever questions we might ask about language are embedded in a social analysis, though he fails to supply a methodology to apply his theory to real-life situations.

Our discipline aims to deal with language in society. Coupland and Jaworski (1997) refer to the view of Joshua Fishman that:

...in multilingual communities, questions of nationalism, group equality, dominance and political change have a strong basis in attitudes to language, language choice and language policies. The sociology of language therefore needs to concern itself with psychological (or, more appropriately, social psychological) questions of attitudes, beliefs, stereotypes, allegiances and antipathies. Its range of research methods needs to be broad enough to give us access to cognitive processes as well as to the facts of linguistic distribution and patterns of use (Coupland and Jaworski 1997: 7).

Romaine points out that 'sociolinguistics attempts to make a coherent statement about the relationship between language use and the social patterns or structures of various kinds' (Romaine 1982a: 1). Trudgill writes that 'sociolinguistics is that part of linguistics which is concerned with language as a social and cultural phenomenon' (Trudgill 1974: 32).

The common thread running through all of these is the emphasis on variation and diversity, the socio-cultural nature of language, and that the focus of sociolinguistics should be on *parole*/language use, interaction and meaning (Figueroa 1994: 2). Sociolinguistics can be seen as a special type of linguistic method, an application of existing linguistic theory, an interdisciplinary field, a sub-field of sociology or anthropology, or a separate linguistic paradigm (p. 3). The two types of linguistic framework are the formalist and the functionalist. Lass (1980) has called these 'speaker free' and 'speaker centred'. Formalists in the Chomskian paradigm tend to regard language primarily as a mental phenomenon, while functionalists, for example Labov, tend to regard it primarily as a societal phenomenon. Labov in fact resisted the term sociolinguistics for years, as he felt it implied there could be successful linguistic theory or practice which is not social. He writes:

There is a growing realisation that the basis of intersubjective knowledge in linguistics must be found in speech – language as it is used in everyday life by members of the social order, that vehicle of communication in which they argue with their wives, joke with their friends, and deceive their enemies (Labov 1997, cited from Coupland and Jaworski 1997: 23).

Most sociolinguists agree with this need for real-life data. Labov points to this rather clearly:

The data that we need cannot be collected from the closet or from any library, public or private; fortunately for us, there is no shortage of native speakers of most languages if we care to listen to them speak (Labov 1973b: 124).

Historical linguists are concerned with language change, but according to McMahon (1994: 225), the problem of *actuation* remains outside the domain of historical linguistics, and by implication, within the domain of sociolinguistics. The distribution of isoglosses on a dialect map indicates that changes also depend on social, political and environmental factors. Sound changes seem to originate in cultural centres or areas of political dominance, or focal areas, and diffuse outwards, but may not affect relic areas, which are isolated for geographical or social reasons (McMahon 1994: 229).

Dialect and language *variation* is a continuum on regional and social dimensions, as has been shown by geographical and social investigation. There is a growing body of evidence that language *change* is also predominantly gradual. Observing changes in progress can help us to understand completed changes, if we accept the Uniformitarian Principle:

> ...the claim that the same mechanisms which operated to produce the large-scale changes of the past may be observed operating in the current changes taking place around us (Labov 1972: 161).

Sociolinguistic studies have now convincingly shown that sound changes in progress *can* be observed, by carrying out 'apparent-time' studies[1] of speakers of different classes and ages within a speech community.

While Labov's methodology concentrates on social class, others have looked elsewhere for explanations of variation, such as social networks. As Chambers points out, the difference between these two

> has to do with their proximity to the individual, or the immediacy of their influence. The class structure of a town, city or nation is a confederation of an unbounded number of networks. 'Network studies' as Guy (1988: 54) says, 'are microsociological in focus, while class studies are macroscopic' (Chambers 1995: 68).

As the network framework is the main subject of this study, a comprehensive overview of it will now be given. Following that, I will examine how it has been adapted for sociolinguistics by Milroy, among others.

2.2   Social networks

The concept of *social networks* was first introduced by Radcliffe-Brown in 1940, and elaborated by Barnes in 1954, and others later. I will here examine some of the viewpoints of researchers in the field.

2.2.1   Social networks in social anthropology

The concept of social networks, in its early stages, focused on 'interacting people engaged in actions that could alter the institutions in which they participated' (Boissevain 1987: 164). A network of interconnected people can be seen to have a definite structure, with patterns of regularities. Boissevain makes the important distinction between *interactional* and *structural* criteria for the network:

Interactional

1. Multiplexity. How multiplex are the strands that connect the members of the network?
2. Transactional content. What are the goods and services, messages, emotional involvement, information which move between the members?
3. Directional flow. Is the flow of the above items mostly uni-directional?
4. Frequency and duration. Do people meet often and for long periods?

Structural

1. Size. How many people are in the 'first-order' and 'second-order' of the network?
2. Density. How many of the members also interact with each other?
3. Centrality. How central is the member in the network?
4. Clusters. How many 'clusters', or sub-units are there in the network? These can function like mini-networks, and have their own norms. This can cause weak links between the clusters, and the member may feel the need to keep the clusters separate.

A network that scores low on multiplexity, transactional content and density is called 'loosely knit' (Boissevain 1987: 166). It is believed that the relative density and multiplexity of the network have important implications for the social, including linguistic, behaviour of the person.

Potential Pitfalls

Boissevain believes that social network analysis should only be used to answer *specific* research questions. According to him, this form of analysis is not over-complicated: it simply asks who is linked to whom, the nature of that linkage, and how it affects behaviour (Boissevain 1987: 166). It does, however, have some potential for over-analysing. Network analysis can be too mathematical and remote from human interaction. It can become an object of study in its own right, sterile and remote. It can be used to attribute specific characteristics to people. He also believes that attempts can be made to explain too much, using networks (p. 164). As will be argued in this book, the analysis of the Huntly data would seem to support this criticism. A person's position in a social network could reflect that person's social choices, and be correlated with that person's linguistic choices in some cases. However, such a social network structure is not necessarily the *cause* of such a person's linguistic choices. Both may simply reflect other, as yet unidentified factors, such as underlying attitudes to the local group. This may apply more to rural than to urban speech communities, though the concept may be generalisable to include urban centres, as will be discussed below.

Social structure 'is best understood in terms of a dynamic interplay between *relations* between and among persons... and the *positions* and *roles* they occupy within a social system (Berkowitz 1982: 3, cited from Stokowski 1994: 56). Stokowski agrees with Mitchell's definition of a network as 'a specific set of linkages among a defined set of persons' (Mitchell 1969: 2, cited in Stokowski 1994: 56). She goes on to say that though networks may be invisible even to the participants related within the structures, researchers believe that networks exert influence directly and indirectly on social behaviour.

Studying social networks leads researchers to analyse patterns of social relationships within social structures, and in doing so to account for social behaviour at both the macro- and micro levels (Stokowski 1994: 58). It has a developmental history starting in 'sociometry',[2] as this extract shows:

> Sociometry was the direct ancestor of today's social network analysis...
> [and] the second coming of network analysis began [with] the invasion
> of social science by computers (Rogers 1987: 287, cited from Stokowski
> 1994: 58).

In terms of the social network framework, social actors are seen as 'nodes' in a network, and are tied by what are called 'links'. The network 'map' which we draw shows the relations between the members, and is used to answer questions and test hypotheses about patterns in social behaviour. The following is a table of criteria for networks, taken from Stokowski 1994: 61:

Table 1   Social network criteria (Stokowski 1994: 61)

Interactional criteria

1. Frequency of communication. (Number and continuity of interactions over time)
2. Content of ties. (Purpose and function of relation; types of relational tie, i.e. exchange, obligation, sentiment, power)
3. Multiplexity. (Redundancy of relationships: number of contents combined in a relationship)
4. Reciprocity. (Degree of symmetry in relation, i.e. if A chooses B, does B choose A?)
5. Strength of ties (strong, weak). (Relative measure of time, affect, intensity, mutuality)

Structural criteria

1. Size. (Number of people or relationships in network)
2. Density. (Connectedness of network; actual links computed as proportion of total links)
3. Distance or proximity. (Number of links between any two nodes in network)
4. Centrality. (Adjacency and influence of nodes and subgroups in network)
5. Clustering. (Partition of ties into network subgroups and cliques)
6. Network roles:
   a) Isolate. (Peripheral node in a network)
   b) Bridge. (Group member who provides link to another network subgroup)
   c) Liaison. (Node that links several groups without being a member of any group)
   d) Star. (Node with largest number of communication links)

Stokowski notes that there is little consensus in the literature concerning which criteria to select for different circumstances (p. 62). Those selected for the Huntly study are elaborated in chapter 3.

Scott (1991) writes that the early forms of social network analysis were rather non-technical. They resulted from the theories of the anthropologist Radcliffe-Brown, whose concept of 'social structure' was elaborated by later anthropologists and sociologists. From the textile metaphors of 'interweaving' and 'interlocking' relations came the notion of social 'network'. Sociometry was developed in the US in the 1930s by theorists such as Lewin, Moreno and Heider. Moreno devised a 'sociogram', or diagram in which individuals are represented by points, and their relationships to one another by lines. Lewin saw a social group as existing in a 'field', or social space, which comprises the group together with its surrounding environment. These ideas appear throughout the literature on social networks. Barnes claimed that 'the whole of social life' could be seen as 'a set of points, some of which are joined by lines' (Barnes 1954: 43, cited from Scott 1991: 29).

Scott refers to Granovetter's notion of 'weak ties'. This concept, also elaborated by James and Lesley Milroy (see below), states that, though the influence of strong ties is more obvious, there is also a strong influence on a network from weak ties. People to whom one is closest (family and close friends, work-mates etc.) have many overlapping contacts with one another, and tend to possess the *same* knowledge about things. Information which reaches one is also likely to reach the rest of them. They are therefore less likely to be the source of new information from distant parts of the network. New information is likely to come into the network from the relatively weak ties of less frequent contacts and people in different work situations (Scott 1991: 36). In his study on job information, Granovetter concludes that 'acquaintances are more likely to pass on job information than close friends' (Granovetter 1974: 54).

This has important implications for the bringing in of linguistic changes from outside a network, or speech community. The concept is rather similar to that of 'linguistic missionaries' (Steinsholt 1962) who, after a period of residence away, return to a speech community, bringing with them innovations from outside the network. They are seen as 'insiders', and as such the innovations are accepted, but it is also possible that the changes are brought in because they have weak ties as a result of their period of absence.

Scott writes that the principal types of data used in social science are 'attribute data' and 'relational data'. The first type includes attitudes, opinions and behaviour of agents. These are mostly collected through surveys and interviews, and can be quantified and analysed through statistical procedures. In the Huntly study, the social scores MENURB (mental urbanisation), ATTDIA (attitude to the dialect), and NATPRI (national pride), and the linguistic scores PHOVAR (phonetic variable score), SSSCOR (spontaneous speech score) and LEXREC (lexical recognition) are examples of this type of data (these terms are elaborated in chapter 3). Relational data, on the other hand, is about:

> the contacts, ties and connections, the group attachments and meetings, which relate one agent to another and so cannot be reduced to the properties of the individual agents themselves. Relations are not the properties of agents, but of systems of agents [...] (Scott 1991: 3).

In the Huntly study, this relational data is measured. It is felt, however, that a person's social networks are not simply the result of arbitrary factors external to that person, but also reflect personal choices which he or she makes. These may be based on mental orientation to the local group, and a desire to be relatively less or more integrated. The Huntly scores for social networks therefore are also a measure of *attribute* data. According to Scott, it is possible for one to undertake quantitative and statistical counts of relations; however he feels that network analysis consists of a body of qualitative measures of network structure (p. 3).

2.2.2   Social networks in sociolinguistics

Lesley Milroy's (1980) book *Language and Social Networks* has been an important contribution to our understanding of language variation. In it she proposes that the notion of social networks be used as an analytic device which can explain linguistic variation in a more sophisticated way than simple social stratification. The view is that understanding more about the social network structure and interaction of a particular individual can help the investigator understand more about the maintenance of vernacular norms. She attempts to show how the network concept can be used as an analytic tool, rather than simply a 'metaphoric device' (1980: 45). By this she means that the network can be used for quantitative analysis. The basic theory is that people interact meaningfully as individuals, as well as forming parts of structured, functional institutions such as classes, castes, or occupational groups. One of the potential benefits of this concept is to help us understand more about how language change is retarded.

Problems with social class

Milroy sees social class as a large-scale category; one which is difficult to pin down. The idea is that people can be ordered with respect to the rest of society by quantifiable characteristics like income, education, occupation, residence or life-style, which are evaluated by society at large. Society can be ordered into strata, or classes, with as many subdivisions as the analyst wishes to make (Milroy 1980: 14). Trudgill has referred to the difficulties in assigning individuals to specific social groups, in the light of the fluidity and abstractness of the latter. His Brunlanes study (1983) ignores social class, as most of the informants were from farming families, forming a socially rather homogeneous group. In the Huntly study, social class was initially considered less important than in an urban study, but this variable has proved to be more significant than was expected from a rural community.[3]

In his 1961 study of Martha's Vineyard, Labov proposes that there is an 'in-group', which he calls 'Vineyarders', and that members use linguistic variability to indicate their affiliation with the group (cited in Milroy 1980: 14). There, social class is less useful in explaining the linguistic patterns than the less abstract concept of what Milroy calls *community*. This is generally seen as a cohesive group to which people have a clear consciousness of belonging (p. 14). Working-class communities generally have more social interaction patterns in the local area, while middle-class communities lack local loyalties and characteristically dense patterns of interaction within a limited area (p. 16). Middle-class people may never speak to their neighbours, but may interact a great deal outside the neighbourhood (Frankenburg 1969, cited in Milroy 1980: 16).

There are also accounts of tensions between old established communities and 'new people' moving in from outside, who do not share local
norms and values (p. 16). The informants in the present study often
mentioned the in-migrants from 'down south',[4] who bring with
them southern varieties of English, and who stuck out like sore thumbs
in the beginning, but are becoming more plentiful now. As Milroy
(1980: 16) says:

> Knowledge of community patterns and conflicts of this kind can be
> extremely useful to a linguistic investigator; some will argue that
> such knowledge is essential. [. . .] in Belfast as we shall see it has been
> possible to use this kind of knowledge to account for systematic dif-
> ferences in language use between individuals, and between sub-
> groups in the population of communities which, in terms of social
> status, are relatively homogeneous.

Seen in terms of Milroy's concept of social networks, the people in
this study mostly have what she calls high-density networks, that is,
they interact within a defined territory, and their contacts nearly all
know each other. Also, as in Blom and Gumperz's (1972) Hemnesberget
study, there is a fluidity of class structure where extremes of wealth and
poverty are absent. Of course, the notion of high- versus low-density networks is a heuristic idealisation, and the reality is more like a continuum
between the two, along which an individual can roughly be placed.

Blom and Gumperz have proposed that the elites (perhaps urban
upper middle class people) have network ties which are 'largely impersonal, focusing around *single tasks*'. In contrast, most low-status speakers
(here, perhaps something like the farmers) 'live, marry, and earn their
livelihood among others of their own kind' (1972: 433). Since most
Hemnesberget natives live, marry and work in the area, their values are
rarely challenged.

The ties between them reinforce the social meanings ascribed to the
dialect, and contribute to the maintenance of the separateness between
the dialect and the standard, or at least the maintenance of the dialect.[5]
It is therefore the *social* (non-referential) meaning in the study of
language that is important, according to the writers (p. 434).

According to Milroy, the *density* of a network can be calculated by
using the formula:

$$D = \frac{100 \ Na\%}{N}$$

(Where D = density, Na = number of actual links, and N = number of possible links.)

This expresses the ratio of the actual links to the total number of all possible links. She later admits, however, that the total number of links is virtually impossible to determine:

> [...] we cannot use multiplexity and density scores directly. As we have seen, both of these can be measured quantitatively. But the formulae require a quantitative statement of the size of a *total* personal network, which very few researchers are in a position to provide. For the purposes of this study therefore, multiplexity and density are expressed indirectly only by indicators which are *readily verifiable from field data*, while at the same time reflecting a number of observations recurrent in a wide range of relevant network studies (Milroy 1980: 141).

Milroy also admits that it is both network patterns and complex *attitudinal factors* which act as a basis for the measurement of degree of integration into the community, and, as will be seen later, the Huntly MENURB score is just such a measurement. The survival and transmission of a vernacular is partly due to important values of local loyalty and solidarity, often seen as opposites to institutionalised provincial or national values. There is a constant tension between these values, and the vernacular and the standard each have prestige[6] associated with them. This often corresponds to what is referred to as covert and overt prestige.[7]

The other characteristic of networks is the *content* of the actual link. If a person is linked to the anchor in a single capacity only, the relationship is seen as *uniplex*, otherwise it is *multiplex*. A score can be allocated to this in the same way as for density:

$$M = \frac{Nm \times 100\%}{N}$$

(Where Nm is the number of multiplex links and N the number of actual links.)

High multiplexity and density scores often co-occur, and both are seen to increase the norm-enforcement mechanism in the network. For high-density networks, Milroy proposes:

[In this network type], each individual is likely to be linked to others in more than one capacity – as a co-employee, a kinsman and a friend, for example. This kind of network tie may be said to be *multiplex* [...], and to contrast with the *uniplex* ties of the elite who tend to associate with the local people in a single capacity only (Milroy 1980: 21).

The *volume* of exchanges and therefore of shared knowledge within a dense, multiplex network is great. Speakers are therefore likely to use their most casual and intimate speech styles, at least for a greater proportion of the time than are people in loose-knit networks. They are also more mutually accessible than if the link is uniplex, and therefore susceptible to the obligation to adopt group norms. Extreme density also produces homogeneity of norms, and consistency of loyalty to vernacular[8] speech forms (Milroy 1980: 61). She believes that a speaker's network ties can change over time, and that this will affect the amount of influence the network has over the speaker. If an individual's network structure becomes less close-knit, it follows that the mechanism of non-standard norm maintenance will no longer be so influential, and that he will be free of the constant supervision and control that the network exercised (Milroy 1980: 182).

Individual speakers in large-scale studies

Milroy believes that there is no reason why a single speaker's output should be viewed as unstructured and unworthy of study (1980: 184). The practice of grouping informants to show patterns of linguistic variation is of course a valid procedure; however, much systematic individual variation is left unaccounted for by this method. She believes that the network of relationships in which an individual is embedded, and the social group to which he or she belongs, can reveal much about such individual variation. Networks can be seen as the main large-scale parameter affecting speech, forming as they do a buffer between the macro-sociolinguistic factor of abstract social group and the micro-sociolinguistic one of interaction (Kerswill and Williams 1994: 12).

Structural features

The main component in the network is the *anchor*, or the one at the 'centre'.[9] From this individual, lines radiate outwards to *points*, or people with whom the anchor is directly linked. These make up the *first-order zone*, and people with whom the anchor comes into contact via his first-order zone make up his *second-order zone.* A social network acts as a mechanism for exchanging goods and services, as well as for imposing obligations and conferring privileges (Milroy 1980: 47). It seems generally true that tribal societies, villages and traditional working-class communities usually have dense multiplex networks, while geographically and socially mobile societies usually have sparse uniplex networks (Milroy 1980: 52).

Milroy believes, therefore, that in order to apply any sort of quantitative analysis to the data, a network *strength scale* must be allocated to each speaker. A five-point scale was used in her Belfast study:

1. Membership of a high-density, territorially based cluster.
2. Having substantial ties of kinship in the neighbourhood (more than one household, in addition to his own nuclear family).
3. Working at the same place as at least two others from the same area.
4. The same place of work as at least two others of the same sex from the area.
5. Voluntary association with work mates in leisure hours (from Milroy 1980: 54).

According to Milroy, condition one is an indicator of density, while conditions two to five are indicators of multiplexity. Allocating a network index score allows the network patterns of individuals to be measured and possible links with linguistic patterns to be tested. Milroy claims that the scale is

capable of differentiating individuals quite sharply. Scores range from zero for someone who fulfils none of the conditions (although a zero score is rare) to five for several informants who fulfil them all (Milroy 1982, cited from Romaine 1982a: 144).

Some critics (Maehlum 1987) have noted that social network criteria are biased towards males, especially in working-class and traditional, rural communities. This is likely to cause a 'gender effect'. Questions 3 to 5 above are not appropriate for women who manage homes and children, and their answers yield low network strength indices, yet they may interact strongly with locals in a non-working environment.

Milroy's research in Belfast hoped to show a link between the nature of a speaker's network and his or her language use, using group as well as individual analyses. Cheshire (1982) points out that group analysis and individual analysis are complementary, and reflect different levels of abstraction. The former is more abstract than the latter, and is the primary objective of sociolinguistics, since explanation of individual variation is impossible without first establishing the social significance of linguistic features (1982: 137). Her study of the vernacular speech of Reading confirms Milroy's (1980) findings, that different linguistic features fulfil different social functions. She questions Labov's concept of style, which says that the more attention is paid to speech, the less vernacular style will be used. Her data shows that sometimes an increase in attention to speech yields an increase in non-standard speech. This is due to the speaker's use of linguistic features as markers of vernacular loyalty. It is the speaker's response to the social occasion. Such use represents a *choice* being made in favour of one linguistic form over another, a fact which will be investigated in detail in this book.

In sum then, Milroy claims to find strong evidence to support the notion that a dense, multiplex network structure will predict relative closeness to vernacular norms. She believes that this is because a close-knit network has the capacity to exercise close supervision and control over its members. This concept will become one of the central issues in this book. Milroy's *data*, however, does not show such strong support for the network framework. In the Clonard, only one of the nine linguistic variables correlate with network, in the Hammer two, and in Ballymacarrett, two. In Ballymacarrett, male networks seemed more close-knit than female networks, a difference which did not show in the other two areas. There is, therefore, an interaction between gender and network in her results. Milroy admits that 'a close-knit network structure is not observable in Ballymacarrett independent of other social variables' (Milroy 1982, cited from Romaine 1982a: 151). Taken as a whole, the data for these three areas in Belfast will be discussed in chapter 7.

Other views on networks

Later studies have not always been uncritical of network research:

> [...] neither stratificational analysis nor network analysis *alone* is capable of answering all questions; they must be considered as two approaches to quantifying certain aspects of a complex picture which includes subjective evaluation and other (perhaps as yet unidentified) socio-cultural factors (Lippi-Green 1989: 215).

An important point to remember is that in any attempt to demonstrate a reliable correlation between social and linguistic behaviour, the interpretation and manner of quantification of the social structure will determine the degree of success attainable (Weinreich, Labov, and Herzog 1968, cited in Lippi-Green 1989: 215). Lippi-Green is also critical of class-based studies:

Early sociolinguistics was constrained by its own (admittedly successful) concentration on socio-economic measurement of status. Initial attempts to transfer this methodology to smaller communities in German-speaking Europe usually failed, primarily because of what seems to be a lack of familiarity with methodology for *non-urban* communities (Lippi-Green 1989: 215, my emphasis).

According to Lippi-Green there are three criteria to measuring communication networks:

• Is the network *closed* or *open*? This tests whether ego's networks extend outside the established networks in the community.
• The *density* of the network. Do the relevant contacts all know each other?
• The *multiplexity* of the network. What is the nature of the links? Are two contacts colleagues, relatives and friends, for example?

She does believe that in the idealised small, bounded community with high degrees of multiplexity and high-density ratios, everyone has a conception of everyone else's social network. Following Boissevain on social networks, she agrees that there is often a homogeneity of values, and the degree of consensus on norms is high, all resulting in a high level of social control (Boissevain 1974: 72, cited from Lippi-Green 1989: 217). The inability of the fieldworker to deal with whole networks for mechanical reasons does not impair the calculation of such strength scales. On the contrary, it brings into focus the distinctions between whole network density and 'key *sectors* or *clusters* of the network – that is, compartments associated with specific fields of activity' (Milroy 1980: 137, in Lippi-Green 1989: 217).

Lippi-Green notes of Milroy's work in the urban neighbourhoods of Belfast that, while it provides a departure point, there is still a 'practical and methodological gap between a study of this type and one of an isolated mountain village of 800 persons' (p. 218). As I shall later show, the Huntly data supports this cautious viewpoint of the social network framework for rural communities.

She maintains that age and sex are indicators of group allegiance about which the individual has no choice, and within which one must function. However, the openness, density and multiplexity of one's social networks are more about the individual as a relatively free agent. One participates in the social life of a community to the extent one wishes, but one cannot control the family or community into which one is born. Of course, one can decide whether to stay in the community and about strengthening ties with it. This viewpoint supports what has been said in this study about the freedom of choice available to individuals. People are born in a certain generation, and belong to one of the two sexes, but have a lot of say in the extent to which they build community ties and conform to community language norms.

On the subject of networks, it seems from Lippi-Green's data that integration in the *workplace* may be more significant than in the 'involuntary' groups such as age and sex. Perhaps this is because workplace networks seem to be stronger norm enforcement mechanisms than families, as they are a better indicator of voluntary community integration (Lippi-Green 1989: 225).

Lippi-Green finds that those males who are best integrated into the community are most loyal to its conservative language norms. She also finds that social network integration alone, or the interaction of integration and age and sex, cannot explain or predict linguistic behaviour, and that subjective evaluation from the perspective of the individual can clarify many of the problems of the quantitative analysis of group behaviour. She finds that integration into the network, when considered along with age and education, was a significant predictor of whether women's speech would be conservative or innovative. Men's speech, however, correlated mostly with the sub-part of voluntary associations.

She notes that previous insights into the social matrices of rural communities were constrained by the urban model, causing theoretical and methodological hindrances. She does not clarify what she means by 'subjective evaluation from the perspective of the individual', however. Perhaps asking the individual questions about his or her mental orientation to the local speech community, in order to try to see things from his or her perspective would help a researcher to do just that. This is what has been done in the Huntly study.

Later revisions: the concept of 'weak ties'

In a later paper, J. Milroy and L. Milroy (1985) write that variability of a structured and regular kind is normal in language use, and is critical to an understanding of language change. They refer to two of Labov's claims:

1. Speakers who lead sound change are those with high social class scores.
2. Among persons of equal status, the most advanced speakers are those with the largest number of local contacts within the neighbourhood, yet who have at the same time the highest proportion of their acquaintances outside the neighbourhood.

The Milroys disagree with the first point. They focus almost entirely upon the position of linguistic innovators in localised networks which are made up of persons of roughly equal status (1985: 343). They do agree with the second point, as the following extract shows:

the diffusion of change is accomplished by those people who have many ties within the close-knit community, and also a relatively large number of outside contacts (Milroy and Milroy 1985: 343).

They do not rely, as Labov does, on the notion of status or class. Their framework suggests that 'innovations flow from one group to another through "weak" network links' (Milroy and Milroy 1985: 344). This framework offers a practical solution to an aspect of the actuation problem, and as such is concerned with *speaker* innovation.

They go on to say that sociolinguistics, like historical linguistics, uses a type of comparative method, though at a micro-, rather than macro-level. The important difference is that sociolinguistics is fundamentally rooted in the present, and it is therefore possible, in principle, to observe more easily both the linguistic and social embedding of observed changes.

There is a tradition in some branches of linguistics of separating languages from speakers, and looking for explanations for change in languages as systems. Sociolinguistics starts from the standpoint that 'the study of social motivations constitutes an important part of any possible explanation of change' (Milroy and Milroy 1985: 345). The Milroys claim it is 'not languages that innovate; it is speakers who innovate' (p. 345). A change brought into a language system by a speaker may then go on to impact the whole system, like the Great English Vowel Shift. Here movements in other vowels were motivated by the language system, but it could also be said that it is the speakers who are motivated to keep vowels distinct within the system (p. 348). This is the point where there is least support in the paper for the influence of the network, which is effectively a speaker-external factor. If, as the writers state, it is speakers who innovate, and other speakers who adopt[10] innovations, then surely this allows that they have the power and the desire to do so, which is a speaker-internal factor.

The writers re-iterate their earlier findings that, generally, the closer the individual's ties to a local community network, the more likely he is to approximate to vernacular norms, as a close-knit network functions as a norm-enforcement mechanism. In their data from Belfast, a tendency to select vernacular (often conservative, rural Ulster Scots) linguistic variants is associated with a relatively high level of integration into the community, at least in one of the suburbs studied. However, as was pointed out above, the causal link which is proposed may not hold absolutely. Speakers have a great many linguistic intuitions and abilities, and are able to control a wide range of dialect, accent, and style variation. There may be other important preconditions involved in the process of language change, and speakers have the ability to use various linguistic forms.

The Milroys believe that social network structure is implicated in processes of linguistic change in at least two ways:

> First, a strong close-knit network may be seen to function as a conservative force, resisting pressures to change from outside the network. Those speakers whose ties are weakest are those who approximate least closely to vernacular norms, and are most exposed to pressures for change originating from outside the network. Second, [...] the vernacular speakers associated most strongly with the innovation are [...] those for whom the vowel functions least prominently as a network marker (Milroy, and Milroy 1985: 362).

They do admit that:

> ... there must be additional conditions, and at least one of these is psycho-social: this is that speakers from the receptor community want to identify for some reason with speakers from the donor community (Milroy and Milroy 1997: 205).

The Milroys also concede that social network analysis is limited by its superior ability to handle close-knit ties as opposed to weak, diffuse types of network structure, because of the fact that personal networks are in principle unbounded. Close-knit networks are located mainly at the top and bottom of society (at least in Britain), with the majority of socially and geographically mobile people located between these two points. For close-knit, territorially defined groups, however, they write that it is possible to treat personal networks as if they were bounded groups, and these close-knit ties are an important mechanism of language maintenance.

The Milroys make a distinction between *innovators* and *early adopters* of an innovation. They refer to other studies, linguistic and non-linguistic, which show that innovators are marginal to the group adopting the innovation. It is the very weakness of their ties that allows marginal members to bring in the innovation. They do not strongly experience the norm-enforcing effect of the group, whereas they are more likely to be susceptible to outside influence. Early adopters, on the other hand, are central to the group, have strong ties within it, and conform highly to group norms. As a general condition, the Milroys propose:

Linguistic change is slow to the extent that the relevant populations are well established and bound by strong ties, whereas it is rapid to the extent that weak ties exist in populations (Milroy and Milroy 1985: 375).

Their conclusion is that innovations are transmitted from one group to another by persons having weak ties with both groups. Furthermore, where the proportion of weak links in a community is high, linguistic change is likely to be rapid. It is also necessary to distinguish between *innovation* (which is the act of one or more speakers) and *change* (which is the reflex of a successful innovation in the language system).

Social class and social network: an integrated framework?

The Milroys' later paper (1992) supplies an explanation for how it comes about that people find themselves in certain types of social network. The argument is that people are precipitated into modes of production by macro-level social, economic and political factors, and that these modes of production then yield different strengths of community-based ties, which in turn cause differences in language use. In this view, the network becomes the 'all seeing eye', exerting a controlling and supervisory influence over its members' behaviour. The power of people to make choices in all areas of their lives, including language use, is not given much attention.

The Milroys argue that a *conflict* model is necessary in order to explain the process of linguistic change. They posit that linguistic variation and change are best accounted for by a framework that emphasises competing social values, and in this paper they attempt to integrate the social network framework with the social class model. They argue that the structure and social function of both strong and weak network types needs to be considered in order to do this. Their conclusions from their Belfast work are discussed above. They feel, however, that analyses of variation based on social class are limited when the sub-groups are economically marginal, not distributed evenly with respect to class, or live in territorially well defined neighbourhoods (1992: 6). The original (1980) work has been refined somewhat in this paper. The Milroys acknowledge that some studies (e.g. Cochran *et al*. 1990) have shown that close-knit networks are found mostly in rural areas nowa-days, with urban (especially middle-class) areas having more loose-knit networks, with impersonal ties and greater social distance. While they do not oppose this view, they do point out that, while the networks of socially and geographically mobile persons are more geographically dispersed and less kin-based, they can also paradoxically be larger, more supportive and more affectively satisfying (Milroy, and Milroy 1992: 7). Moreover, highly educated and mobile persons can be more selective in their choice of contacts than those embedded in a localised solidarity network, which can be oppressive as well as supportive. Though they re-iterate their belief that in any close-knit network, a weakening of the structure will allow more outside innovation and influence, they acknowledge the problems involved in trying to *demonstrate* the effect of weak ties. They claim that network analysis is effective at explaining the effects of strong ties, though they concede that it cannot easily demonstrate the effects of weak ties using quanti-tative methods.

The theoretical implications of the weak-tie framework are numerous. Mewett (1982) argues that class differences in small communities begin to emerge over time as the proportion of multiplex relations declines. This suggests the development of a sociolinguistic model with two levels: one where small-scale network structures have individuals embedded and acting 'with intent' in their daily lives, and the other where large-scale social class structures determine relationships of power at the institutional level (Milroy and Milroy 1992: 16). This model proposes local stability and cohesion at the network level versus overall fragmentation and conflict at the social-class level, and that the two types of analysis are in fact complemen-tary. The Milroys do admit that the model is more suited to urban communities (p. 17).

Life Modes

The Milroys introduce Thomas Højrup's (1983) concept of 'Life Modes', and attempt to integrate it into their framework, together with social class. It will be useful to summarise Højrup's paper at this point, before going on to examine how the Milroy's have incorporated it into their framework. Højrup's (1983) notion of 'Life Modes' was developed in Denmark for social anthropology, but can be useful for sociolinguistics. This concept sees all people belonging to one of three modes of production or 'life modes':

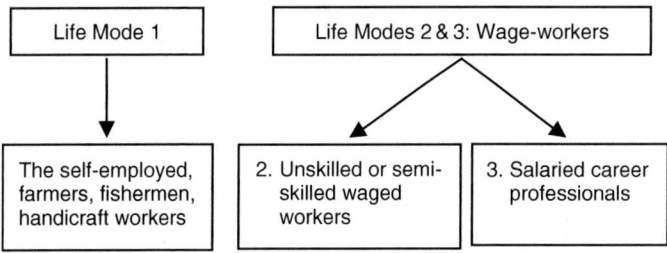

Figure 1   Højrup's (1983) concept of Life Modes

The first is that of the self-employed, where the person is involved in what he terms 'simple commodity production'. This includes farmers, fishermen, 'liberal trades', handicrafts, and partnership companies (Højrup 1983: 20). The second and third form part of what he terms the 'wage-workers' life modes. Life Mode 2 has to do with wage-earning workers in the capitalist mode of production. These people possess neither the means of production as property, nor the qualifications to begin and control the production process. Included in this category are unskilled and semi-skilled workers, who work only in order to obtain the means with which to live a meaningful life during their free time. The third type includes qualified, educated people, responsible for other workers, those who monitor and control the production process, and who attend to organisation, management and marketing. These people are not paid according to an hourly rate, but usually a salary for their abilities. In this career- or success-oriented life mode there is less sense of solidarity with colleagues than is found with the wage earners of life mode two (I return to this notion below). The Milroys refer to Højrup's notion of life modes as a theory:

which can explicitly link a network analysis of subgroups within society to an analysis of social structure at the political, institutional, and economic levels (p. 19).

Højrup's life modes theory sees subgroups as the effect of 'fundamental societal structures which split the population into fundamentally different life modes' (Højrup 1983: 47). The Milroys suggest that the different types of network structure seem to *arise from* the differences in life mode of individuals. Højrup's concept of life mode, like that of network, is a structural one, and the characteristics of one life mode are determined by its contrast to the others (Milroy and Milroy 1992: 22). The Milroys emphasise the conflict-based notion of class, rather than the Labovian notion, which is consensus-based. The main thrust of the article is therefore that there are macro-level social, political and economic structures in society, which *produce* different modes of production, or life modes, and that these in turn *produce* different types of network, and that these then *produce* different types of social (including linguistic) behaviour. The earlier absent explanation for just how a person 'falls' into a particular type of network is now supplied, but whether this framework has adequate explanatory power is not clear. This question is taken up in chapter 7.

Other social factors

Eckert (2000) writes about her long-term study of the speech of teenagers in Belten High School. While acknowledging the importance of social networks, she believes that the notion of *community of practice* is more important. Social meaning is made as people construct social relations and views of the communities and people around them, and this meaning-making takes place both within and beyond dense networks (Eckert 2000: 35). Eckert finds Lave and Wenger's (1979) construct community of practice a valuable analytical tool.

A community of practice is an aggregate of people who come together around some enterprise. United by this common enterprise, people come to develop and share ways of doing things, ways of talking, beliefs, values – in short, practices – as a function of their joint engagement in activity. [...] The value of [this concept] is in the focus it affords on the mutually constitutive nature of the individual, group, activity, and meaning (Eckert 2000: 35).

Eckert believes that this concept will replace current constructs, as it focuses on the day-to-day co-construction of individual and community identity, emphasising common practice as an explanation for linguistic behaviour.

One of the first points Eckert makes about the 'Jocks' and 'Burnouts'[11] in her Belten High study is that

> representing opposing *orientations* to school and to the local area, the jocks are an institutional, corporate culture while the burnouts are a personal, locally oriented culture (Eckert 2000: 3, emphasis mine).

This notion of 'orientation' has shown itself to be very important in the Huntly study. The jocks and burnouts 'embody opposing class-related ideologies, norms, trajectories, and practices of all sorts' (p. 3). These 'ideologies', though probably not class-related, are essentially what have been measured by the MENURB score in the Huntly study. Not only are people involved in social network structures of differing densities and multiplexities, but they also have orientations to these networks or groups, and the latter also seems to have important implications for social behaviour. Eckert makes it clear that variation is a social *practice*, rather than a structure:

> A theory of variation as social practice sees speakers as constituting, rather than representing, broad social categories, and it sees speakers as constructing, as well as responding to, the social meaning of variation (Eckert 2000: 3).

Eckert also refers to the important notion of *linguistic market* (Bourdieu and Boltanski 1975, cited from Eckert 2000: 13). In this concept, the value of a speaker's 'verbal offerings', and how much they will be noticed and heeded, depends very much on which linguistic variety they are encoded in. The production of a particular language form, in order to maximise one's value in the 'marketplace', is central here. A speaker may produce standard or near-standard language in order to gain employment in a company in a city, but in the same way, another may produce a local vernacular in order to be accepted as one of the in-group. Again, this has links with the notion of overt versus covert prestige (see 2.6).

On the subject of the 'speech community', Eckert agrees with Mitchell (1986: 74) that we should avoid seeing the community as a static unit, a view which precludes change. Such a community is simply created by individuals, in order to provide them with a framework in which to solve day-to-day problems. These problems change, and so do the communities. Eckert sees networks as fluid and ever changing:

> But networks are only more or less dense or multiplex, and 'leakage' is no doubt crucial to the formation of the vernacular. For while people may concentrate their social and linguistic activity, they also get around, engaging in a variety of endeavours and in a variety of communities (Eckert 2000: 34).

As we saw above, Milroy and Milroy (1985) have focused on weak ties as a source of linguistic innovation across community boundaries. Eckert claims that the linguistic influence in such contacts depends on the perceived identity of the speakers and on the social significance of their speech features. This perception is in turn mediated by the hearer's closer contacts. This has implications for the framework. A condition, or conditions, would have to be built in, that allowed for a more complex view of weak ties as automatic sources of innovation. Perhaps they should be seen as *potential* sources of innovation from outside the network, but that the acceptance of such innovations would be conditional.

On the subject of style, Eckert emphasises that it is

> at the same time an individual and communal endeavour. It is a tangible means of negotiating one's meaning in the world. And it relies on, and contributes to, the styles and meanings of groups and categories in the world (2000: 41).

In other words, stylistic variation is where social meaning and identity are negotiated. Your place in relation to others, your perspective on the world, your view of your value in the system, are 'constructed collectively, even as others are involved in the same construction themselves' (Eckert 2000: 39). Engagement in the world, for Eckert, is a constant process of identity construction, and variationist studies should focus on the relation between variation and identity. Importantly, she goes to the heart of the matter as far as fieldwork and research analysis go:

> While the ethnographer does not have access to identity, we do have access to some of the practices that people attend to in working out their meaning in the community. Individual identity is not constructed in a vacuum; it is co-constructed with group identities (Eckert 2000: pp. 41–42).

The north-east identity is very important to locals in the Buchan and Gordon areas, as Macafee and McGarrity's (1999) research on attitudes shows. The concept of constructing individual and group identities is extremely valuable in making sense of the sociolinguistic variation we as researchers find. Eckert calls for a greater focus on the individual, rather than on groups and group norms, and on social *practice*, rather than on structure. Variationists have seemed to concentrate on the significance of groups of speakers who have been judged to be similar according to selected criteria, where the individual is seen to represent the group or category, and to be a 'performer of group norms'. She feels that a speaker should not be seen as a clone, but as an *agent* in a process of convention-making (Eckert 2000: 44, and see Sealey and Carter 2001 in section 2.9). This agrees with the view promoted in this book, that individuals have choices of which linguistic style to use, and of which identity to construct.

In suggesting a focus on communities of practice, Eckert claims not to be proposing a new social variable to be included in analyses of variation, but rather a 'different way of seeing the relation between social meaning and human aggregations' (2000: 172). She feels that it is not merely engagement in day-to-day activities, but attitudes towards these activities that construct identities and links between people. Relations with others in a community are negotiated jointly within the community of practice, and it is in this process of negotiation that linguistic style is constructed and refined (p. 172). She sees the network *cluster* as being the place where people are more intensively engaged in the construction of meaning with each other than with those outside. In these meaningful interactions and construction of identity and style, 'peer pressure', including linguistic pressure, is found (p. 177).

The Belten High data shows that it is those girls with the highest level of involvement in the institution (and less social involvement) who are the most conservative in their speech style (p. 192). In other words, when the direction of change is towards the (normally urban) vernacular, as in Belten High, access to the vernacular can only be gained through integration into local social networks. Lippi-Green's data from the Alps, where the direction of (slow) change is *away* from the vernacular, leads her to posit that integration in the workplace is more significant as a conserving force than integration in the 'involuntary' groups such as age and sex. As was mentioned above, perhaps this is because workplace networks are stronger norm enforcement mechanisms than families, as they are a better indicator of *voluntary* community integration (Lippi-Green 1989: 225). Indeed they are communities of practice (Eckert 2000: 193).

In sum then, Eckert finds that 'the knowledgeable construction of local styles is a function of integration into local networks and access to local information' (p. 210). She also finds that, in general, linguistic influence takes place without explicit comment, although there is a certain amount of conscious negotiation, where metalinguistic comments are made, such as high school students discussing 'cool' ways to say things. This influence must rely on access to changing styles, and a sense of entitlement to adopt them. Those speakers in her study who do not have access to information from the dominant people in the school are likely to be conservative or anomalous in their speech.

There are some variables in her study which carry no urban associations and which are widespread in the region. These carry a more general style, and are available by virtue of their widespread distribution, to all speakers no matter how marginalized. Those speakers willing to use a more flamboyant style (normally girls) are the ones who use these the most. This has important implications for the concept of 'access to local information' mentioned above. The availability of particular features to the individual may differ in certain types of community. This is discussed further in chapter 7.

2.3   Life Modes updated

Most of the people in the Huntly study belong to (Højrup's) Life Mode 1 or 3. The question is: what are the implications of Højrup's concept for studies of language conservation and change? In its original form, it is mainly sociological. If we take the model a step further, and ask *what effect* these life modes may have on the mental orientation[12] of individuals to their local communities, and, by extension, on their language use, it may take on greater significance. The Danish linguist Inge-Lise Pedersen has done just that.

Pedersen's (1994) notion of life modes is particularly useful for comparing the Danish situation with that in Scotland. Denmark has developed from a dialectal society into a relatively uniform linguistic community, *viewed from the outside*. Prior to industrialisation and urbanisation, the country could be divided into a number of fairly homogeneous dialect areas, each diverging greatly from the others (Pedersen 1994: 87). Today the geographically determined differences have diminished, and instead there is much linguistic variation within individual areas. Marx's concept of class distinction and the traditional model of social stratification are both unable to account for the variation within these areas, and the connection between educational background/ occupation and language use provides no clear picture either.[13]

Pedersen therefore, like Milroy, has searched for other ways of grouping speakers in an attempt to explain the phenomenon. She believes that *urbanisation* is the major factor determining language or register choice, even more than social stratification. She uses this term in the sense of 'mental urbanisation', i.e. the spread of a specifically urban *pattern of behaviour* that extends beyond physical urbanisation (Pedersen 1994: 87). She claims to rely upon the nature of the network in order to measure the degree of urbanisation, since it is a common assumption that the networks of those who live in cities are of a different nature from the networks found in rural societies. However, it is not clear how she justifies this, as social networks are a structural concept, whereas mental urbanisation is subjective: surely individuals with similar network structures will have differing degrees of mental urbanisation? At the level below the network, that of the individual, she finds the concept of social network to be inadequate. She claims to rely on the notion of life mode as an *analytical tool* to show that language variation at the individual level can be accounted for as 'an expression of the tensions which exist between the person's life mode and his or her objective social status', though it is not clear exactly how she goes about this in any rigorous manner.

In the Huntly study, it has become clear that Pedersen's notion could be useful, providing it is developed in such a way as to move beyond the subjectivity it clearly involves. Whereas before the building of transport links such as the railway line from Aberdeen to Inverness and the A96, many villagers seldom, if ever, journeyed into Aberdeen, many do nowadays. The friction of distance, a term discussed in 1.3, has been reduced, and people may be more open to mental urbanisation. Their earlier conceptions of cities and their inhabitants may change as a result of this mobility, and they may become less resistant to the social behaviour patterns emanating from the city. The resulting process of mental urbanisation may mean that the individual becomes less resistant to urban speech norms, and even comes to favour them over local norms, which may take on increased connotations of rural backwardness. Those individuals who resist such mental urbanisation have proved to be more resistant to linguistic influence from the city as well, as will be shown in chapter 5.

Urbanisation, in the mental sense, has been transmitted by means of mass communication, such as television, to the population in the rural areas. Cultural uniformity has been advanced as the culture of the city/metropolis has spread and dissolved the rural communities with their local ties (Pedersen 1994: 88, although see also Trudgill 1986 below). Pedersen has compared this degree of mental urbanisation with the linguistic variation that is found in communities which were once purely rural, and found a correlation, although she has not quantified this. In this study, mental life mode has been quantified and used as an independent variable for the analysis of the linguistic data.

Rural life modes

The traditional agricultural family with its rural life mode is character-ised by integration in production and a lack of sharp distinction between work and leisure time. Survival and the possibility of passing the productive mechanism to the next generation are highly important. Kinship ties often exist with other families in the area, and goods are often exchanged. There is an orientation towards a nearby town, par-ticipation in local club activities, and local friends and acquaintances. The entire family ideology is one of mutual responsibility, and qualities such as endurance, responsibility, independence and co-operation are highly valued. The farm is what life revolves around, and what gives independence to its owners.

Urban life modes

Urban life modes are tied to a means of industrial production. Here work is detached from family life, and separated from the home spatially and temporally. Leisure time is spent in the home, and the family has no function in the organisation of the productive apparatus. The family delegates tasks such as child-minding and food production to outsiders, and one does not have to associate with one's neighbours. The worker and career person share these aspects. The two are differ-ent in that the *worker* (especially the man) sharply divides working and leisure time, and the latter gives life its meaning. People at work do not usually form part of one's social group, or meet one's family for social activities. At work, one's ideal is 'solidarity' with the other workers against the 'others', the bosses. The *career life mode* lacks these sharp contrasts between work and leisure. Here people refer to themselves as part of the company, and often work overtime without extra pay. It is their work which makes life worth living for these people, and they are reasonably free to manage their affairs *in* their work. Here dedication and ambition are highly important (Pedersen 1994: 90).

Composite life modes

The changing material circumstances of rural people have been seen as the cause of their mental urbanisation. Life mode analysis shows that it is not the case that these people are passive recipients of this influence. Many commuters take a job in an urban centre in order to maintain a rural lifestyle. This is when their life modes become complex and *composite*, even if they are still ideologically determined by the rural life mode (Pedersen 1994: 90). The impression gained is that Pedersen does not successfully marry the structural and subjective elements involved, but the message is clear: individuals, regardless of where they have been placed in society by macro-level socio-economic factors, retain a subjectivity, which will influence their social behaviour at the individual level.

Pedersen goes on to say that these people with composite life modes are more reliable at work and less supportive of pay disputes. They are farmers and remain so. This may be a transitional stage in which more and more of the rural lifemode will be displaced by the urban one, but Pedersen suspects that it is a reasonably stable situation which can last the lifetime of the individual and even be passed on to the next generation. She believes that life modes are not specifiable to the point where one can measure them directly, but they can illuminate linguistic and other behavioural patterns within sociologically defined groups. Below is a diagram of Pedersen's concept of the different life modes, with Højrup's given in brackets:

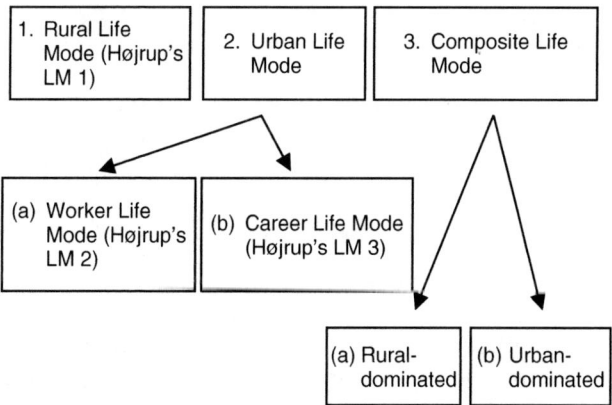

Figure 2   Pedersen's 1994 concept of life mode as mental orientation

Most of the boxes represent structural entities. Boxes 3(a) and (b) represent a subjective evaluation. In the Huntly study, most people have either Pedersen's life mode 1 or 3(a) or (b), and the effect of this upon their use of the dialect will be examined in detail below.

Language and network

Pedersen does not dispute the results of other network studies, which show that networks can function as norm-reinforcing mechanisms (especially in urban settings), but otherwise claims to use the notion of network differently (Pedersen 1994: 99). L. Milroy's (1980) concept of network is that the very *structure* of the network is significant, and she estimates the relative density and multiplexity of the network to show that they correspond to the local linguistic characteristics of the speaker. For Pedersen, it is partly the structure of the network, but mainly the influence of network *interaction* on language use that is most important, seen from the perspective that rural and urban societies differ in their network structure. She claims to place more value on the interactional criteria of the network than Milroy, but her network indicators are not significantly different from those of Milroy, as can be seen below (the scores allocated are either zero or one).

1. Family relationship with at least two other households in the parish.
2. Work within the parish or together with at least two others from the parish.
3. Membership of a local group (organised or non-organised).
4. The cultivation of leisure activities together with at least two others from the neighbourhood or with at least two colleagues.
5. Both parents raised in the parish.

This leaves Pedersen's position rather unclear, although the basis is provided for a model to be developed around the concept of mental urbanisation as a contributory factor in the process of language change.

The implications for language use

Pedersen differentiates between urban, rural, and composite life modes (Pedersen 1994: 106). The latter can be dominated by either a rural or an urban mentality or orientation plus the usual structural criteria. In her study, the informants who, in her opinion, have rurally dominated composite life modes (a subjective phenomenon) generally have higher dialect scores than other informants with *the same network scores*. There are many such cases in the Huntly data, as will be seen in chapters 5 and 6.

Pedersen's data show (at least as far as the men are concerned) that there is a connection between dialect use and mental urbanisation, or at least the way a speaker feels about the local versus the supra-local group, which cannot be explained by network indicators (p. 107). She posits that life mode cannot be quantified, nor analysed quantitatively as a variable, but rather she sees it as a picture one can build up of an informant by using an extended interview. In this study I have designed a questionnaire, and shown that one can in fact arrive at an index score for life mode and use it effectively as an analytical tool for language change. The degree of mental urbanisation of a speaker can be measured by asking specific questions, the answers to which are graded along a five-point scale. The resulting index score can then be tested against dialect maintenance, just as with social network indices.

Pedersen concludes that linguistic standardisation is a 'mechanical' consequence of the transition from a rural to an urban occupation (p. 112). She believes that the degree of mental urbanisation can, to a certain extent, be understood through an analysis of the speaker's network character. She notes that this, however, does not always suffice, as some variation is left unaccounted for. Some speakers choose to signal their rural ties by using dialect features in a handful of words, where others with the same network indicators, but urban-dominated composite life modes, do not. She is convinced that linguistic groups are not automatically the same as social groups, and that her notion of life modes, with its emphasis on both a material and an ideological aspect, can lead to a better understanding of the relationship between language and social identity (p. 113). This concept of including a mental component in a quantitative analysis of dialect loss has becomes important for the Huntly study, as the data will show in chapters 5 and 6. For the purposes of discerning between Højrup's Life Modes and this concept, the term mental urbanisation will be used in this study. In order to ease the handling of the variables in the spreadsheet programme, the names of the variables have been contracted; mental urbanisation becoming MENURB.[14]

2.4   Exocentric and endocentric change

Røyneland (2000) argues that language change in cities is endocentric, or internally generated, while that in peripheral areas is exocentric, or contact-induced. She writes that the role of adolescents differs in the two sorts of area: in cities, adolescents are more non-standard than older generations; in peripheral areas they are more standard.

This agrees with what has been shown in many urban studies, and in the Huntly data, as will be seen in chapters 4 and 5.

Andersen (1988, 1989) distinguishes between 'innovation' and 'change'. He believes that any element of usage which differs from previous usage is an innovation, and that the term 'change' has become confused in linguistics. He believes that initial innovations can be divided into three categories: *adaptive* (including contact innovation), which is externally motivated, *evolutive*, which is internally motivated, and *spontaneous* innovation, which is internally motivated. In the Huntly study, innovations in the form of Scottish Standard English variants of (morpho-) phonological and lexical items have been entering the dialect as adaptive innovations for generations now, as will be seen in chapters 4 and 5. As Romaine (1989) puts it:

> The introduction of a new variant into a speech community does not in itself constitute a change; it is only when others adopt it that it spreads and is transmitted from one generation to the next, and change takes place (1989: 201).

Central and peripheral areas

Central and peripheral areas have different patterns of adoption and diffusion. The 'centrifugal' force favours the levelling of differences between speech areas, and the 'centripetal' force favours the elaboration of local features (Andersen 1988: 39, cited from Røyneland 2000). Andersen calls communities characterised by centrifugal forces *exocentric*, and those characterised by centripetal forces *endocentric*. Peripheral areas are mostly exocentric, while urban areas are mostly endocentric (Røyneland 2000). The changes under way in the Doric are system-externally motivated contact innovations. The role of adolescents in endocentric urban areas is different from their role in exocentric peripheral areas. Adolescents in rural areas use more standard forms than their elders, because of dialect levelling, whereas those in urban areas use fewer standard forms, experimenting with features which challenge standard norms, and which in time can become accepted as standard norms. This is supported by Røyneland's data from Røros and Oslo.

2.5   Cognitive Dissonance

The mental component introduced above is similar to some of the concepts introduced in the theory of Cognitive Dissonance (Festinger 1957,

Omdal 1994). This states that when attitudes and behaviour do not match up in a particular individual, with time one of these factors must be changed in order to re-establish 'harmony' (Omdal 1994: 144). Therefore, if an individual has a negative attitude towards a local linguistic norm, or towards the rural area lived in, or towards the local people, he or she may consciously or unconsciously try to modify his or her speech in the direction of the standard. Should this prove difficult due to linguistic features of one or both of the varieties, the speaker may later abandon these linguistic efforts and slowly change his or her attitude in favour of the local norm or area lived in, thus achieving harmony'.[15]

Problems

Omdal (1994) writes about the relationship between the various types of language attitude and language use. He finds it difficult to make straightforward statements about the strength of the relationship between these two. In Wales, for example, Mees and Collins (1999) show that there is a large difference between reported attitudes and actual linguistic behaviour. This mirrors Hindley's (1990) study in the Republic of Ireland, where attitudes are reported as being highly favourable to Irish Gaelic in all surveys conducted, and there is overwhelming support for the continued government support of the language. People want the continuation of the Gaelic final year school requirement into all public sector posts, but most parents recognise the need for pragmatism over patriotism, and send their children to English-medium schools. Fluency in English means they will have a better chance at 'getting on' in life. Despite the fact that real, unmediated attitudes will probably never be truly accessible to us, the theory of Cognitive Dissonance can still help our understanding of attitudes and language use.

The route to harmony

Omdal writes that, for a person to establish harmony at the linguistic level, he or she must have the ability to *implement* the necessary linguistic changes. Should the speaker be unable to do this, then the attitude will have to be changed in the direction of language use (see figure 3 below). For there to be a change in *language use* in the direction of attitudes therefore, the person must be able to identify and control the linguistic features to be acquired, and these features must be 'above the level of conscious awareness', and not too complex (Omdal 1994: 147).

Omdal's study was conducted in Kristiansand in Norway, and is about the speech of migrants from Setesdal, which is an area of archaic dialect speech. Setesdal dialect has not moved as far as other dialects in their development towards phonologically and morphologically simpler systems. Setesdal dialect has prestige for its speakers, but it is a different type of prestige from that associated with Kristiansand speech. Although Omdal finds age to be the strongest predictor of language use, the relationship between language modification and attitude to language modification does exist, if weakly. In his opinion, attitudes would seem to change before language use.

2.6   Language attitudes and language behaviour

Giles et al. (1987) write that

> evaluations of language varieties do not reflect either linguistic or aesthetic qualities so much as the social conventions within speech communities concerning the status and prestige associated with speakers of the varieties (1987: 585).

This is critical to our understanding of the choices people make when evaluating and using particular language varieties or codes.

The authors also write:

> It seems reasonable to propose that when a non-standard speech style is, or becomes, a valued symbol of in-group pride (be it working class, ethnic, occupational), individuals who are strongly committed to their social group membership display evaluative preferences for their own variety (Giles et al. 1987: 587).

This notion will prove important in the discussion of the results of the present study in chapter 7.

As Löw (1997) points out, social psychologists and sociolinguists alike have been very interested in the study of *attitudes*. Although the concept *attitude* has been defined in various ways, a fundamental distinction is the one made between the *mentalist* and the *behaviourist* view of the concept. Mentalists see attitudes as a 'readiness to respond', i.e. an underlying, intervening variable between a stimulus and a response (Agheyisi and Fishman 1970: 138; Fasold 1984: 147, cited from Löw 1997: 6). A typical mentalist definition is the one by Williams (1974: 21): 'Attitude is considered as an internal state aroused by stimulation of some type and which may mediate the organism's subsequent response'. If one adopts this view, attitudes have to be inferred indirectly from actual behaviour or to be elicited via questions. However, as Fasold points out, the first possibility can be criticised for its subjectivity and the second one because the validity of self-reported data is often questionable

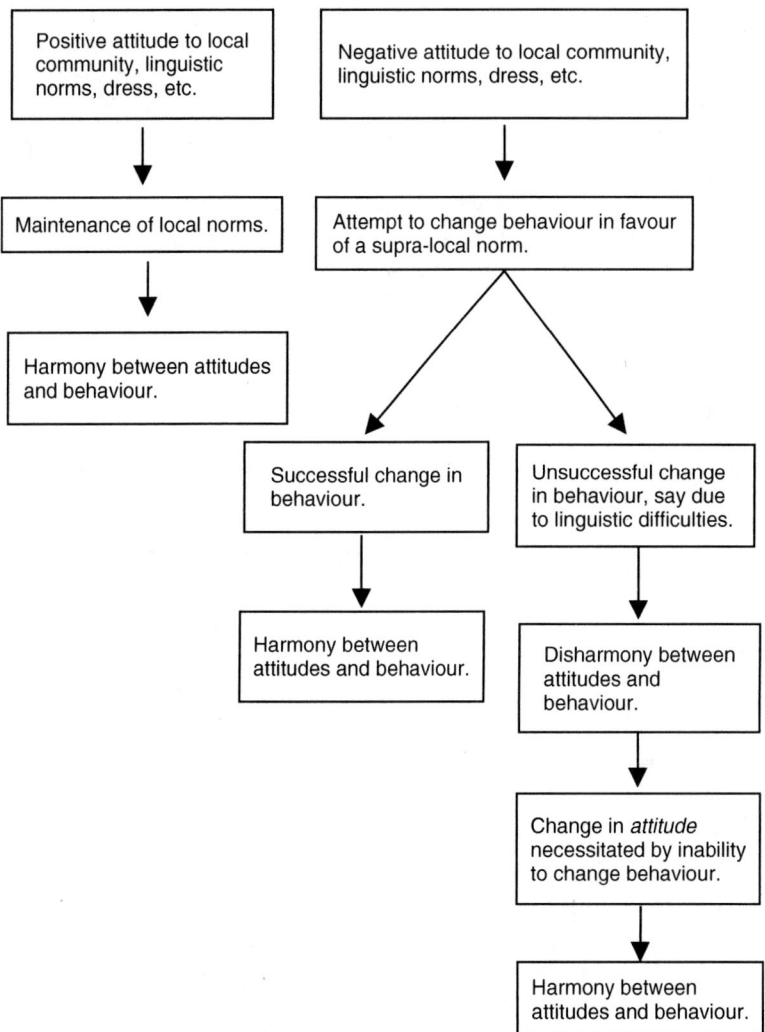

Figure 3 Omdal's concept of the resolution of Cognitive Dissonance

(1984: 147), and so the links between the two are not clear cut. Standard varieties in Britain are usually perceived as reflecting high status and competence, whereas regional (rural) accents score high on integrity and attractiveness, which apparently is linked to a feeling of in-group solidarity they seem to reflect (Edwards 1982: 25, cited from Löw 1997: 7). In the Huntly study, attitudes have both been inferred from behaviour (language use), and elicited via questions.

As mentioned, the link between language attitudes and language behaviour is complex, and many factors may be at play. Ladegaard (2000) has written about the methodological problems faced by researchers. He points to a lack of agreement on the subject, citing Cohen as saying that in most work on attitude-behaviour relations, 'attitudes are always seen as precursors of behaviour, as determinants of how a person will actually behave in his daily affairs', a view which concurs with Fasold (1984) (Cohen 1964: 138, cited in Ladegaard, 2000: 214). He also cites other researchers, such as Wicker (1969: 65), who have an opposing view: 'it is considerably more likely that attitudes will be unrelated or only slightly related to overt behaviours than attitudes will be closely related to actions' (cited in Ladegaard 2000: 215). Ladegaard refers to the notion of the three components of an attitude (see also Breckler (1984)): cognition, emotion and behaviour, calling for experiments to validate this tripartite model. The first component deals with the knowledge of the language varieties concerned, the second with the evaluation of the varieties and their speakers, and the third with variation in linguistic behaviour. Ladegaard questions the validity of the assumptions that some researchers have made, such as 'because subjects co-operate and comply with specific requests given in high prestige speech styles, this is an indication of positive attitudes' (p. 215).

Ladegaard's study attempts to test whether there is a correlation between sex and language use, between sex and attitude, and between attitude and language use. The results of the tests show that the first correlation is statistically significant, and follows the normal pattern: females use more standard language than males. The second test shows a clear relationship between attitudes and linguistic behaviour, looking at the open-ended responses in the attitude questionnaire: males express more positive attitudes to the vernacular than females, and they also use the vernacular more. The third test compares reported attitudes to the recorded speech of an unidentified speaker of the local vernacular, and actual use of the vernacular in the respondent's own speech during the interview. Here there is no correlation at all. This accords with the result for the Huntly study, as will be shown in chapter 4. The correlation between reported attitudes to the dialect, and actual, measured use of the dialect in varied situations is not significant. Ladegaard believes that the questions linguists ask, as well as the methodologies we adopt, are of paramount importance for the results we get (p. 227). His data suggests 'that subjects may have positive attitudes towards a particular variety of speech which, for some reason, they choose not to speak, at least in certain contexts' (loc. cit.). People may feel that the speaker of a vernacular is to be trusted, or has a friendly nature, but may not themselves use the same style, because it would not be socially advantageous. This phenomenon is discussed below in 2.11, which deals with Hindley's (1990) study of language loss in Ireland.

In the Huntly study, many speakers report highly positive attitudes to the vernacular, but the question of whether they actually use it in their own everyday speech will be answered by the data. The section of the questionnaire which deals with mental urbanisation deals with the degree to which the (rural) speaker has become mentally 'urbanised'. The answers to these questions reveal a type of attitude, as one with a negative attitude to the urban centre would most likely not allow himself/herself to become as mentally urbanised as another with a more positive attitude to the city. This may be a way around the problem of trying to test for correlations between attitudes and behaviour, at least for rural studies: a speaker may be asked for his/her attitudes to a local vernacular. S/he may report certain attitudes, but the response may be influenced by the interview context, by *competing motives* (see below), and other factors, which result from, among other things, the way the questions are posed. The focus of the questioning is on language, and this very focus may produce answers which do not reflect the real attitude of the respondent. On the other hand, if the questions posed relate to attitudes to the local community more *generally*, the speaker's underlying attitudes may be obtained more accurately, because the focus is not on language, and the competing motives and other factors mentioned above may not come into play.[16] These attitudes, however, relate to the community as a whole, including the language used, and may give us insights into the speaker's underlying, unexpressed attitudes to even the local vernacular. This may be useful in explaining results of the Huntly study.

Many important factors that may affect behavioural patterns are listed by Ladegaard, following Wicker (1969), who suggests that personal and situational factors are also important. Among *personal* factors Ladegaard lists:

(a) *The subject's verbal, intellectual and social abilities.* A person may express positive attitudes towards a particular variety of speech, but feel (or be) unable to change his/her speech style accordingly.[17]
(b) *Competing motives.* The person may want to be associated with the peer group, but also with the norms of the institutional power structures.[18]

The *situational* factors he lists are:

(a) *Actual or considered presence of peer group members.* Members of the peer group may influence a speaker even when they are not present in the speech event.
(b) *Normative prescriptions of proper behaviour.* These are present in society at all levels, and may influence boys and girls differently.
(c) *The availability of alternative behaviours.* A speaker may be required by, for example, the school system, to use a standard form that s/he has a fairly negative attitude to.
(d) *Expected and/or actual consequences of acts.* How do others perceive the speaker if s/he uses the standard/vernacular?

(adapted from Ladegaard 2000: 228).

The point is also made by Le Page and Tabouret-Keller (1985), who write about the concept of speech as *acts of identity*. The authors see speech acts as acts of projection:

> . . . the speaker is projecting his inner universe, implicitly with the invitation to others to share it, at least insofar as they recognise his language as an accurate symbolisation of the world, and to share his attitude towards the world (Le Page and Tabouret-Keller 1985: 181).

They write that there are constraints upon the individual's ability to create the patterns of linguistic behaviour which resemble the group with which he wishes to be identified (Le Page and Tabouret-Keller 1985: 181). The authors believe that we can only behave according to the behavioural patterns of groups we find it desirable to identify with to the extent that:

1. we can identify the groups
2. we have both adequate access to the groups and ability to analyse their behavioural patterns

3. the motivation to join the groups is sufficiently powerful, and is either reinforced or reversed by feedback from the groups
4. we have the ability to modify our behaviour (p. 182)

The authors write that the third point is by far the most important of the constraints governing linguistic behaviour. Motivation is the area in which the individual has the 'greatest appearance of choice' (p. 184). They write that

> ... there are always linguistic changes in progress, and it is possible for the individual to adopt or not to adopt these changes, to practise identification with some, and distancing from other, perceived groups (Le Page and Tabouret-Keller 1985: 184).

I return to this point throughout this book.

Ladegaard justly points out that correlation does not automatically mean causation. Other factors may be at work, which cause a person to behave in a certain way (2000: 228). He believes that correlations suggest that attitude is a predictor of behaviour, but that research still has a number of problems. Researchers should not rely on self-reported language use, but should endeavour to record actual language use. The context of the interview should be taken into account, as people accommodate to their audience, and bilinguals or bi-dialectals can code-shift. Language attitudes are able to predict at least broad behavioural patterns, but the link between the two is complex (Ladegaard 2000: 230). It is very important for researchers in the field to take this into account. In this study, correlations, even though statistically significant, between sociological factors and language use, will *not* be seen as *causes* of language change or lack of it, but rather as some of the necessary preconditions for allowing change. The actual changes will probably be caused by a number of preconditions operating together, such as language-internal, phonetically natural causes, language contact phenomena, etc.

Macafee and McGarrity (1999) attempt to correlate language attitudes in Aberdeen with social variables and with language maintenance. The experiment is limited to a test of lexical recognition of 96 weather-related items, which the authors admit is a rather crude proficiency test. The authors write that Scots has low status[19] in Glasgow and Edinburgh, but that as we move north the anglicising influence is felt less. People in the north east are proudly Scottish, and the local Scots dialect is held in high esteem, being spoken, at least on some occasions, by individuals at all social levels (Macafee and McGarrity 1999: 166). Scots is perceived as a separate entity from English, not just 'incorrect' English. Their experiment yields three attitudinal scores for language: defensiveness, positiveness, and participation. The lexical scoring system was as follows: 0 = no knowledge, 1 = passive knowledge, 2 = rare use, 3 = occasional use, 4 = frequent use. Of course, the weakness in this type of questioning is that the researcher cannot know whether *reported* use is an accurate reflection of *actual* use.

The analysis reveals only a few correlations, all of which are positive:

- Use with Positiveness (0.333)
- Use with Participation (0.509)
- Occasional use with Participation (0.440) (Macafee & McGarrity 1999: 174)

Their conclusions show very few significant relationships between attitude and the pre-determined social factors of age, sex, education and occupation. They feel that this could be because *unidentified extra-linguistic factors* are at work, and that their experiment also measures 'some unknown aspects of life experience that do not coincide neatly with age, education or occupation' (Macafee and McGarrity 1999: 174). The language attitudes, too, do not explain lexical decline. Attitudes are largely positive, yet the traditional vocabulary is rapidly disappearing from use. The authors believe that this may be due, at least in part, to the fact that the respondents were urban Aberdonians, and that attitudes were reported relative to the idealised rural dialect. Language loyalty, therefore, they find particularly strong in the north-east of Scotland, but the correlations between it and language use are not significant. This will be compared with the results of the questionnaire on attitudes to the dialect in the Huntly study. The unidentified extra-linguistic factors referred to above have been tantalisingly out of reach for researchers.

Macaulay (1997) writes about the importance of language attitudes in sociolinguistic research, but acknowledges the problems faced by researchers in determining these attitudes accurately. Various methods have been applied, such as Labov's (1966a) Index of Linguistic Insecurity, those that elicit forced, or scaled choice responses, and those that use the responses to open-ended questions (Macaulay 1997: 45). He admits that none of these is completely reliable, and obtaining reliable information about a speaker's attitude towards his or her own speech remains critical for research. Macaulay seriously doubts Labov's assertion that New Yorkers have 'linguistic self-hatred', and that the city is a 'sink of negative prestige'. Macaulay finds it paradoxical that a community should hold such a negative view of its speech, while *maintaining* a form that asserts their community identity (1997: 47). This is again evidence of the covert/overt prestige dichotomy at work. In Macaulay's Glasgow study, remarks on language, which were elicited or freely volunteered, were used in the analysis. These revealed clear attitudes that a broad Glaswegian accent was unlikely to get one a good job, but that a medium Glaswegian accent was more appropriate in Glasgow than an English one (one speaker commented that English accents sound daft). The point is, the target form is *not* RP, but a local form, somewhere along a continuum from 'broad' to simply clearly recognisable Glaswegian, depending on what the situation calls for.

Hendry (1997) writes that the north east has been one of the last areas of Scotland to experience radical changes in its traditional industries, employment patterns, and living conditions, at least until the last two decades. As a result, the local language and culture have survived further into the twentieth century (and the twenty-first) than elsewhere in the country (1997: 2). Nevertheless, the vast changes brought about by the oil-related industries since the 1970s have brought about changes in the attitudes and experiences of the local population to their speech.

He believes that distinctive Scots, as it was spoken from the fourteenth to the sixteenth centuries, will never become widely used again. He suggests that Scottish people could, however, be persuaded that they have, as a unique national possession, a 'highly distinctive and expressive spoken language which is also the vehicle for a literature of great antiquity, merit, and durability' (McClure 1988: 31, cited from Hendry 1997: 13).

Hendry refers to attitudinal surveys done with working-class Glasgow secondary school children and with Aberdeen University students. The Glasgow children showed strong positive attitudes to their Scots nationality, but strong negative attitudes to their language. They also showed a strong dislike of RP and in fact, more positive attitudes to their dialect were emerging by the end of the study. The Aberdeen students showed far more positive attitudes to the dialect, and expressed a desire to see an official policy which encouraged the use of Scots alongside Standard English. Hendry asks what possible effect negative attitudes, political opposition, and recent sociolinguistic changes, brought about by technological developments, could have on the dialect traditions of Scotland.

Throughout Hendry's study, attitudes to the local dialect were shown to be very positive. This is borne out by other attitudinal studies (Macafee and McGarrity 1999, Löw 1997). There is considerable enthusiasm for the use of Scots both in and out of school (Hendry 1997: 91). He does not perform any quantitative analysis on these attitudes vis-à-vis language use, though. This is something which has been considered very important in the present study, and is quantified and analysed statistically in chapters 4 and 5.

Cheshire et al. (1999) comment on how adolescent attitudes in urban areas tend to show strong in-group allegiance, a scorn for 'posh' people, and anxiety about sounding 'country'. The uniformity of attitudes they find across schools in Hull, Milton Keynes and Reading shows that at least part of the mechanism involved in dialect levelling lies in subjective parameters. These subjective parameters will also prove important in the present study.

2.7   Linguistic choices and their results

An increasing number of researchers now point to the *social meaning*, or *social consequences* of code choice. Labov writes that the functions of these sound changes:

> cannot be limited to the communication of referential information, [but that they have to do with] the emblematic function of phonetic differentiation: the identification of a particular way of speaking within the norms of a local community (1980: 262, cited from Romaine 1989: 206).

In *Codes and Consequences* (1998), Myers-Scotton focuses on the selection of one linguistic code over another, and its consequences. The consequences considered here have to do with either effects on ease of cognitive processing or social/psychological effects. Myers-Scotton sets her discussion within the framework of the markedness model, and regards choices within a set as a system of oppositions. The basis for this is that all linguistic codes have *social and psychological associations* in the community in which they are used (Myers-Scotton 1998: 5). What community norms would predict is unmarked, what is not predicted is marked. These oppositions are not categorical, but rather fall along a continuum as less or more marked. As part of our language faculty, we are all predisposed to view linguistic choices as marked or unmarked. We all have the innate competence to assess linguistic choices. These are marked when they can be viewed as negotiations to invoke a set of rights and obligations *other* than the one for the context (p. 6). Myers-Scotton deals with choices between available styles, rather than languages. She believes that

the concept of markedness contributes to the social or psychological message in different choices of linguistic form. [...] Many messages of intentionality in conversation are about a speaker's view of his or her own persona or social group membership and relationships to other participants [...]. [...] The notion of speakers as *rational actors* is developed [in the book] (1998: 7, my emphasis).

The model of people as rational actors attempts to explain why actors (in this case speakers) choose the linguistic forms they do. The view is that such choices are the means by which actors try to 'achieve their goals as well as possible, thereby optimising the outcome' (Myers-Scotton 1998: 8). Linguistic choices are seen as being very similar to how social choices are made. This strongly supports the results of the analysis of the Huntly data, which will be presented in chapters 5 and 6. Macaulay (1997) agrees with Myers-Scotton's notion that speakers are free to make choices, but that the manner in which their choices will be interpreted is not free (Myers-Scotton 1998: 8). The question he asks is: what do people stand to gain or lose by using language in different ways? Myers-Scotton sees

features of the social context, including the speaker's social identity features, [as] structural constraints that determine an opportunity set; in the case of linguistic choices, the opportunity set is a speaker's linguistic repertoire (1998: 8).

In other words, a speaker makes the 'best' selection, given the level of internal consistency of desires, values, and beliefs and the available evidence. In most communities, more than one style or dialect is spoken, even if not by all members of the group. Individuals exploit the differences and relationships between who uses a variety and when, that become established in their community. The Markedness Model in other words:

accords to language users the ability to *make choices* regarding the varieties they employ, choices that necessarily involve cognitive calculations about their potential effect. [...] Approaches based around the Markedness Model see such choices as intentional in the sense that they are made to achieve certain social ends. Further, not only are speakers' intentions behind choices, but speakers make choices with the expectation that addressees will recognise a choice as carrying a particular intention. On this view, *speakers' choices are not determined by their social group memberships* – although their individual linguistic repertoires (what varieties are available to each individual) *are* very much so determined. Unfortunately, some researchers mistakenly equate limitations on *choice* with limitations on *repertoire* (Myers-Scotton 1998: 19).

What goal do speakers have when using the social and psychological relationships of varieties in a speech community? The Markedness Model (MM) sees their goal as to optimise rewards and to minimise costs. Speakers therefore make linguistic choices because they expect the benefits to outweigh the costs. Myers-Scotton does not claim that the rational actors model *always* sees speakers as *always* being rational in their choices, but that seeing choices as rationally based can account for the phenomenon (1998: 20). She sets it out thus:

> While the MM definitely recognises the crucial role of the speaker's actual experience with social factors, the model argues that speakers do not make choices of linguistic varieties on the basis of such direct linkages in a cause-and-effect fashion. Instead, the Markedness Model builds in a device that will prune multiple options and multiple future outcomes in some way. This device is a cognitive device, the markedness evaluator (1998: 23).

Myers-Scotton argues against the view that social norms are the major mechanism in choosing among possible varieties, or that choices are made merely to support norms. She asserts that, while norms designate marked and unmarked choices, speakers do make choices (1998: 31). Norms do influence speakers; that is why unmarked choices are the most frequent. A major reason to make the unmarked choice is to avoid group disapproval and personal distress. Yet, speakers *do* make marked choices at times. The aim of such a choice is to establish a new Rights and Obligations (RO) set as unmarked for the current exchange. It is therefore a negotiation *against* the unmarked RO set, and a call for another RO set in its place, in which it will be unmarked (1998: 32).

In the Huntly study, it is clear that the dialect is being lost rather rapidly, and that younger speakers are using it far less than older speakers. This is to be expected, given changes taking place all around the country. But, as the analysis will show, there is a pattern to the early adopters of standard forms, and the resistant types (McIntosh 1961).

If, as the data shows, change is the norm, then the standard forms are rapidly changing from being the marked forms (the dialect has been shown to be conservative until recently) to becoming the unmarked forms in a new RO set. Therefore, those who continue to use dialect fórms are now in fact living in a community where the older RO set has been displaced, and their choice now represents the marked one. *Yet they continue to make those choices.* The question of why they do so is what I will consider throughout this study.

Andersen (1989) also writes about individual choice as one of the factors involved in linguistic change. He refers to the confrontation between two views on the matter, that of Bloomfield, and that of Coseriu. Bloomfield's view is as follows:

> Although many sound changes shorten linguistic forms, simplify the phonetic system, or in some way lessen the labour of utterance, yet no student has succeeded in establishing a correlation between sound-change and any antecedent phenomenon: the causes of sound-change are unknown (1935: 385, cited from Andersen 1989: 6).

Coseriu has a different viewpoint:

> In one sense, the most general one, the so called 'causes' are actually not unknown, but perfectly well known and observable every day, for they coincide with the very conditions of speaking, and are part and parcel of every speaker's experience. In another sense – as cultural and functional determinants – the 'causes' of change derive from the general conditions of language and are, whenever a given language is adequately documented, by and large open to investigation (1952: 83, 1967: 123f, Andersen's translation, 1989: 6).

The latter takes a rather cautious view of the 'causes' of language change, preferring to use the term 'conditions' which are favourable for language change. According to Andersen, this view sees change (or absence of change) as being part of the speaker's own free will. He believes that, when speaking, an individual may be motivated by the different circumstances in which the speech event is located, to deviate from the usage that is normal in that particular speech community. Such a motivation is not the *cause* of such deviation and change, however:

> Change in language, as well as absence of change, is produced by its speakers as part of that exercise of their free will which speaking is.

In speaking, they may be motivated by the diverse circumstances under which they speak to deviate from the usage that is traditional in their community. But such a motivation is not a *cause* in the sense in which Bloomfield and his predecessors understood the word, for the individual speaker is free to let himself be moved, or not be moved, by the given circumstance or circumstances. In Coseriu's view, the only true 'causes' of changes are the speakers, who use their language – and in doing so, observe or neglect their linguistic traditions as they see fit (Andersen 1989: 7).

This notion assumes that any change may be conditioned by a number of coexisting circumstances. It also assumes that speaking has an intentional character, whether it is in the process of change or relative stability. The implication is that there is an element of intention in both stability and change.

Nevertheless, if we are to explain and account for *all* the different kinds of change that are to be found in the historical record and around us now, we must also consider changes which are *not* intentional on the part of the speakers.

Sealey and Carter (2001: 1) argue that 'the constitution of independent variables based on social categories is itself a task of theoretical description'. In other words, they would like to call into question the practice of using social aggregates, or 'involuntary-membership' groups as de facto categories of analysis in sociolinguistics. They also argue against the 'additive', or linear view of variable correlations popular in modern sociolinguistic research. This is a process which sees the language use of speakers who do not conform to predicted age- or sex-group patterns as *deviations*, which need to be explained by the 'leftover' factors, such as local networks, peer groups, attitudes, etc. They call for a view of language variation as complex and emergent (that is, the product of earlier engagements between people and their world). They acknowledge that the linear model of variation can indicate empirically the 'traces' of causal relations, but propose that a realist epistemology can improve sociolinguistic methodology.

Sociolinguists are often concerned with social categories, such as age, sex, social class, and ethnicity as independent variables. The authors call the validity of such categories into question. They propose that 'the social world is not fully or directly intelligible to its inhabitants' (p. 2), saying that such categories as 'class' or 'ethnic group' are not brute facts. Age too, is regarded with caution, as a category which is largely a theoretical construct. Such constructs, the authors argue, are not *presented* to us by the social world (p. 2).

Sealey and Carter (2001) make a distinction between two types of social category: involuntary and (at least partly) voluntary (p. 3). The first type consists of 'social aggregates' (Greenwood 1994), or groups such as the poor, females, people over 50, etc. These do not imply shared norms to which members can be party. The second type of social category is 'social collectives'. Members of these groups must be party to a set of conventions and norms (Sealey and Carter 2001: 4). Membership is therefore indicated by an awareness of, and some kind of commitment to, the conventions that are found in the group.

Sealey and Carter (2001) point to the use by researchers of social aggregates, such as age group, to show correlations between the use of linguistic variables and (involuntary) membership of the category. The authors write that these findings are more descriptive than explanatory. They believe that, in order to *explain* why, for example, most adolescents are in the vanguard of linguistic change, we need to acknowledge that speakers have some degree of choice over how they use language (p. 5). Social choices may not cover an infinite range, but even binary choices are choices, and reflect the actor's own understandings. Any investigation into why certain speakers use marked forms, while others do not, must involve recognising the fact that the speakers themselves have a role in the process. Using language in a certain way is not simply the result of an irresistible pressure from outside, but rather the result of the social actor's adoption and maintenance of certain distinct linguistic features (Sealey and Carter 2001: 7). This point is important when considering the results of the Huntly data analysis. As will be seen in chapter 5, the theoretically predicted pressure from local social networks to conform is not apparent, and the view of speakers as social agents appears to have far more validity in considering the social factors which may facilitate or retard the spread of contact-induced language change.

The main point made by the paper is that there can be no *logical* necessity between belonging to a social aggregate and using language in particular ways. Language features themselves cannot have or lack inherent value. The use or rhotic speech is seen as indicating ruralness, perhaps backwardness, in England, but in Scotland and Ireland it is used categorically, and in the US it connotes education and prestige. It is not that speakers are *bound* by their membership of any social category to use certain language features rather than others. The theories that use this hypothesis 'fail to distinguish between culture, structure and agency' (Sealey and Carter 2001: 9).

Individuals are born into contextual social conditions, which are temporally prior to their existence, and offer to them involuntaristic and reasonably predictable options in terms of access to wealth, education, and employment. These options are, however, conditioning, rather than determining, and the individual has a degree of choice in responding to the options (loc. cit.). The cultural resources, including language, which are available, are subject to this agency on the part of individuals. Language as a resource system constrains the number of choices available to speakers, in terms of the *standing constraints* in the system, but not in terms of the *emergent constraints* decided at the discourse level (de Beaugrande 1999: 131, cited from Sealey and Carter 2001: 9). This means that, while a Scots speaker cannot say *[kʉ es] 'cow this', instead of 'this cow' (a standing constraint within the language), she may choose between saying [es kʉ], the Scots form, and [ðɪs kəʉ], the Scottish Standard English form (an emerging constraint). The authors write that 'language change is brought about by the engagement of *human purpose* with an independent and antecedent body of linguistic resources' (p. 11, my emphasis).

In sum then, Sealey and Carter's view of the linear model is thus:

If membership of an age group, say [+ adolescent], correlates with use of particular feature:

explained by the antecedent hypothesis, based on membership of social aggregates. Thereafter, any individual deviation:

is explained by means of membership of social collectives, the 'leftover' categories, such as social networks and attitudinal factors.

As can be seen, the model is linear and additive. As such, it fails to take account of the fact that the social world is complex. The authors write that structured social relations are of the type of emergent entities mentioned above, and are based upon individuals' experience of the world in which they find themselves. People, too, have their own emergent properties, and as such are not puppets of structures (Sealey and Carter 2001: 15).

In sum, Sealey and Carter believe that the effect of multiple independent variables should not be seen as the sum of their separate effects, but rather that the relationship between the variables alters their causal properties in complex ways. The 'social mechanisms' involved in language variation are therefore seen as complex and multiplicative, rather than linear and additive (p. 15).

One way around the problem is to gather the data without pre-existing notions about social categories and how they will behave, then to use cluster analysis, which identifies sets that emerge from the data when subjected to post-hoc statistical testing.

Lüdtke (1984) believes that linguistic behaviour is goal-directed, that is, governed by principles that ensure successful performance (Lüdtke 1984: 131). By this is meant the social benefits of using one particular form over another, whether for prestige or solidarity. There are, however, *unintended side-effects* to this behaviour, and to other human behaviour. These are neither independent of human action, nor due to people's intent, but make up a third set of phenomena, sometimes referred to as 'invisible-hand processes'. These are not planned as such, but are due to 'the involuntary combined effect of a great number of single individual acts' (p. 131).

He believes that language change is a subset of variation, and that a prerequisite of variation is redundancy in performance. While one's qualitative decisions depend on free choice, and are therefore statistically speaking random, these same decisions become subject to calculation, *when taken by many people on the same issues.*

He points to three quantitative processes that are universal:

1. items, or meaningful elements become shorter and shorter, as regards their phonic representation,
2. longer items replace shorter ones, and optionally added ones become necessary,[20] and
3. syntactically adjacent items become merged or fused (Lüdtke 1984: 13)

These are the processes of the 'invisible hand'.[21]

Lüdtke writes that speech is a continuum, and that *change* in speech is one too. It is therefore artificial to mark the beginning and the end of a process, and to call such a process 'a change'. He believes that it is important to distinguish between observed features of speech performance, changes taking place in a single speech item, and overall results, which alter the state of a language in a significant way.

2.8 Age and language change

Earlier concepts of the sharply defined differences between child and adult language acquisition and use may be over-simplistic. For example,

Aitchison (2001) writes a convincing critique of the critical period hypothesis (Lenneberg 1967), in which she discusses evidence that adults can acquire languages with near-native fluency (Aitchison 2001: 204). But since we are dealing with change rather than acquisition, I concentrate here on age as a factor in that process. Aitchison believes that young children have little of importance to contribute to language change (p. 209), though the same is not true for adolescents, as Kerswill (1996) and Kerswill and Williams (1994) show. Age will be compared with language use through-out this study, though the focus will be more on other sociological factors.

Most studies of language variation and change look at variation between age groups, on the assumption that diachronic change can be observed synchronically in the generational differences (Weinreich, Labov and Herzog 1968). Gauchat (1905, cited from Romaine) proposed that sound change could be 'observed' in progress by doing apparent-time studies. One methodological problem with this notion is that of *age grading*. The differences between age groups may be due to other factors, such as adjustments made by individuals as they move through life and the linguistic market. Age graded changes are regarded as changes in the use of a variant that recur at a particular age in successive generations. These therefore represent developmental stages in the life of an individual. Evidence shows that children are 'more likely than adults to restructure certain aspects of their grammar in more far-reaching ways, particularly under the influence of their peers (Romaine 1989: 200). From this we can infer that children may be the locus of language change, or at least that the process of acquisition 'involves certain natural processes which have been found to apply in language history' (p. 200).

In a forthcoming paper, 'Is age grading always a potential problem in apparent-time studies?', Røyneland argues that the 'problem' of age grading in apparent-time studies is more pronounced in system-internally motivated (endocentric) innovations than in innovations which are primarily motivated by system-external forces. Speakers in areas which involve endocentric innovation are not normally exposed to as much contact with speakers of varieties external to the group. Those innova-tions which are attributable to dialect levelling (contact innovations) are less exposed to age grading than other kinds of innovation, such as evolutive or spontaneous innovations (Andersen 1988, 1989). Dialect levelling is considered to be a dynamic dialect contact phenomenon which leads to the gradual abandonment of local dialect features in favour of more regional or standard ones (cf. Hinskens 1996). This term is used for both horizontal dialect/dialect convergence as well as vertical dialect/standard convergence.

Røyneland writes that individuals may want to re-adopt vernacular features as they get older, and as social pressures upon them change, and this will result in a small amount of age grading. Most linguistic features are, however, unlikely to be changed back, as they become relatively fixed as part of the person's linguistic repertoire, and also because of socio-psychological reasons for *not* re-installing them. Røyneland's conclusion implies that apparent-time methodology is a valid representation of real-time changes in language. In the Huntly study, as in any other, repeated interviews over an extended period would have allowed for a more complete picture to be built up, but this was not possible because of time constraints. In Hatch and Lazaraton's (1991) terms, the Huntly study therefore uses a 'one-shot' research design. Chambers (1995: 194) writes that, 'since age-grading is relatively rare and is realised in a distinctive, identifiable pattern, it does not refute the hypothesis but is a codicil on it'. Various studies show that adolescents lead such convergence (e.g. Kerswill and Williams 1994).

Lane's (1997) study of a changing rural dialect in Thyborøn, Denmark shows another important aspect to the question of age and speaker orientation. She aims to show that

> it is possible to conduct research which focuses on the documentation of the development and synchronic status of a dialect through the implementation of a multidimensional (i.e. interdisciplinary) model of change in dialects. This model involves the combining of ethnographic, sociolinguistic and historical data with theories of variability, then couples the data with studies into the social network ties of the informants. [...] Only by including external evidence can we gain insight into what causes linguistic change, i.e. the actuation problem raised by Weinreich, Labov and Herzog (1968) (Lane 1997: 144).

Lane believes that the 'life-stage' which a speaker is at when experiencing socio-historical events is important when a researcher considers the group's as well as *the individual's orientation to the events and also the effect which those events may have on their orientation to the community.* The various age groups in a study belong to different 'life-stages'. As younger speakers become more active in society, their life-experiences and attitudes become reflected in the evolving dialect and social norms. She believes that the social history of the community, the 'identifying power' of the dialect, and the self-consciousness of the residents must be considered together (Lane 1997: 151).

Lane writes of the *different choices* which individuals in the Thyborøn fishing community make when it comes to modes of production. She shows that, in her 16- to 40-year-old men, there are *some who choose the traditional modes of production* in the fishing industry (the normal choice for those men in the 40- to 65-year-old, and over 65-year-old age groups), whereas *others choose less traditional modes* of production. These 'exemplify the social differences and network patterns which have arisen out of the change in economy and educational opportunities' (Lane 1997: 152). This again shows that there is a large amount of *leeway open to individuals*, who are born into the same sex and age groups in a particular community, *to choose modes of production and other things, such as language*. Her data shows an inverse correlation between age and network symmetry across sex, meaning that the older one is, the more likely one is to favour same-sex network ties. Younger people may feel more at liberty to foster opposite-sex ties, due to changing opportunities for contact with the opposite sex through education, sport, etc. The notion of individual choice is central to my argument.

The youngest women in the sample (16–40 years old) have more uniplex social network ties, and are breaking with the traditional wage-earner mode of production, in order to follow career goals. They do not feel a need to stay in Thyborøn, although they report that the town is important to their identity. Their network ties are the same as those associated with urban life modes. This has important similarities with the results of the present study. The Huntly SOCLAS index has built into it a measure of career goals, and the effectiveness of this line of questioning will be shown below. In the Thyborøn study, Lane notes that the 16- to 40-year-old women report consciously regionalising their speech as a result of contact situations in which they have to accommodate away from the local dialect. Breaking with the traditional wage-earner mode of production will result in more frequent contacts of this nature, and lead to accommodation.

Lane's data shows an age effect in language use and ideological orientation to the community, and her point is that we should include such considerations in a sociolinguistic model of language change. Her analysis, however, does not go as far as testing whether the latter two are correlated or not. She does, however, show that the older people are more positively oriented to the local community, more bound up in its traditional modes of production and network structures, and use the dialect more. A statistical model which tests whether people who are more positively oriented to the local community, and who do not fall into urban-dominated life modes (Pedersen 1994), use the dialect more *regardless of age* would be even more useful. The model used in the Huntly study has been designed to do just that.

Romaine (1989) points to the similarities between children's language acquisition and language change. Acquisition is seen as a developmental process which proceeds in real time. She writes that, traditionally, historical linguists have taken a long-term view of change, ignoring the changes which take place within a life span, and how these may relate to long-term changes in a language system (Romaine 1989: 199). The focus of the paper is the role of children in the overall communicative structure of a speech community. A question asked is whether the deviation of children's speech from adult norms contributes to long-term restructuring of the language system.

An Example from Edinburgh

Romaine (1989) writes that irregularities in class and style variation, and unusual patterns of age and sex differentiation are important indicators of sound change in adult populations (Romaine 1989: 203). In her 1989 Edinburgh study, Romaine examines the variants of post-vocalic /r/ in children's speech. She finds a great deal of sex differentiation, with the males using [r] more, and the females [ɹ]. There is another realisation of the phoneme, namely Ø, which is rather unexpected for Scotland. The males use Ø quite extensively, as can be seen in table 2. The youngest females are starting to use the feature a little, but the oldest ones hardly use it at all (1%).

Table 2 Age-grading post-vocalic /r/ (from Romaine 1989: 204)

Age	10		8		6	
Variant	M	F	M	F	M	F
[r]	57	45	48	40	59	33
[ɹ]	15	54	37	54	16	50
Ø	28	1	15	6	25	17

She concludes that r-lessness is an example of change from below: 'It manifests itself as a gradual shift in the behaviour of successive generations well below the level of conscious awareness of the speaker' (Romaine 1989: 204). The other variant, [ɹ], seems to be an example of change from above the level of consciousness of speakers. Its use is being spread by overt social influence from prestige groups, as it is associated with middle-class female speech in Scotland. Therefore, it seems that both sexes are innovating, but the females are moving towards the supralocal form, as is normal. These conclusions are, however, based upon a rather narrow age range of 6, 8 and 10 year-olds. She summarises thus:

1. The process of acquiring grammar involves internalising the norms of the models one is exposed to. This involves a certain amount of restructuring and over-generalisation of rules. These can be seen as changes in apparent time.[22]
2. In some cases there is a regular relationship between change in apparent time, i.e. age-grading, and change in real time, such that synchronic variability represents a stage in long-term change (p. 212).

She refers to the opinion of some researchers, which holds that children have little of importance to contribute to language change. Aitchison writes that 'Babies do not form influential social groups; changes begin within social groups, when group members unconsciously imitate those around them (1989: 180). While Romaine concedes that very young children cannot be the main instigators of change, she maintains that 'children's innovations could still lead to cumulative change, providing that they were maintained into adulthood, i.e., are not purely developmental' (1989: 213). Kerswill (1996) shows that the truth lies somewhere between apparent and real time. Certain types of change are adopted by older speakers, while others seem only to be adoptable by children (1996: 179). In fact, the 'adoption' may be misleading, as some features are more a case of L1 acquisition, rather than a change as such.

2.9   Dialects in contact

Trudgill (1986) refers to Weinreich's (1953) book on languages in contact and the processes of individual bilingualism that go with it. These processes can also be seen in the light of *dialects* in contact. Speakers of mutually intelligible dialects seem to transfer items from one variety to the other, which can lead to language change. He also refers to Giles' Accommodation Theory (1973), which says:

> ... if the sender in a dyadic situation wishes to gain the receiver's approval, then he may adapt his accent patterns towards that of this person, i.e. reduce pronunciation dissimilarities (Giles et al. 1973, cited from Trudgill 1986: 15).

It is likely that situational factors alone will not determine choice, but that interpersonal relations have an effect. The theory is based on the socio-psychological concept of similarity-attraction, which proposes that an individual can and will induce another to see her or him in a favourable light by reducing the number of dissimilarities between her- or himself and the other, whether consciously or subconsciously. This may involve expressions, mannerisms, gestures, body language, and speech style.

Giles et al. (1973) look at convergence and divergence in terms of social factors, but accommodation also takes place between speakers of *regionally*, rather than socially different varieties. This can be long- or short-term accommodation, and the former is what Trudgill focuses upon here. Long-term accommodation may occur when regionally mobile individuals or minority groups come to live among a non-mobile majority. Our task is to determine how speakers accommodate and why accommodation varies between situations and individuals. Trudgill notes (1986: 9) that 'during accommodation between accents that differ at a number of points, some features are modified and some are not'. An example is Trudgill's own accommodation to his informants in his (1974) Norwich study. A quantitative analysis shows that he accommodated to his informants in respect of the variable (t), but not in respect of the variable (a:). The reason for this is that some variables are subject to both social class and stylistic variation (Labov's *markers*), while others are simply subject to social class variation (Labov's *indicators*). The latter are not changed by speakers during style-shifting, as they are below the level of consciousness for them. He emphasises that one of the origins of linguistic change is in numerous acts of 'accommodation' on the part of speakers talking to people with other dialects (see the discussion of the notion of *salience* below).

In their (1972) Hemnesberget study, Blom and Gumperz found that choice among dialect variants is normally restricted by sociolinguistic selection constraints: if a standard form is used at the beginning of an utterance, the rest of the utterance will be in that dialect (p. 416). In-migrants who do not learn the local dialect are seen as distancing themselves from the locals and their community spirit. Some may want to appear as part of the local team on some occasions, but to identify with middle-class values on others.[23]

The decision as to whether a speaker is code-switching or merely style-shifting in Huntly is a difficult one, as there is no clear point at which Scots stops and Scottish Standard English begins.[24] There are, however, some morpho-lexical variables which are clearly Scots, and these are the ones singled out for the study.[25]

In the Huntly area there seems to be a stable local population with a slow but steady influx of 'outsiders' from other parts of Aberdeenshire, Scotland generally, and from England and abroad. The short-term accommodation seems to be on the part of the *locals* more than the outsiders. This is explained by the locals as arising from intelligibility problems; they are able to accommodate, whereas the outsiders are not. The reason for this is probably that the locals are exposed to the standard,[26] whereas the outsiders (especially non-Scots) are not familiar with the local variety, though there are also complex issues of identity and prestige operating. If the encounter takes place with a foreigner, speech accommodation is likely (the shift will be in the direction of SSE). If the outsider is English, the reaction may be less favourable, and the insider may want to create social distance, otherwise known as *divergence* in Giles's terms (1973: 67). Long-term accommodation seems to be on the part of the in-migrants, though, as Scots has been maintained rather well in the face of this influx of outsiders and dialect contact which has existed for centuries, as the following extract shows:

> The language spoken in this parish is the broad Buchan dialect of the English, with many Scotticisms, and stands in much need of reformation, which it is hoped will soon happen, from the frequent resort of polite people (sic) to the town in summer (minister of Peterhead, in *The Statistical Account of Scotland*, 1795, 'Peterhead', cited in Aitken 1979: 97).

In considering issues involved in dialect contact, it is worth looking at Labov's (1972) concept of linguistic variables, which can be subject to both class and stylistic variation (markers), or only to class variation (indicators). He suggests that markers are relatively high in a speaker's consciousness, whereas indicators are not. When speakers are highly aware of a feature, they are led to modify it in a situation where they are monitoring their speech, say, in a formal situation or when they are accommodating to an interlocutor. Trudgill (1986) is interested in the notion of *salience*, and how it is that certain features are modified instead of others. The idea is that some features are more salient or striking than others to the speaker, and lead to accommodation. According to Trudgill (p. 11), increased awareness is attached to variables

- that are involved in the maintenance of phonological contrasts
- when the forms are overtly stigmatised in the community

- when the feature is involved in a current linguistic change
- when the variants are phonetically radically different

Factors which inhibit accommodation are:

- extra-strong stereotyping or salience or negative attitude; 'Greater awareness attaches to forms which are overtly stigmatised in a particular community [...]'.
- presence of phonotactic constraints in the receiving dialect
- possibility of homonymic clash

Kerswill and Williams (2001a forthcoming) have criticised the concept of salience, saying that it could be circular. A feature is readily adopted, and this is ascribed to its degree of salience, but the notion itself is defined on the basis of which features are (or are not) readily adopted. Also, Trudgill claims that some features are too salient, and that this in fact inhibits accommodation. Kerswill and Williams ask why a factor should facilitate a change in one case and hinder it in another. They believe that salience must be taken together with language-external factors which may be linked to the salience. Of Trudgill's five factors, they believe that only two of the language-internal ones (phonetic difference and phonological contrast) fully avoid circularity (Kerswill and Williams 2001a: 26). The authors point out that either of these two factors could be the cause of salience or the *result* of prior salience.

While the salience of a variable is crucial in accommodation, the picture is more complicated, as other factors can impede or prevent accommodation. For example, Trudgill (1986: 16) cites the non-accommodation by English speakers to non-prevocalic /r/ in American English. He suggests this is due to phonotactic constraints in the non-rhotic speaker's phonological system, which allows /r/ to occur only before a vowel. The potential for homonymic clash can also prevent accommodation.

Accommodation often leads to linguistic change, which may manifest as dialect levelling, which takes place within a context of economic, social, and regional differences, degree of contact between regions, and social and geographical mobility in individuals (Kerswill and Williams 1994: 12). If a variety is associated with a 'desirable' group, it is more likely to be adopted, although this can be complicated by the fact that there is often covert prestige in using vernacular forms, and social pressure to maintain them.

The 'route' of long-term accommodation is often different for different speakers, as Trudgill's data on two 7-year-old British twins who moved to Australia for a year seems to show. Speakers are relatively free to adopt different strategies of accommodation. Accommodation by children seems to be a different process to that by adults, and children are vital to the process of dialect-mixture and formation. Children use the dialect and accent of their friends, and not of their parents and teachers, and this is probably why regionally distinct dialects do not survive in the face of geographical mobility (Kerswill and Williams 1994: 15).

We understand much about how linguistic forms are transmitted or diffused geographically from one area to another at the macro level, but not much about the micro level, i.e. from speaker to speaker at the individual level. Trudgill's view of accommodation is that it can only take place when there is face-to-face interaction (p. 40). In other words, he does not believe that the electronic media are very instrumental in the diffusion of linguistic innovations, as people do not speak to TV sets, nor accommodate to them. He cites the fact that linguistic innovations in Britain spread outwards like ripples from a stone dropped into a pool, yet if they were to be the results of diffusion influenced by TV, they would diffuse throughout the country simultaneously. He allows that there are exceptions to this, mainly lexical items that are copied from American English on TV, but states that the phonology and grammar of British English are almost totally unaffected. He does later concede that television programmes can act as a softening-up process for change (p. 41).

Trudgill writes that locals who move away from the area to an area where a prestige variety is spoken, and return later with some features of that speech, may cause them to be incorporated in the speech of locals because they were seen to be more sophisticated than the stay-at-homes. These have been called 'language missionaries' by Steinsholt (1962). Trudgill's point is that, if particular individuals are *perceived* as being insiders by a certain group of speakers even though they are linguistically distinct, then they can have a considerable linguistic influence through face-to-face contact in spite of being heavily outnumbered, providing attitudinal factors are right (1986: 57). This agrees with the notion of weak ties, as discussed above.

2.10   Language standardisation

James Milroy (2001) makes a great contribution to our understanding of the processes and ideologies involved in language standardisation. He explores the effects of the standard language ideology on attitudes to language of non-linguists and of language specialists, and considers how far linguists themselves have been affected by – and have contributed to – this ideology. He takes the primary definition of standardisation to be *the imposition of uniformity upon a class of objects*. He also reviews attitudes to language within standard language cultures and contrasts these with un-standardised situations, in which the boundaries of languages are indeterminate. He writes that widely used languages such as English, French and Spanish are believed by their speakers to exist in standardised forms, and that this kind of belief affects the way in which speakers think about their own language and about 'language' in general. Speakers of these languages live in what we may call standard language cultures. He gives a broad definition of what standardisation is: 'in respect of the internal form of language, the process of standardisation works by promoting invariance or uniformity in language structure' (J. Milroy 2001: 531). He goes on to problematise the notion that prestige and standard forms of language are automatically the same. Indeed, the standard/non-standard dichotomy is itself driven by an ideology – it depends on prior acceptance of the ideology of standardisation and on the centrality of the standard variety. He writes that an extremely important effect of standardisation has been the development of consciousness among speakers of a 'correct', or canonical, form of language. In 'standard-language cultures', virtually everyone subscribes to the ideology of the standard language, and one aspect of this is a firm belief in correctness. This belief takes the form that, when there are two or more variants of some word or construction, only one of them can be right.

Milroy believes that this ideology requires us to accept that language (or a language) is not the possession of the native speakers: they are not pre-programmed with a language faculty that enables them to acquire (or develop) 'competence' in language without being formally taught (if it is conceded that they are equipped with such a faculty, this is treated as unimportant). What they do acquire in an informal way before school age is not reliable and not yet fully correct. In this general context 'native speaker intuition' means nothing, and grammatical sequences are not products of the native speaker's mind (2001: 537).

Milroy writes that the linguist has not been free from this ideology. Much of descriptive and theoretical linguistics, together with much of historical linguistics, has depended on, or modelled its methodology on, the study of major languages (i.e., widely used ones) in standard language cultures – in which a language has been regarded as existing in a standard, classical, or canonical, form (2001: 543). He does believe that there is no reason why accounts of standard English should not be relied on for various purposes, provided that arguments are put forward to justify the use of the standard, and not other forms, in some given instance, and so long as we can be assured that it is appropriate to do so in such an instance. However, he is critical of the fact that that virtually all quantitative investigations have been carried out in standard language cultures and, moreover, mainly in monolingual situations. His conclusion is that determinate languages, such as English, may be defined more by ideologies than by their internal structures.

These points are of great importance to the present study and its findings. The changes in language use in progress in Huntly are clearly the results of language standardisation. The reference point throughout has been Scottish Standard English, but this variety has not been seen as in any way linguistically superior to Scots. In fact, during the quantification process detailed in later chapters, the numerical bias has been placed *in favour of* the Scots forms, so that, for example, if a speaker uses a Scots form, a point is allocated, and the use of a Scottish Standard English form attracts a zero. While it may be impossible to conduct a quantitative sociolinguistic study that does not fall into the standard/non-standard ideological framework, it is hoped that the present study does not fall into the familiar traps associated with it.

2.11   Geolinguistics

According to Trudgill (1983: 52) and Chambers and Trudgill (1998: 166), the notion of the linguistic variable, taken together with insights from human geography about methodology and theory, can help us understand how the relationship between language and geography works. Trudgill cites Hägerstrand (1952) as saying that the diffusion of an innovation is the result of a complex interplay of, on the one hand, exposure to information about the innovation, and on the other hand, factors leading to resistance to its adoption (1983: 61). Geophysical barriers such as lakes, forests, difficult terrain and distance impede communication, and are, according to Trudgill, functionally rather similar to social barriers (1983: 62). Diffusion processes need to be explained in terms of the spatial patterns they take, and Trudgill proposes a model which will be able to accurately predict diffusion patterns, based on finding out the relative significance of geographical and social barriers, helping us to understand why speakers adopt or reject linguistic changes, though he does not give details of such a proposed model until 1998 (see below). The *Gravity Model*, taken from the physical sciences into human geography, investigates the interaction of two or more centres, and could be adapted to cope with the complexities of language (1983: 73). Trudgill's version of the model therefore attempts to explain and predict the geographical diffusion of linguistic features, and is the spatial counterpart of other models.

The city of Aberdeen is the urban centre which possibly has the most 'gravitational pull' on the people of Huntly, by virtue of its proximity (see below under Hernández-Campoy). Presumably, Edinburgh, as the capital city and cultural centre of Scotland, also has a substantial influence. In terms of the gravity model, the greater size of its population gives it the power to influence even those smaller centres further away. London obviously has a great influence on the whole of Britain by virtue of its great population, and the fact that it is the capital city and cultural centre of the United Kingdom, mean its effect will be felt to the far reaches of the country. But of course it is also associated with *Englishness*, and all the related stereotypes that go with that, so attitudes are bound to be complex, affecting the influence that it may have on Scottish people. The gravitational pull of the various centres upon Huntly would be something like the diagram on the following page.

But any calculations based upon these facts must surely also take into account intervening topographical features, such as mountains and lakes. It is not clear how these factors could be accounted for by a geolinguistic model.

Chambers and Trudgill (1998) detail a geolinguistic model which takes population and distance into account, but not intervening geomorphology. A map of the area under investigation is covered with a hexagonal grid. Linguistic fieldwork is then carried out in each cell, and the mean scores for the linguistic variables in each cell are then calculated, with isoglosses drawn linking areas with similar scores. These actual linguistic scores can then be compared with the results of the predictive model based on population and distance. The formula used in this model is:

$$I_{ij} = S \times \frac{P_i P_j}{(d_{ij})^2} \times \frac{P_i}{P_i + P_j}$$

I_{ij} = Influence of centre i on centre j
P = Population
d = Distance
S = Index of prior-existing linguistic similarity (the higher the index the greater the similarity) (From Chambers and Trudgill 1998: 179).

The factor S is included to account for the fact that 'it seems to be psychologically and linguistically simpler to adopt features from a dialect that closely resembles one's own than from one that is rather different' (p. 179). The authors go on to apply the model to predict the influence

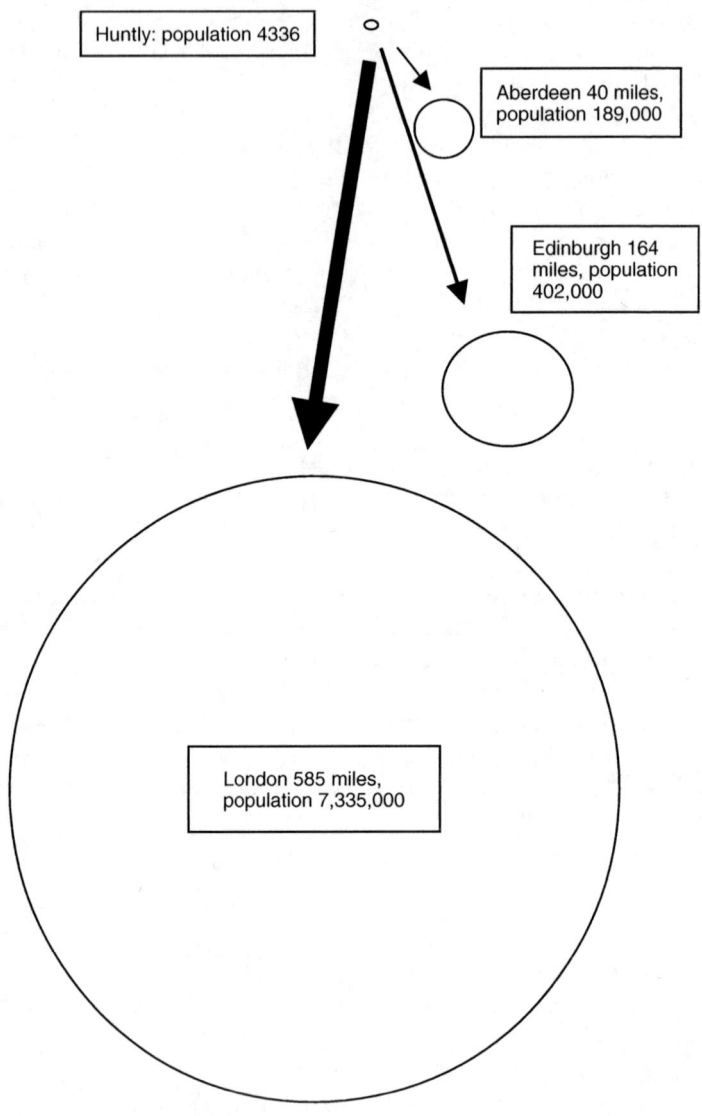

Huntly: population 4336

Aberdeen 40 miles, population 189,000

Edinburgh 164 miles, population 402,000

London 585 miles, population 7,335,000

Map 2 Gravitational pull on Huntly

of London, Ipswich, Norwich, Lowestoft, King's Lynn and Great Yarmouth on each other, and to compare the output of the model with actual linguistic data on /h/ dropping in these centres, taking the origin of the feature to be London. The model produces a high correlation with the linguistic data, and so seems to be well designed:

Table 3 Data from Trudgill and Chamber's model (1998: 183)

Order predicted	Centre	(h) index
1	Ipswich	56
2	Norwich	44
3	Lowestoft	40
4	G. Yarmouth	33
5	K. Lynn	21

The linguistic scores for the different urban centres will conceal a wealth of individual variation, but their model does achieve its goal: to account for population and distance as factors involved in the linguistic influence of urban centres upon each other. As the authors point out, the model does not cover all variation (for example in Illinois), but at least this leads the investigator to consider what *other* factors may be involved (1998: 183).

Hindley's (1990) study of the survival of the Irish language in the *Gaeltachtaí*[27] is pertinent to the present study, as the areas in question share with Scotland a proximity to England and the English language and media. More importantly, they are contiguous with English speaking Ireland. In the past, the agrarian nature of society in the Gaeltachtaí and the absence of electronic media and private cars prevented much contact with the outside world (though of course there is no easy way to measure the influence of the media, as the ongoing debate surrounding this matter shows). The insular nature of the communities ensured a high rate of endogamy, and migration in and out of the areas was low (Hindley, 1990: 214). Factors such as the sea and the geographically insular nature of the islands and peninsulas that make up the Gaeltachtaí have been one of the greatest aids to survival. The sea is a linguistically neutral neighbour, and the English-speaking communities adjoining the Gaeltachtaí do not have extensive borders along the Irish-speaking areas because of the geomorphology of the peninsulas.

Hindley writes that in the last forty years the introduction of the electronic mass media, personal transport, the building of roads and harbours in the three areas and diverse employment have reduced the social and geophysical isolation and brought English in via television,[28] travellers and migrant workers. Hindley's study focuses mostly on language planning, and the efforts by the Irish government to maintain Irish, but does contain some interesting geolinguistic information which suggests a strong correlation between the social and geographical isolation of the people in the Gaeltachtaí and survival of the vernacular.

Hernández-Campoy's (1996) study aims to show the influence of space, in addition to the social, context, and time dimensions, in the geographical diffusion of linguistic innovations emerging from linguistic change. He sees linguistic variation as being not only conditioned socially, but also spatially. He claims to use statistical data such as population, distance, communications and connections (provided by human geography) empirically, but does not do so in a rigorous manner in this paper. He mentions how human geography regards urban centres as each having an *inter-urban* status that is dependent upon its form, size, function, historical transformations, etc. (Hernández-Campoy 1996: 51). The inter-urban status of a centre is a measure of its demography, area of influence, and flow systems between the different settlements. The larger a centre, the greater its population, and normally the more activities and functions it monopolises, giving it a wider range of influence. The extent of influence of a settlement is directly proportional to its mass (population size), and inversely proportional to the distance between it and the centre it influences (p. 54).

Distance has a retarding effect on human interaction (often called the friction of distance). However, the advent of public transport and the private car are causing 'the contiguous physical expansion of the cities into the surrounding countryside' (Hernández-Campoy 1996: 104). The building of roads and the rise of affordable air travel will mean that the friction of distance and the retarding effect of geomorphology will have a declining influence on mobility and speaker contacts, leading to more rapid diffusion of linguistic changes (Hernández-Campoy 1996: 117). The effect of geomorphology in the area under investigation in this study has long been recognised as important, however:

> Pope Alexander VI, in founding the University of Aberdeen in 1494, attributed the 'rude and ignorant' character of the people [...] to the fact that they were cut off from the rest of the kingdom by 'firths and very lofty mountains' – 'per maris bracchia et montes altissimos' (Buchan et al. 1924: 135).

In this study I have considered the geographical isolation of the farmers and the geomorphology of the region important factors in the maintenance of the dialect, though I will not attempt to quantify them, as the model needs to be developed to include geomorphological factors. In addition, such calculations would rely on many subjective evaluations of the factors at hand, and would not offer any real benefits to our understanding of the language use of the area. The specific focus will be the possible *sociological*, rather than geographical, factors operating on the process of change.

Conclusion

In this chapter I reviewed the literature dealing with the social factors operating on the process of language change. I examined the theoretical background to sociolinguistic studies of language change, covering some of the major studies in this area. I covered the more general theoretical issues surrounding the phenomenon of language change, after which I reviewed the social network framework. Next I summarised Højrup's (1983b) notion of Life Modes, the concept of exocentric versus endocentric change, Cognitive Dissonance, attitudes and language change, language choices and their results, age and language change, dialects in contact and geolinguistics. Having covered these approaches and indicated where the models may be improved, I now move on to the research design. I will specify the research question, detail the pilot study and first impressions from the sampling area, give an overview of the descriptive material, supply a detailed list of linguistic and social variables selected for the study, with explanations of how they were elicited. I will then give details of the methodology used, and how the indices were calculated. Lastly, I discuss the individual informants recorded for the study.

Notes

1. This concept will be discussed in more detail below.
2. For a more detailed discussion, see below.
3. This is discussed in more detail in chapters 5 and 6.
4. England.
5. Blom and Gumperz's work has been criticised by, among others, Maehlum (1987). She notes that the results of their work are highly uncharacteristic of Norway, and that this deviance is left unexplained. She criticises the fact that their data collection methodology is based on a dichotomy between the standard and local varieties which is predetermined by their hypothesis, and the fact that the data is collected without recording equipment.

6. The question of whether a social group, language variety or linguistic form has prestige or not is rather difficult to answer. Some researchers prefer to use the term 'supralocal' for language forms that are not used in the speech community being studied. The latter will be used wherever possible here.
7. I return to this concept below.
8. Though see chapter 7 for a critique of Milroy's use of the term.
9. Though not in the absolute sense. This should be taken as the centre of that particular person's network, not of a larger, community network.
10. See below for a discussion of this.
11. The 'Jocks' are children who attend school regularly, and who work hard. The 'Burnouts' are those children who attend school as little as possible, take drugs, etc.
12. By this is meant the person's attitude to the local group. It is a measure of how much solidarity the individual feels with his or her speech community. In the case of rural people, I will use the term 'mental urbanisation', taken from Pedersen (1994). A rural speaker's relative degree of mental urbanisation will be closely related to his or her mental orientation to the local rural group, since a high degree of solidarity with the local rural group will inhibit mental urbanisation.
13. As we shall see, however, the Doric data *does* show a correlation between social class and language use.
14. The variables and their contracted forms are detailed in chapter 3.
15. It should be kept in mind that, in the Doric study, as in all such studies, the scores represent *reported* attitudes. One can never be sure if the speaker's real feelings are accurately reported, as the presence of an age-mate, colleague or spouse (and indeed the interviewer), may cause attitudes to be differently reported, in order to present the speaker in a better light, for example. There is no easy way around this problem, but at least the problem is common across all such studies. I return to this problem below.
16. Although it must be born in mind that *other* competing motives may operate during such questioning.
17. This is discussed in 2.5 'Cognitive Dissonance'.
18. This phenomenon has been identified by many researchers, e.g. Trudgill (1974), who refers to it as covert versus overt prestige. Wicker's (1969) notion of *competing motives* is also pertinent here.
19. Corrigan (1992) writes: 'Language death at the community level is due to the loss of prestige status of the language in question. This can occur for a variety of reasons, but case studies in the field appear to suggest that external factors such as modernisation are the root causes' (Corrigan 1992: 143). This concept can equally be applied to dialect loss.
20. Though it is not made clear what is meant by this.
21. See also Keller (1982).
22. Presumably she means between young children and others.
23. The findings have not been well supported in later studies, though. Maehlum (1987) questions the findings of the Hemnesberget study. Blom and Gumperz are criticised for failing to differentiate between active and passive competence, and also for attributing discrete code-switching strategies to the local population, yet asserting that interference is a salient factor in local language use.

24. In fact, it is probably more a case of a levelled urban Scottish English, than true Scottish Standard English, a point to which I return in chapter 7.
25. These will be discussed in chapter 3.
26. In this case, Scottish Standard English, or SSE.
27. The last three Irish-speaking areas in Ireland.
28. The rise of the mass media is often cited as being responsible for the erosion of several minority languages. Radio and television facilitate contact between isolated rural areas and the majority (usually urban) language and culture (Corrigan 1992: 146). The debate surrounding this issue continues, however.

3
The Research Design

Sociolinguistic theory has been developed to account for, among other things, language change (or maintenance), though most of the research has been conducted in urban speech communities. Pedersen's (1991) and Lippi-Green's (1989) studies of rural communities have not yielded the same results as, for example, Milroy's (1980) study of urban Belfast speech. The Huntly study was conceived as a test of the various social factors involved in language change. The question of whether an individual's degree of integration into social networks is a reliable predictor of language maintenance in rural speech communities has been asked, as well as whether attitudes to the local variety, national pride, and orientation to the local speech can throw more light on the problem of accounting for resistance to change.

3.1 Research questions

1. In a rural dialect, such as that of Huntly, currently undergoing rapid levelling and standardisation, what are the speaker characteristics that seem to be most clearly correlated with those changes? In particular, how important is a speaker's integration into local social networks? Or are more subjective factors, such as a speaker's orientation to/away from the local community of greater importance?
2. What are the linguistic manifestations of this levelling and standardisation?

3.2 Pilot study

The aim of a pilot study is to obtain a small sample of sociolinguistic data, in order to formulate some ideas about the direction the main study should follow. The pilot study for Huntly was conducted in the Strathbogie Valley during December 1997.[1] The aim was to record a small database of local speech, from which observations could be made about which features of the local dialect were still in everyday use. These were checked for naturalness with the study's 'insider', a woman of 69, who is the mother of the 'nuclear' family sampled in the main study. In addition, the Doric column in the Aberdeen Press and Journal acted as a reference, as did Kynoch's (1994) book *Teach Yourself Doric*. First impressions of age grading were formed. The linguistic features observed were used to design the elicitation aids for the main study.

Four 8-year-olds, two boys and two girls, were interviewed in the school in the presence of the head teacher, and because of time constraints only one hour could be allocated. The boys were given a task and left to collaborate on that while the girls were interviewed, and then the process was repeated, with the boys being interviewed. A social profile was obtained by informal questioning about the occupations of parents, area of residence, friendship groups, aspirations, etc., after which a number of elicitation exercises were performed, using pictures and word lists. The children were asked if they could recite any poems or rhymes, and these were recorded as well.

The rest of the interviews included informants aged nine, eleven, thirteen, sixteen, thirty-seven, forty-four, and a married couple aged seventy and seventy-five. There is also a family recording, in which sixteen people were present. The database consists of at least an hour recorded with each informant, and in the case of the old couple, the interview extended to informal narratives lasting three hours. The total for the database is around nine hours, and has been manually transcribed in its entirety using the IPA. On the basis of this database, the linguistic variables for the main study were selected.

3.3 Descriptive material

Romaine points to a problem in sociolinguistics: that many researchers assume that all varieties of a language have an underlying unity, and that the standard language is to be taken as the point of reference in describing other varieties (1989: 215). 'Notions such as deletion or addition of rules and grammar simplification or complication make certain assumptions about the starting point of the analysis' (p. 215). There is no easy way around this problem, and any references to Scottish Standard English or Standard English will simply be made because they are convenient reference points, and it is not implied that they are in any way 'better' or form a linguistic point of departure for the variation observed.[2] Comparisons will be made with Urban Scots where there is descriptive material with which the Doric can be compared, though such material usually focuses upon urban Glasgow or Edinburgh Scots.

Below are some of the main linguistic features of the Doric. A subset of these has been chosen for the study,[3] based on the results of the pilot study, which showed them to be in general use. All transcriptions are phonemic, unless otherwise stated. I begin with a discussion of the vowels, following Wells' (1982) lexical sets, expanded, following Chirrey (1999), to allow for the differing lexical sets in Scots.

Wells's lexical sets

KIT	ë	DRESS	e
HEAD	i	NEVER	ï
TRAP	a̠	LOT	o
STRUT	ʌ	FOOT	ë
BATH	a̠	AFTER	e
CLOTH	o	NURSE	ʌr
FLEECE	i	FACE	e
STAY	e	PALM	a̠
THOUGHT	o	GOAT	o
GOAL	o	MORE	e
GOOSE	ʉ	PRICE	əi
PRIZE	a̠i	CHOICE	oi
MOUTH	ʉ	NEAR	iɐr
SQUARE	eɐr	START	er
BIRTH	ë	BERTH	er
NORTH	or	FORCE	or
CURE	jʉɐr	happY	ë
lettER	ɐr	horsES	ɪ
commA	ɐ		

Comments

KIT

Lowered /ɪ/ is a feature of General Scots (Jones 1997: 301). Adams (1799: 152, cited from Jones 1997: 300), refers to Scots *hell, mell, tell* matching English 'short i' in *hill, mill, till*. The feature is still present in Urban Scots, as Chirrey (1997: 225) shows /ï/ in Edinburgh Scots. In the Huntly area this feature is strongly present.

1999

DRESS

The Scots vowel in this set is higher than the one found in English south of the border:

> It is in his CLEMENCY entry that Sylvester Douglas shows most forthrightly the salience of a Scotch predilection for using an [e] vowel in contexts where low front mid vowels might be expected (Jones 1997: 298).

Chirrey (1997: 225) shows /ɛ/ for Edinburgh Scots.

TRAP

Unlike in southern varieties of English, there is no distinction between TRAP and BATH (see phoneme inventory below). In a restricted set, a different lexical incidence is evident, where the vowel is [e].

glasses	glesɪz
Aberdeen	ebɐrdin
arse	ers
apple	epḷ
ladder	ledɐr
after	eftɐr

There is evidence in the historical record for this vowel.
Quhill efter for hym prowisioune we may mak.[4]

When preceding /n/, the vowel is mid-high back in a small set of words, possibly restricted to just the following items, again a different lexical incidence:

many	monë
any	onë

Non-backing of /a/ before /l/

call	ka̠
all	a̠
ball	ba̠
wall	wa̠
small	sma̠

The backing of /a/ before /l/ in most varieties did not take place in the north-east, as /l/ had already been deleted, though it did in most traditional Scots, as is shown in the writings of Robert Burns, for example.

The alternation between the retained and the backed variant has been commented upon since at least the eighteenth century.

> Adams (1799: 152–3) asserts [...] that 'When coalescing consonants preserve the long, or broad sound of preceding vowels, then the vowel is changed [...]', listing as Scots usage *caw, faw,* or *câ, sâ* for English *call, fall,* where it is possible that his <aw> symbol represents [ɔ] [...], while <â> probably realises [ɑ] (Jones 1997: 319).

In the Doric, therefore, the /a̱/ vowel retains its phonetic shape before /l/, whereas in general Scots it would be backed to assimilate with the vocalised /l/. For example, a word like 'all', in general Scots would be pronounced something like [ɔ:], whereas in the Doric it would be [a̱:].

LOT

The vowel is higher than in the Standard English /ɒ/. In fact, the merger of /ɔ/ and /o/ in Scots has been overtly commented upon since the eighteenth century (Jones 1997: 303):

> The Scotch, after they get rid of the more barbarous pronunciation in which the *gh* is pronounced as a strong guttural, generally fall into the mistake of using the long close sound of *o,* and making (for instance) *bought,* and *boat,* the same word to the ear (Sylvester Douglas, in Jones 1991, cited from Jones 1997: 303).

LOT, THOUGHT and GOAT therefore rhyme (see also Grant and Dixon 1921: 50 and Aitken 1984: 100). Chirrey (1997: 225) shows the same is true for Urban Scots. In Huntly, when /o/ precedes a historically pro-nounced /l/, the vowel is fronted, and the /l/ is vocalised as /y/:

roll   rœy

FOOT

Wells's lexical sets do not always apply to Doric lexical items. Different lexical items in the set behave differently from each other:[5]

foot	fët	good	gwid
out	ʉt	book	bjʉk
hood	hʉd	food	fʉd
house	hʉs		

Chirrey (1997: 225) shows /ï/ for FOOT in Urban Scots.

NURSE

In RP, all vowels except /ɑ/ and /ɔ:/ are pronounced [ɜ:] before a historic-ally pronounced /r/ followed by a consonant. The Doric vowels before /r/ are pronounced as they are elsewhere in stressed positions:[6]

nurse	nʌrs	word	word*
heard	herd	bird	berd*

*These two are often pronounced with the [ʌ] vowel, especially by younger speakers. Chirrey (1997: 225) shows very similar vowels in Urban Scots.

FLEECE

The Standard English long/short vowel distinction does not hold for Scots. The difference between vowels in words such as 'sit' and 'seat' is more one of height than of length:

sit	sët	seat	sit

Chirrey (1997: 225) shows the same vowel in Urban Scots.

FACE

The quality of this vowel in Scots is not discernibly different from that in the DRESS set.

> [...] in James Robertson's 'sounding alike' list in his *The Ladies Help to Spelling* 1722, [...] we find pairs such as *age/edge, abate/abet,* and *bacon/beckon* (Jones 1997: 298)

This is shown in Chirrey's (1997: 225) lexical sets.

PRICE

The first mora of this diphthong is central, very short and unstressed, representing a very early post vowel-breaking diphthong [ᵊi].
Chirrey (1997: 225) shows /ʌi/ in Urban Scots.

PRIDE

When followed by a voiced consonant or zero, the diphthong is lower [ai]. This is one of the conditions of the Scottish Vowel length Rule (Aitken 1979).

lettER /ɐr/

The schwa in the Doric is rather lower than that in Scottish Standard English, when it appears before /r/, /n/, /m/ and /l/. However, before /z/, /k/ and /t/, it is similar to SSE. Chirrey (1997: 225) shows /v/ in Urban Scots.

horsES   horsɪz

Chirrey (1997: 225) shows /ï/ in Urban Scots.

Phoneme inventory

A phoneme inventory will augment the lexical sets given above, as the standard lexical sets do not capture the groupings in the Doric.

Monophthongs

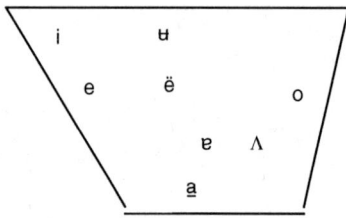

/nid/	'need'
/bed/	'bed'
/hạn/	'hand'
/fʉd/	'food'
/hël/	'hill'
/horsiz/	'horsES'
/betɐr/	'bettER'
/kvp/	'cup'
/lot/	'lot'
/dʉn/	'down'

Outward-gliding diphthongs

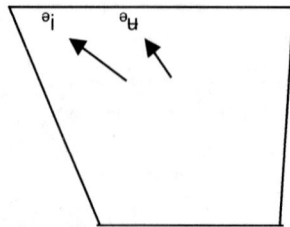

/tʲit/   'tight'
/fʲʉnd/   'found' (almost the same as SSE)

Inward-gliding (centring) diphthongs

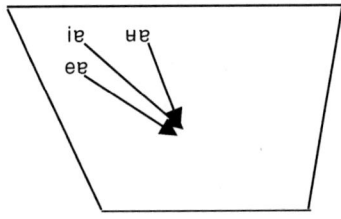

/hiɐr/   'here'
/meɐr/   'more'
/kjʉɐr/   'cure'

Upward-gliding (rising) diphthongs

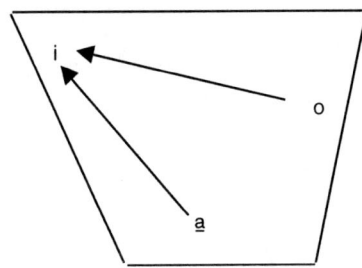

/dɐvaɪd/   'divide'
/noiz/   'noise'

Forward-gliding diphthongs

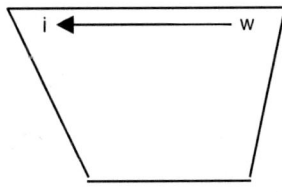

/gwid/   'good'

Backward-gliding diphthongs

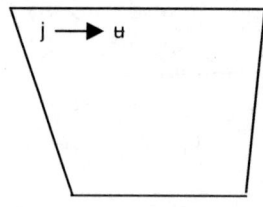

/bjʉk/   'book'

More vocalic features

It has already been noted that /e/ is higher than in other varieties. However, certain lexical items have merged with the FLEECE set, so words such as 'head' and 'dead' rhyme with 'heed' and 'deed'. In other lexical items, it is [e], so <u>aneth</u> 'beneath' rhymes with 'death'.

In the Doric a mid-high or high front vowel in a restricted lexical set corresponds to southern English varieties in [əʊ~ɔ]. This is a matter of lexical incidence, rather than being found throughout the vocalic system.

home   hem
stone   stin
more   mer
sore   ser[7]
only   enlë
no   ne[8]

Diphthongs

A feature of certain northern English varieties is different glide paths for the diphthongs in certain lexical items, such as the South Yorkshire [kɔɪl] 'coal', and [gʊət] 'goat', where Standard English has [əʊ]. In the Doric, diphthong-like glides, starting with bilabial and palatal approximants, are found in some lexical items:

our   wir
school   skwil
good   gwid

This pronunciation, with a fronting diphthong, is a strong feature of the Doric, often used in pantomimes and jokes. Instead of the original high back vowel simply being fronted, as in General Scots, a diphthong, with its first mora something like the original high back vowel, glides into a high front unrounded vowel. In another set, a high front back-ing/lowering diphthong is found:

duck	djʉk
cake	kjạk
book	bjʉk

This has not happened in all words. Historically, /u/ was fronted else-where, followed by loss of rounding, to yield [i]. Again, this is restricted to a small lexical set. It is not clear why FOOD, FOOT, and FOOL have each ended up in different, and apparently fossilised, sets.

fool	fil
do	di[9]
boots	bits

(Historically) long monophthongs

A well-known feature of Scots is its retention of the high back monoph-thong in words like:

brow	brʉ
mouth	mʉθ
town	tʉn
house	hʉs
down	dʉn
round	rʉn
out	ʉt
pocket	pʉtʃ

While many regional varieties in Scotland now have a diphthong [ᵊʉ] here, corresponding to southern /aʊ/, the Doric retains the monophthong. However, the *high front* monophthong is now mostly diphthongised:

| find | fᵊin |

Though before /x/ the vowel appears not to have broken, but simply lowered:

| night | nɛxt |
| right | rext |

In some words, the monophthong survives:

| fly | fli |

This is even pronounced this way in compounds such as 'butterfly'.

Non-backing of /a/ before /ŋ/

wrong	raŋ
long	laŋ

The Northumbrian and Scots varieties retained the low front vowel, while southern varieties rounded and backed it before /ŋ/.

Lowering of Middle English /u/

bull	bʌl
pull	pʌl

The vowel is the result of the ME, MSc lowering of /u/ to /ʌ/ working through the lexicon in the Doric, leaving no fossils, as Standard English has in 'bull', 'pull', 'push', 'bush'.

The diphthong /oi/

boil	ba̱il
spoil	spa̱il
pay	pa̱i
way	wa̱i

The diphthong in this lexical set has a low front vowel for the initial mora, perhaps as a result of a merger with the PRIDE set. This is a case of lexical incidence, though, as not all /oi/ words have merged with PRIDE:

boy	boi
noise	noiz

Consonants

The inventory is:

p b t d k g f v θ ð s z ʃ ʒ x ʍ j l m n ŋ r w

Non-affricated plosives in a restricted lexical set

church	kërk
chest	këst
bridge	brëg
stitch	stik
britches	brëks

Most historical linguists accept that the plosive forms are a Norse influence (for example Johnstone 1997), though for the alternative view that Scots conserves older (northern) plosives in these lexical items, see Taylor (1974).

Denti-labials for /hw/

A characteristic feature of north-east Scots is the denti-labial onsets in 'wh-questions', where Scottish Standard English has /hw/. This feature is also found in the adjective 'white':

what	fët
who	fa̱
when	fa̱n~fɐn
which	fëtʃ
where	fa̱r
why	fët wa̱ɪ[10]
how	fʉ
whose	fa̱z
white	fʰit

Rhoticity

General Scots still displays rhoticity, and the north-east conserves the alveolar trill or tap, except in younger (especially female) speakers.

Elision of ð and θ

this	ës
that	a̱t

This only happens in initial position. In medial position /h/ is substituted.[11]

Deletion of /v/

/v/ is often deleted (or substituted by /w/) in medial and final position:

over	a̱wɐr
give	gi
have	he~hɐv

For 'have', the first form is used in negation: 'I dinna hae ony' [a dënɐ he onë]. The second is used in question-formation, where the 'do' auxiliary is not used: 'Hev ye a car?' [hɐv jɐ ɐ kar].

Fricatives in temporal deixis

The lexical form of a small set of temporal deictics preserves an older fricative onset, resulting from the cliticisation of the definite article 'the' to the noun:

today	ðɐde
tonight	ðɐnɛxt
tomorrow	ðɐmorᵊn

The fricative represents the same archaic form which gave us the standard form in [t].

Consonant clusters

hand	han
find	fain
cold	kal
old	al
self	sel

Under a final consonant-cluster reduction rule, the plosive (or fricative in 2nd position) was lost.

The 'extra' phoneme

The presence of the velar fricative is unique to Scotland among all the anglophone countries, and the north-east is the most conservative with regard to this feature. /x/ survives only as a fossil elsewhere in Scotland, in lexical items that are high in the consciousness of speakers, such as 'loch'.

daughter	doxtɐr
bright	brɛxt
night	nɛxt
right	rɛxt
bought	boxt
thought	θoxt

The glottal stop

This feature is increasingly being used as a variant of /t/ across the country, and north-east Scotland is also showing this trend. However, unlike, for example, Glasgow, the feature shows signs of only recently reaching the north-east. This is discussed in 4.3.

Lexical features

above   ɐbin

These two are simply different lexical forms of the same word. The presence of the final nasal is a remnant from the Old English form a-bufan. Fronting and unrounding of the vowel, as detailed above, along with /v/-weakening and deletion yielded the modern Doric form abi : n.

ankle	kwit[12]
ask	spir[13]
at all	ɐva[14]
bathing costume	dʉkɐrz

From the Doric verb [dʉk] 'swim'.

big/great/much   mʌkɐl

The Old English form was micel, and the Middle English forms were mukil, mekil, meikill, mikil 'large, great, powerful, important, much, great amount'.

boy	lʉn[15]
broom/brush	bizɐm
child	berɐn[16]
cover	hap[17]
cry	grit
damage, handle roughly	blad[18]
daze	dwam[19]
dig	hœyk[20]
muddy, sticky	klartë[21]
dust	stjʉr~stʉr[22]
every	ëlkë[23]
few/couple	pʌkɐl[24]
fool	gʔip
frog	pʌdëk

From Old English padde. The plosive at the end seems innovative.

frozen   dʒɛlt

This comes from Old Scots and northern dialects gell, geal (unknown origin) 'tingle, ache with cold'.

fuss (verb)   faʃ

From Old French se fâcher.

girl   kwain

From Old English cwēn, and of course spelt 'queen' in Standard English now, with its semantic narrowing.

hit/pat/slap/clap   klap
[al gi jə ə klap on ə lʌg]   'I'll give you a clap on the ear'
[hizklapənədog]   'He's patting the dog.'
if   gën

The form and meaning are unchanged from Old Scots.

knock/tap/chop   tʃap
[ərz sʌmbdë tʃapən on ə duər]   'There's somebody knocking on the
                                  door'
know   ken

This is another well-known Scots lexical item. In Old English the verb was cennan, Middle English kenne(n), ON kenna 'to know, recognise, acknowledge, perceive, teach, tell'. In some areas of England the Old English cognate cnāwan was used, which is the ancestor of the modern Standard form.

muddy   dʌbë

The origin is Old Scots dubbi 'muddy pool', related to Old Irish dubh linn 'dark pool'.

porridge   broz

From Old Scots browis, Old French broez 'porridge, broth'.

puppy   fʌlpë~felpë

This is the word 'whelp' in its diminutive form. The initial consonant follows the normal [f] for Doric forms of words which have [hw] or [ʍ] onsets in general Scots, such as 'where', 'when'.

ram   tʌp

From Old Scots and northern English dialects tup, tuip, teep (origin unknown).

remember   main

This is the verb 'mind', which used to mean 'think of' (think of the step), and later took the meaning (be careful, watch over). It still exists in the compound 'remind' (make someone think of something again).

shirt   sark

From OSc, Old English 'a man's shirt'.

speak nonsense   hever

This word is not listed in the *Dictionary of the Older Scots Tongue*. It may be the Scots cognate of the Standard English 'hover'. As mentioned, there is a correspondence between southern [əʊ~ɒ] and Scots [e]. In Northern England the word means 'be uncertain'. To hover between two points of view would be similar to this meaning, and the Scots sense is related.

struggle, work   tʃav

The origin may be Old Scots cave 'fall over helplessly' or chave 'strew with chaff'. The hard work associated with agriculture makes the association clear.

sure   sëker

This is related to the word 'secure'.[25] The medial consonant is attested in the 13th-century literature:

> All þat þey moued…was to be secewre of hemself and siris to ben y-callid.[26]

swim   dʉk

This is related to the southern verb 'to duck' (disappear under the water, or behind a wall, for example).

talk   spëk

The word 'talk' is only used when referring to a southern way of speaking, or when a local uses 'posh' language.

that (over there)   jon

From OSc, Old English yon, yun, yahn, indicating a person or thing at some distance (third position deixis).

then   sain

From Old Scots syne, sine, saen 'thereupon, directly after, next, hence, ago, since'.

through, along   ben

From Old Scots <u>ben</u>, <u>bein</u>, adverb, preposition 'in or towards the inner part or end of a house'.

tidy up   red ʌp

From Old Scots <u>red</u>, <u>reid</u> 'debris, rubbish'.

to   tël

This is used invariantly, unlike in Standard English, where there is an alternation between 'to' and 'till'. The latter is the Old Norse form.

[hë gɐd ʌp a̱ntël ɐ rif]   'he went up onto the roof'

vest   semɪt

From Old Scots <u>semmit</u>, <u>seamit</u>, <u>semat</u> 'undervest', 'shirt', Old English <u>samite</u> 'fine silk cloth undergarment'.

> Cesar brocht with him nouthir wapyn na armuris na othir defence bot in his <u>semat</u>.[27]

wall   dᵊik

This is from the Old English <u>dīc</u> 'ditch', 'wall', now with the palato-alveolar affricate in Standard English, with its current meaning.

yes   a̱j

This is a well-known feature of not only Scots, but also of northern English. Its origin is OSc, Old English <u>ay</u>, <u>ai</u>, <u>ei</u>, ON <u>ei</u>, <u>ey</u> 'always, ever, at all times'.

Morphological and morpho-phonemic features

An orthographic system is difficult to achieve for Scots. Writers such as Robert Burns made popular a system which tried to show the differences between Scots and English pronunciation, so 'have' was written 'hae'. Here I have chosen a more phonetically based orthography, with IPA transcriptions where necessary.

Verbal paradigms for the Doric

'Go'

Infinitive	Preterite	Present continuous	Perfect	Imperative
gʲaŋ	gëd	ga̱ɐn	gin	gëŋ

The word 'been' is therefore not used in locative expressions as a quasi-perfect of 'go', as is done in Standard English.

'Have'

Infinitive	Preterite	Present	Perfect	Imperative
he	d, hɐd	v, hɐv, hənɐ (neg)	hen	he

'Do'

Infinitive	Preterite	Present	Perfect	Imperative
di	dëd	di~dëv, dëz (3rd sg.)	din	di

'Be'

Infinitive	Preterite	Present	Perfect	Imperative
bi	wëz	ëz, a̱m	bin	bi

[ëz] for all persons and numbers except first singular, which is [a̱m]

Preterite forms of certain verbs

There are more verbs that follow the regular (weak) pattern than in Standard English. There is therefore an absence of stem-vowel changing in certain preterite forms, as can be seen in the following:

blow	bla̱	blew	bla̱d
sell	sel	sold	selt
tell	tel	told	telt

The devoiced final consonant is a normal feature in other preterite forms:

covered   kʌvɐrt

In Standard English its distribution is phonetically governed: voicing is determined by the preceding consonant, for example in 'picked' [pɪkt] and 'rigged' [ɹɪgd]. In the Doric, in the phonetic environment of a non-alveolar consonant, the preterite ending is fuller:

kick	këkɐt
pick	pëkɐt
catch	ka̱tʃɐt

The rule is therefore:
{-ed} → [d], V __
　　　 → [t], /l, r/ __
　　　 → [ɐt], everywhere else

Prefixes

The prefix 'a-' is used with prepositional forms that have 'be-' in Standard English.

beneath	ɐnɛθ
below	ɐblo
before	ɐfor
above	ɐbin
behind	ɐhain
between	ɐtwin

There was dialectal variation in OE, Middle English prepositional forms beginning in <u>a-</u> and <u>be- ~ bi-</u>. Both had the sense 'by, near, about'.

Cliticisation of main verbs

The verb 'have' is reduced to [v], not only as an auxiliary in perfect tense constructions, but also as a main verb:

'I've a dog'

The same applies to the past tense of this verb:

'I'd [tw<u>a</u>] goats'

This is also a feature of Northern English varieties.

Negation

The negator is [-nɐ~-ne], and is used uniformly, without any regressive vowel assimilation in the verb.

Standard English	Scots
can't	k<u>a</u>nɐ
haven't	h<u>a</u>vnɐ
don't	dënɐ
won't	wëlnɐ
wouldn't	wʉdnɐ

Diminutives

Diminutives are common in the Doric:

man	mạnë
woman	wᵓifë

Pronouns

everybody	ạbdë
everything	ạhën

These words are a compound of 'all' and 'body', and 'all' plus 'thing'. The negative and general forms are given below:[28]

nobody	nebdë
nothing	nehën
anything	onëhën

3.4 Choice of variables

Language variation research is centred on the notion of the linguistic variable, 'an element which has a number of realisations, or variants, in speech, but a constant meaning' (McMahon 1994: 235). Hatch and Lazaraton's definition is rather more general, applying also to other types of research: 'a *variable* can be defined as an attribute of a person, a piece of text, or an object which "varies" from person to person, text to text, object to object, or from time to time' (1991: 51). The second definition is useful in a study such as the present one, where non-linguistic variables are included. When analysing the data, the experimenter often assigns a score to each occurrence of the variable, say 1 or 0. The resulting figures are then plotted against age, sex, and so on, to see whether any significant pattern emerges. This kind of quantitative, statistical approach is necessary because most speakers will use both variants, but the frequency of use will vary according to non-linguistic factors (McMahon 1994: 235).

After transcribing the recordings made during the pilot study, a number of linguistic variables were identified as being clear features of the vernacular. These were identified by comparing their use with equivalent forms in Scottish Standard English (SSE). Some of them are found in general Scots, but others are unique to the north-east. These will be identified below. It is realised that Scottish Standard English is not spoken even in the city of Aberdeen as it is in, for example, Edinburgh. Aberdeen urban speech has distinctly north-eastern characteristics. Phonological items are included as a category of analysis, as they

> are high in frequency, have a certain immunity from conscious suppression, are integral units of larger structures, and may easily be quantified on a linear scale (Macaulay 1991: 4).

Morphological and morpho-lexical variables were also used. Although fifty lexical variables were used to arrive at a lexical score for each speaker, it was initially felt that these may not be very reliable as indicators of dialect maintenance. Passive recognition of lexical items does not imply active use. The results will show that this view is over-cautious, however, as will be seen later.

3.4.1   Phonological variables chosen for the study

Using the term 'phonological variable' for the following features of the Doric sound system is not entirely without problems. For some of the variables, the vernacular vowel is only found in a restricted set of lexical items nowadays, and can therefore be said to be a case of lexical incidence, rather than a phonological feature. This is what Kerswill (1987) found in Durham. There, a large number of words exist in two lexical forms.

> One form is as close to standard English as the Durham phonological inventory and its phonetic realisation will allow, while the other form is lexically distinct from standard English while remaining identifiable as the 'same word' as its standard counterpart (Kerswill 1987: 28).

In Huntly, whether we choose to view the variation as phonological or morpho-lexical, the use of the local variant shows a manifestation of vernacular versus standard use, and as such effectively allows us to answer the research question. The variables chosen have for all practical purposes two variants: the clearly (north-eastern) Scots variant and the Scottish Standard English one.[29] The binary nature of the variables means that each variant can be allocated a score. As the present study is concerned with the social factors involved in retarding language change, it was decided that use of the Scots variant would attract a score of 1, and use of the Scottish Standard English variant a score of 0.

Choosing a writing system is not easy for studies of Scots. A system based on that of the poets was rejected, on the basis that it would have left room for confusion. The IPA will therefore be used throughout, as the Doric forms are often so phonetically different from SSE. All transcriptions are phonemic, unless otherwise stated.

(1) Initial /f/ where Scottish Standard English has /ʍ/ in 'wh-questions'. This is, by all accounts, unique to the north-east. Both Scottish Standard English and Urban Scots have /ʍ/ in conservative speakers, but in younger speakers, there is evidence of a merger between /ʍ/ and /w/ (Chirrey 1997: 227).

fɑrz ɑt	'where's that?'
fʉ mʌkɐlz ɑt	'how much is that?'

(2) Doric /e/ ~ Scottish Standard English /o/ correspondence, as in [hem] 'home'. This is also found in Urban Scots (Chirrey 1997: 225).

(3) Non-glottalisation of /t/. This feature has a different status in the study. As will be shown in chapter 4, use of the glottal stop is relatively new to the area, and the variant is neither a dialect nor a Scottish Standard English feature. Its use has been quantified as part of the study, but it cannot be regarded as a dialect indicator in the same sense as the other variables. In some urban Scots varieties, the glottal variant has been shown to exist for many years (see, for example, Stuart-Smith 1999: 183).

hi fɑd entël ë wɑtɐr   'he fell into the water'

(4) The presence of /x/ in certain preterite forms and certain lexical items, very rare elsewhere, except for some older rural Ayrshire speakers, (Robert Millar, University of Aberdeen, personal communication). According to Johnston (1997: 505):

> The phoneme /x/ is somewhat recessive in Mid and, to a lesser extent, Southern Scots. Even in these areas, however, many speakers retain it variably in place-names like *Auchtermuchty*, personal names like *Lachlan*, and words without true English cognates like *pibroch*, while replacing /x/ in all 'ordinary words' like *right, bought* with /x/-less Scottish Standard English forms.

The absence of /x/ in this study attracts a score of 0.

boxt	'bought'
nɛxt	'night'

(5) Consonant-cluster reduction. This feature is found in Scots generally (Jones 1997: 327), and also to a certain extent in all English speech. It is more marked in Scots, however, and the presence of the cluster attracts a score of 0.

grʌn	'ground'
hʌnɐr	'hundred'
han~hanz	'hand ~ hands'

(6) /v/-deletion or -substitution. This is found in Scots generally (Stuart-Smith 1999: 209). Presence of the /v/ attracts a score of 0.

gi	'give'
he	'have'
owɐr	'over'

(7) Full rhoticity with a trilled or tapped realisation. In the Doric, /r/ is realised in all positions, either as [r] or [ɾ]. The use of [ɹ] or zero has been regarded as non-dialect, and attracts a score of 0. The alveolar approximant has been equated with speech in urban centres, such as Edinburgh,[30] and is beginning to show signs of increase in the young females in this sample. The allophonic realisation is also phonetically governed, but the elicitation materials took this into account.

Non pre-vocalic [r]

kert	'cart'

pre- or inter-vocalic [r]

karɐvan	'caravan'

(8) [ʌ] where Standard English has a small set of fossilised lexical items in [ʊ]. This Doric feature is rarely found elsewhere in Scotland (Robert Millar, personal communication). Use of the Scottish Standard English [ʉ] attracts a score of 0.

bʌl, fʌl, pʌl	'bull', 'full', 'pull'

(9) [a] where Standard English has [æ] (SSE does have a lower vowel than Standard English here, but the Doric vowel is even lower and more back). This is found in Scots generally, including Urban Scots (Chirrey 1997: 225).

han, badʒɐr, manë	'hand', 'badger', 'manny'

3.4.2   Morphological variables chosen for the study

(1) Preterite endings in /ɪt/ are used where Standard English has /-t/ or a stem vowel change. This feature is still found in Scots generally (Beal 1997: 351).

këk~këkɪt	kick ~ kicked
pëk~pëkɪt	pick ~ picked
k̠atʃ~k̠atʃɪt	catch ~ caught

This ending (or its allophonic variant [-t]) is used also where Standard English has a stem vowel change:

tel~telt	tell ~ told
sel~selt	sell ~ sold
ken~kent	know ~ knew

This is the only morphological variable used in the study, as it proved too difficult to elicit variables of this type generally. Use of a Scottish standard English variant, such as 'sold', attracted a score of 0.

3.4.3   Lexical variables chosen for the study

The list of lexical variables is given below. Those items that are not generally found in Scots elsewhere are marked with an asterisk. The speaker was required to give the equivalent English word, or a Scots sentence using the word correctly. Failure to do so attracted a score of 0.

Table 4   List of dialect lexical items chosen for the study

Word	equivalent
1. mʌkl	big/much/many
2. pʌkl*	few/small/little
3. lʉn*	boy
4. kwain*	girl
5. blad*	damage
6. tʃav*	struggle
7. klap	slam/hit
8. dʉk	swim
9. djʉk*	duck
10. ext	bother/own/eight
11. hap*	cover
12. hevɐr	speak nonsense
13. klartë	dirty
14. red ʌp	clean/tidy up
15. rœy ʌp	roll up
16. ʒik	seek/search/look for

Table 4   (Continued)

Word	equivalent
17. spir*	ask
18. gën	if
19. faʃ	fuss
20. ɐva*	at all
21. ben*	through
22. ɐstrin*	yesterday evening
23. sain	then
24. bizɐm	brush
25. dʉ	dove
26. dwam	daze
27. dˀik	ditch/wall
28. tʌp	ram
29. jaʉ	ewe
30. gˀip	fool
31. sark	shirt
32. spʌrgë~spʌrdë	sparrow
33. ëlkë*	every
34. ɐneθ	beneath
35. ɐbin	above
36. brʉ	forehead
37. broz	meal porridge
38. tʃap	tap/strike
39. krak	conversation/fun
40. dʌbë*	dirty
41. fʌlpë~felpë	whelp/puppy
42. grit	weep
43. hœyk	dig
44. dʒilt*	frozen
45. kest	chest (box/body part)
46. pʉtʃ	pocket
47. kwit*	ankle
48. semët	vest
49. sëkɐr*	sure
50. stjʉ~stʉr*	dust

In sum then, the speaker was tested on his or her knowledge and use of the Doric phonology, morphology and lexis. As far as possible, the speaker's attention was drawn away from the fact that what was being investigated was language. Use of a picture list was found to be very useful, and slight pressure was put on the speaker to quickly say the first word that came to mind when seeing each picture. This made the task seem more like a test of one's ability to recognise what appeared in the (rather badly drawn) pictures. It was found that this elicited more natural-sounding speech, with much laughing as the pictures were deciphered. A scene description and treasure hunt too, drew attention away from the fact that what was being investigated was language.[31] The lexical test was very obviously about language, but came at the end, and seemed to draw out linguistic pride, as it was not about pronunciation, but about a set of lexical items which are very clearly associated with the local vernacular. Each time a speaker used a vernacular phonological or morphological form, or correctly identified the meaning of a vernacular lexical item, he or she was allocated a score of 1. Failure to use such phonological and morphological forms, or to correctly identify the meaning of such lexical items attracted a score of 0.

This leaves the social variables. As Kerswill (1994: 51) puts it: finding a set of extra-linguistic parameters relevant to the informant group is crucial in a sociolinguistic study. For reasons of practicality, these are normally selected from the set of all possible parameters in order to simplify the results, and effective selection requires that the investigator know the community rather well. The social variables chosen for the Huntly study are based on previous sociolinguistic research in the area of language change.

3.4.4 Social networks

Gumperz (1976b: 14) points out that personal network structure is influenced by a very large number of factors. It is therefore not possible to identify and measure all of them, though it is important to be able to justify the approach which has been adopted. The Huntly SOCNET score is a network index score, or a *combination* of interactional and structural criteria (mostly the former), which has been used to test whether a high social network score will predict a high (conservative) dialect index score, as was discussed under 2.1.2. A comparison of the Huntly SOCNET score and Stokowski's (1994) criteria will be useful at this point. I have taken a speaker at random, AM, thirty-two years old, and listened to her answers to the section of the questionnaire on social network again. From these I have built up a table and a network map, or sociogram, set out on the next page. This kind of *structural* information is not available for most individuals in the database, however, as most speakers did not elaborate in such depth. The Huntly SOCNET score, as is discussed below, is a scalar index of network *interaction*.

The sociogram for AM is not maximally dense or multiplex, but it is doubtful whether anyone in fact has such a network. What is, however, clear, is that AM is very well integrated in the local community.

Table 5 SOCNET responses for AM

1. Do your friends generally know each other as well as knowing you? **Density or distance**	yes (B, D, E, G, H, I, J)
2. Do you have family members in this area? How many? **Content**	yes (A, C, F)
3. Do you work/go to school with 2 or more local people? **Number and frequency of interactions**	yes (A, G, I)
4. Do you work/go to school with at least 2 other locals of the same sex? **Number and frequency of interactions**	yes (A, I)
5. Do you spend time with work/school friends after work/school, or during weekends and holidays? **Multiplexity**	no
6. Do you take part in a local group (organised or non-organised) in the area? (religion, scouts, guides, youth groups, DofE, sports, jobs, holiday activities, hunting, cards, Bridge). **Strength**	no
7. Do you take part in leisure/sports activities with 2 or more locals or work/school friends? **Strength**	no
8. Have your mother and father lived here all their lives? **Content**	yes SOCNET total = 5/8

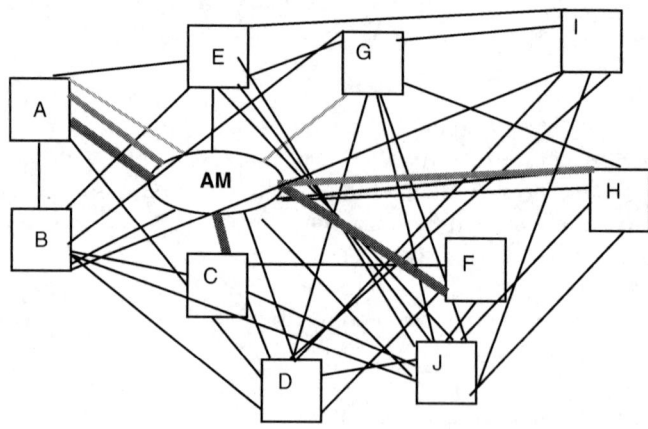

Key:

Friends of yours that know each other.

Work/school with 2 or more locals.

Work/school with 2/more of same sex.

Family members.

Figure 4 Sociogram for AM

AM's answers to questions 5, 6 and 7 were almost uniformly negative, as there are not many such organised activities in the area, and people generally work long hours. In addition to this, one has to consider the distances involved, as many of the farms are quite large. The Huntly SOCNET score clearly has limitations for *structural* criteria, such as the following:

1. Size
2. Density
3. Centrality
4. Clustering
5. Network role of the speaker

It does, however, accurately measure the *interactional* criteria of the network, and as such is similar to Milroy's network strength index:

1. Number and frequency of interactions
2. Multiplexity
3. Strength
4. Content

The Huntly SOCNET questionnaire is based closely on Milroy's and Pedersen's questionnaires, and this makes the scores obtained comparable to theirs. As many of the respondents in the Huntly study are farmers, or their wives or children, numbers 3 and 4 have been slightly revised, and some extra questions added, which also serves to make it statistically more valid. These questions are similar, but more specifically stated. All attempts have been made to keep them locally relevant. The questions were worded specifically to include housewives and children, and the questions were rephrased often during the interviews to tease out such possibilities. A more complex measure, perhaps more structurally oriented, could not have been achieved without spending an extremely lengthy period of time in the fieldwork area, living among, and interacting with local people, and was in any case unnecessary. The norm-enforcement influence of the network is effectively tested by the questionnaire.

3.4.5 Social class

Social class has proved to be a very important factor in our understanding of language variation and change. Since Labov's early work in New York

City, we have repeatedly discovered correlations between social class and language use in various locations around the world (Trudgill 1986, Kerswill and Williams 1997, Chambers 1995). Romaine refers to Labov's (1980) argument that we should tackle the problem of why sound changes by looking for the 'social location' of the originators (Romaine 1989: 206). Labov points to those speakers who have the highest *local* status, and the greatest number of local and supra-local network contacts, as the most advanced in ongoing sound change. Having the highest local status means that their speech will be emulated by others, and being aware of, and having contacts with, the supra-local level of social communication, means that they will not only have access to, but also be more open to, acquiring non-local speech forms.

In a rural community such as the one in the present study, clear social divisions may not exist, or at least, they may be more difficult to access. Within the local rural community in the Strathbogie Valley, there seems to be *some* socio-economic variation, but problems occur when trying to measure this. There are no prestige suburbs or ghettos, as found in most urban centres, and most people have similar levels of education. Those who do decide to study usually move on afterwards to seek employment. Farming and agricultural support industries are the main sources of livelihood.

In urban studies, the researcher can work with predetermined know-ledge about which areas are inhabited by which socio-economic groups, and use visual clues from the types of housing to support this. In rural areas, such neatly packaged categories are not present. One can't easily ask how large the farm is, how many cattle or sheep are owned, and how much the machinery cost. Most of the children were interviewed at school, and such clues as the type of housing lived in were completely absent. The scalar measure of social class used, therefore, measures in a relatively neutral way, socio-economic clues about the individual, which can then be used as an index score, with which other scores can be com-pared statistically. This part of the questionnaire was drawn up with the assistance of Annie Williams, and resembles the one used in Kerswill and Williams's work in Milton Keynes, Reading and Hull.

This by no means represents a comprehensive list of all the possible questions one could ask regarding the social class of a respondent, and some of the questions may not seem specific to social class, though the link is often made. The location and type of housing, and whether it is rented or owned, can give insights into the matter, as can more indirect questions, such as where holidays are spent, for example. Occupation, however, is felt by many to be a reasonably reliable indicator of social

Table 6 Social class questionnaire

Social class
1. What is your occupation?
2. What is/was your father's occupation?
3. What is/was your mother's occupation?
4. What do you think of the standard of education locally?
5. Is it important to have good discipline in school?
6. Do you think a good education is important?
7. Which newspapers do you read?
8. Did you/will you do 'O' Grade, Highers, University or College studies?

class (Reid 1978, Cheshire 1982). As many of the respondents lived on farms, the question of location was not effective, and the houses seemed to be, on the whole, rather similar. The format used therefore represent a set of questions that are felt to be locally relevant.

3.4.6 Life modes: the question of mental urbanisation

Pedersen (1994) believes that her concept of the mental component of life modes is not specifiable to the point where one can measure it directly, but that it can illuminate linguistic and other behavioural patterns within sociologically defined groups. In this study, however, a section of the questionnaire was developed to yield an index score for degree of mental urbanisation, which can be compared with the linguistic scores. This takes the form of a section of questions with gradable answers along a five-point scale (see below). The answers were graded from zero to four,[32] reflecting a mental orientation to either a rural or urban life, or a mental urbanisation index. This index has been called MENURB, in order to distinguish it from the conventional notion of Life Modes (Højrup 1983). An index score was arrived at for each speaker, with a maximum score (40) indicating the greatest *resistance* to mental urbanisation (similar to Pedersen's rural life mode), and zero the greatest level of mental urbanisation. Because of the weighting of the answers, it should be borne in mind that the index actually represents (resistance to) mental urbanisation. There were similar sections assessing attitude towards Scottish identity and the Doric (see appendices). All these scores were compared with the social network scores, to explain linguistic variation between individuals who have the same network scores.

Questionnaire: MENURB

The scale used for this section was graded as follows:

0 str. agree	1 agree	2 neutral	3 disagree	4 str. disagree

Here follows the section of the questionnaire on attitudes to urban lifestyles:

1. I notice what people are wearing in Aberdeen. I like to keep up with city fashion.
2. I mostly watch TV programmes about city life and avoid nature/environmental programmes.
3. I would like to follow a career in a city rather than one where I work in the country or a small town around here.
4. I think it is very important to own a PC or at least have access to one at school/work.
5. I would love to move away from this area to the city.
6. When I am in Aberdeen, I feel at home and unstressed by the crowds and traffic.
7. City folk are just as friendly as anyone, and are basically the same as country folk.
8. I never eat brose or any traditional meals. I prefer modern/international dishes.
9. A good education, getting on in life, and having all the modern equipment and appliances is more important than quietness and having a good family life.
10. I'd rather spend a day in Aberdeen playing computer games and shopping than spend it walking up Bennachie[33] with friends and family.

The number of questions and the grading of the answers is due to the need for comparison with the other attitudinal indices.

Potential problems

There are a number of potential problems with some of the questions asked. For example, questions 2, 4 and 8 could be criticised for not being reliable measures of mental urbanisation. It is easy to imagine the city dweller, tired of the hustle and bustle of city life, relaxing to a television documentary about wildlife. But such a person may have no desire to leave the city and settle in a rural area. A rural person may not like the taste of traditional meals like haggis, but still show high degrees of solidarity with the local rural community. These problems are present in most questionnaires of this sort, and there is no easy way around the problem. There is, however, one factor which operates during the interview to reduce the potential for error. Interviewees are sensitive to the 'message' contained in the line of questioning. They very soon seem to realise what the interviewer is driving at, and answer the questions in a way that demonstrates their feelings on the matter. In such a way, the questions that may not seem to be good measures of what is being investigated, become viewed in the general vein of the line of questioning used.

The reader will recall that Pedersen found that those speakers who have rurally dominated composite life modes generally have higher dialect scores than other informants with the same network scores. Although Pedersen's analysis was impressionistic, it paved the way for a study that could quantify such data for each individual involved. For example, in the graph below, all three speakers belong to the same age and sex group, and have the same SOCNET (social network) scores. The social network framework predicts that the norm enforcement effect of their equivalent networks should operate reasonably uniformly on their language use. In reality they show remarkable variation in their PHOVAR (phonetic variable) scores.

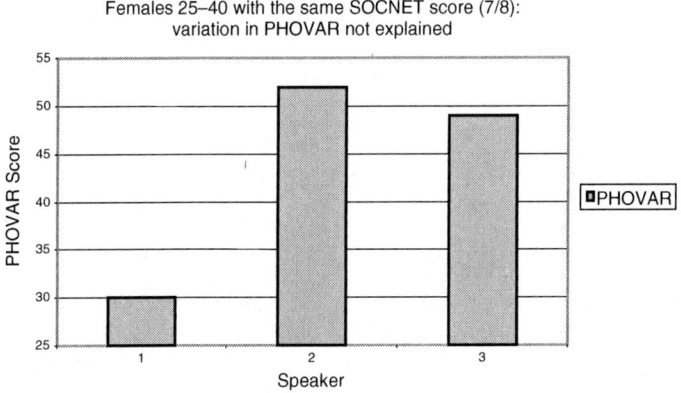

Figures 5   Dialect scores not predicted by social network strength

Examining the other social scores reveals that speaker one has a MENURB score of 21, speaker two 39, and speaker three 24 (the maximum is 40). The correlation between mental urbanisation and language use will be investigated in detail in chapter 4.

3.5   Methodology and data collection

The questionnaire

The most widely used direct approach for gathering sociolinguistic data is the *questionnaire*, which can contain open or closed-question items. In an open-question questionnaire, the respondents can freely express their opinion on topics. The advantage of this approach is that informants' answers are not framed by the researcher's own perception of the issue and may yield different results from what was anticipated. The disadvantage in a written questionnaire is that the informants may not express their opinion in detail because they would have to write it down. In an oral interview, however, they may 'fail to focus on the actual dimension of a question' (Agheyisi and Fishman 1970: 147 and 8, cited from Löw 1997: 9).

A closed-question item makes analysing the data much easier, yet it has the disadvantage of imposing on the informants the researcher's categories and preconceived ideas. Sometimes only a yes/no-answer is required, sometimes five- or seven-point linear scales are used. A frequently used experimental method is the *matched-guise technique*, which was developed in the 1960s. Developed originally for a bilingual setting, it consists of a tape-recording of several bilingual speakers reading a passage and its translation in each of the languages in question. Then the different versions are arranged so that the two guises of each speaker do not follow each other on the tape. Informants are asked to judge each voice on the tape (*friendly–unfriendly, intelligent–unintelligent,* etc.). They are not aware that they are listening to each speaker twice. The ratings for one speaker in his or her two guises can then be compared, and attitude differences towards the one or the other variety are used in the analysis. The method aims at excluding and controlling all possible intervening variables other than the language variety in question, such as voice quality, personality of speaker, and topic. This, however, proves problematic because the fact that translated passages are read out makes the recordings often quite artificial. This applies especially to studies in which standard and non-standard varieties are compared since texts in the vernacular are very seldom written down and read out (Löw 1997: 10).

For this reason, the Huntly questionnaire consists of questions or statements read out to the respondent, who then chooses an answer from the ranked set given (see above, under Mental Urbanisation). The data was collected in much the same way as in the pilot study, with the only changes being to the design of the word-list and personal profile questionnaire. The interviews were conducted informally, but as uniformly as possible. Time was allocated to non-linguistic, as well as linguistic tasks, in an attempt to gather interview speech as well as less formal speech. In Kerswill's (1994) Bergen study, interview speech was chosen, as it was felt that the data would be as far as possible stylistically comparable for each speaker.[34] Macaulay's (1991) interviews were not structured in any consistent pattern, but he claims that his method, and the interview generally, is an effective way of gathering data, despite what some researchers have said. Wolfson, for example, has said that the so-called spontaneous interview is not a speech event, and that it has no rules for speaking to guide the subject or the interviewer, but Macaulay asserts that speakers in an interview in fact do use features of everyday conversation (Wolfson 1976: 202, cited in Macaulay 1991: 7). Pedersen's interviews included the whole household, as it was felt that their presence would have a vernacular norm-enforcing effect (Rickford 1987). As comparisons are to be made between individuals and between groups, the speech samples should be comparable, so the Huntly interviews were designed structurally. Labov believes that the social history of a speaker is important, that is, how they have used language, and with whom (1986: 21), and the questionnaire used in the Huntly study has been designed to take the speaker's social history into account.

Selecting the informants

In the 1960s sociolinguistics broke with the dialectological tradition of excluding the social aspects of variation. It also became clear that informants should not be selected in a subjective way, since the fieldworker's own prejudices could have an unwelcome influence on the results. The informants in the Huntly study were, for this very reason, selected by means of a quasi-random sampling procedure, detailed below, under 3.6.3. Once the speakers have been selected, the problem of overcoming the 'Observer's Paradox' needs to be addressed. There are ways of resolving this problem.

The Observer's Paradox

Various techniques have been used to deal with the Observer's Paradox, the most common in earlier studies being the structured interview, where the speaker is asked to perform tasks at decreasing levels of formality, followed by informal speech where the speaker is encouraged to talk about childhood and emotional experiences. Later researchers have often followed Milroy (1980), who argues that it is easier to access the vernacular if the informant is relaxed, and if the nature of the relationship between the interviewer and interviewee is established as one of exchange and of mutual rights and obligations. This is achieved when the interviewer has a definite role in the speech community (the friend-of-a-friend technique).

According to Milroy, the central problem of the Observer's Paradox seems to be exacerbated by random sampling, because individuals or households are usually recorded out of context of the social networks with which they normally interact (1980: 41). She introduces the notion of *both* the insider *and* the outsider as field-workers, positing that they will between them have greater access to the full stylistic range. The importance of self-recruited groups is stressed, as participants are likely to adhere to obligations and norms of speech that have already been established. The presence of the field-worker and tape recorder are 'components of the total communicative situation' (Milroy 1980: 43), and need to be accounted for in some way. The fieldworker must find a way of establishing exchange relationships. An interested and sympathetic fieldworker will boost the self-esteem of the speaker in return for prolonged interaction. Obligations arise from more valued goods or services being provided by one person, leaving the other under pressure to return them (Milroy 1980: 49).

Milroy writes that she was able to analyse the character of her relationship with the group by using the notion of social network. She set herself up as a friend of a friend, or *second-order network contact* (p. 44). In the Huntly Study, my family ties with one of the families in the valley were brought into play to this end. In order to overcome the Observer's Paradox, a local woman of 55 years was trained as a research assistant. She conducted 90% of the interviews alone, as I was present only at the first six, in order to ensure things went smoothly. It is not likely that my presence at these few interviews would have any adverse effect on the data. Being local, she could also activate network contacts. For the investigator to become a second-order network contact is thought to set up certain rights and obligations, allowing recording to proceed because of obligation to the mutual contact (Boissevain 1974, cited in Kerswill 1994: 65). Thus Milroy was neither an insider nor an outsider.

As no two informants are the same in terms of temperament, it is necessary for the researcher to be flexible and informal, and a rapport should be built up between the two, in an attempt to elicit speech which is as natural as possible. In McIntosh's (1961) opinion, the more rigid method of strict questioning and answering is deceptively simple, and though it may have advantages in certain cases and for eliciting certain types of information, it cannot be regarded as a satisfactory method in general (p. 92). In the Huntly Study, it was felt that, in order to ensure uniformity in the data, questionnaires and elicitation pictures would have to be used for all the interviews. Free narratives and discussions were encouraged only when time permitted.

The fieldwork equipment

The advent of portable recorders has of course made it possible to analyse large samples of continuous speech, giving modern researchers a great advantage. In this study a Marantz C430 portable cassette recorder was used with a PZM Professional desktop microphone, which does not appear as intrusive as a normal microphone, as it is flat. This yielded good results, as it is non-directional, and was able to pick up the interviewer and subject equally well.

Eliciting the linguistic variables

As Lüdtke 1984 points out, there is a difference between changes taking place in a single speech item, and overall results, which alter the state of a language. The methodology used in the present study has incorporated this notion. Each morpho-lexical feature has been observed independently, and the results have been collated, in order to present a picture of overall dialect maintenance. However, the changes at these levels are seen as part of an on-going process of change, with a moving target. Scottish Standard English is itself probably undergoing change, gradually losing its distinctively Scottish features in favour of RP-like features, especially at the top end of the societal scale, in areas such as Morningside, for example, though fieldwork would be needed in order to confirm this.

There are three linguistic scores for each speaker:

1. The phonetic variable score (PHOVAR)

This is a composite index score calculated from the use of dialect phonetic variables during the description of a picture list,[35] where the interviewer was the interlocutor. In fact, it is more accurate to view the variation as morpho-lexical, as it is restricted to small lexical sets. Some of the variables in this category are purely phonetic, though, and as such it was decided to use the term PHOVAR. A picture list has been used to elicit the data instead of a word list. In studies where the dialect is linguistically distant from the standard, use of word lists can trigger code shifting, or at least style shifting in those speakers who do not have a fluent command of the dialect. Besides, there are different cognitive processes involved in, on the one hand, reading words, and on the other hand, saying what one sees in a picture. Reading tasks are, to the respondent, obviously linguistic tasks, and can result in careful speech styles. Describing pictures is not an overtly linguistic task, but rather a general cognitive task, albeit involving language. The focus is on successfully describing the picture, and it was found that the respondents concentrated more on the task at hand, than on their speech. Often the respondent had to be prompted and guided towards the required word, and this is why it was necessary for the interviewer to be the interlocutor. The picture list was designed to test whether the respondent used the Scots or the Scottish Standard English phonetic form of the variable. For example, one of the pictures used was of two glasses, one full, the other empty, shown below:

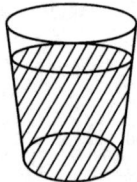 

This picture would elicit a token of the /ʉ/ variable, the variants of which are [ʉ] and [ʌ] in a restricted lexical set, as was detailed above, under 3.3. In other words, the Doric has consistently lowered Middle English /u/, leaving no fossils, like Standard English 'pull', 'full' and 'bull'. For this particular token, if the speaker pronounced the word [fʌl], the dialect variant, he or she was allocated a score of 1, and if the word was pronounced [fʉl], the Scottish Standard English variant, a score of 0 was allocated. All of the tokens for this variable were then added together, and a percentage calculated for that variable. These scores are detailed in chapter 4. In addition to this, the scores for all the variables were added together to yield a composite dialect index score, representing the eleven phonetic, morpho-lexical and morphological scores, as was done in Kerswill's (1994) Bergen study. These composite scores are detailed in chapter 5. For example, a speaker could end up with a score sheet like the following, calculated from all the tokens of the dialect variant of each variable during the picture-list task (data from PG, a female in the 60 plus age group):

1. Denti-labial fricative /f/   100%
2. The mid-high front vowel /e/   100%
3. No glottal stop for /t/   100%
4. The velar fricative /x/   100%

5. Consonant-cluster reduction	100%
6. /v/-deletion	100%
7. Pre-consonantal /r/	100%
8. Pre- and inter-vocalic /r/	100%
9. Lowered Middle English /u/	100%
10. The low central vowel /a̲/	86%
11. Preterite endings	100%
Composite dialect index score	99%

The words given below are the expected answers for the picture list used in the study. From these answers, the scores for PHOVAR were calculated. Given in brackets is the number of the variable being elicited, taken from the list of eleven variables above.

Table 7 PHOVAR: expected results from the picture list

1 ruler (7), (8)	2 three (8)
3 car (7)	4 fall (10)
5 nothing (discard)	6 panda (10)
7 rabbit (8), (10)	8 ladder (7), (10)
9 lorry (8)	10 (hand) bag (10)
11 butterfly (3), (7)	12 'why?' (1)
13 pull (9)	14 badger (7), (10)
15 roller skate (7), (8)	16 horse (7)
17 full (9)	18 polar bear (7)
19 Alford (10)	20 water (10), (3)
21 butter (3), (7)	22 bread (8)
23 old (5)	24 'how much?' (1)
25 more (2), (7)	26 'which?' (1)
27 home (2)	28 a hundred (5)
29 ground (5)	30 'where?' (1)
31 night (4)	32 right (vs. left) (8), (4)
33 bull (9)	34 caravan (10), (8)
35 cart (10), (7)	36 rocket (8)
37 heart (7)	38 everything (discard)
39 nobody (2)	40 Anne (10)
41 eight (4)	42 who? (1)
43 kicked (11)	44 cold (5)
45 stream (8)	46 both (2)
47 rolling pin (8)	48 apple (10)
49 only (2)	50 'when?' (1)
51 call (10)	52 'what?' (1)
53 cat (10)	54 hand (10), (5)
55 gutter (3), (7)	56 give (6)
57 over (6)	58 that (discard)
59 told (11)	60 bought (4)

2. The spontaneous speech score (SSSCOR)

This is a composite index score for phonetic, morpho-lexical and morphological variables used during the collaboration tasks, which involved a partner, such as a spouse, sibling, or friend. These included a scene description and a treasure hunt (see appendices 8 (a) and (b)). These tasks proved very effective, as the focus is on successfully completing the task, and not on one's speech. At every point during the task, where a Doric or a Scottish Standard English form could be used, a score was allocated; 1 for a Doric form, and 0 for a Scottish Standard English form. Any of the Doric forms noted in section 3.3 would qualify for a score of 1. As no two respondents gave exactly the same number of variables, the scores then had to be converted to a decimal, for use in the statistical analysis. A respondent who used no Doric variables would have a score of 1, and another, who used Doric variables at every possible point in the non-linguistic task, would have a score of 1. These decimal scores are comparable, given that the amount of speech obtained for each speaker was similar for these tasks.

There is an important difference between these two sections of the interview. Researchers have often devised linguistic tests which are arranged in order of increasing levels of formality. This is done in order to test whether increased attention to speech will cause style-shifting towards the standard or supralocal norm. Observing such shifts can give us insights into which variables are prominent in the speaker's consciousness as *markers* (Labov 1972). Normally, a general discussion, with details of the speaker's upbringing and childhood experiences will come at the beginning. This will often include narratives about 'danger of death' experiences, which the interviewer will ask about, in order to help the speaker to relax, and speak more naturally. This is often followed by an informal reading passage, since reading will necessarily involve paying more attention to language than speech. Next, a word list is read out. This will again raise the level of formality a level. Finally, a list of minimal pairs can be read out. This will bring the highest level of attention to language use, since it is obvious to the respondent that the pronunciation of each word is being compared and contrasted to the other word in the pair. In the Huntly study, it would seem natural to see SSSCOR, the spontaneous speech score, observed during non-linguistic tasks, as being situated lower in the scale of formality than PHOVAR, which was observed during a more overtly 'linguistic' test. This point will be developed in chapter 5, where the dialect indices for each section will be compared.

3. The lexical recognition score (LEXREC)

This is an index score for the recognition of fifty Doric lexical items read from the list, which appears above, under 3.4.3. The words were read out by the fieldworker in the normal dialect pronunciation, and the respondent was asked to either give the meaning of the word, supply a Scottish Standard English equivalent, or to use the word in a sentence, in order to show that its meaning was known. A correct answer yielded a score of 1, and an incorrect one 0. The maximum possible score is 50. The results of this test are, however, used with caution, as passive lexical recognition does not automatically imply active use in everyday situations (see above, under 2.5, where this problem is referred to in the design of Macafee's study). These three linguistic scores were then correlated with the social factors sex, age, life mode, social network, social class, attitude to dialect and national pride.

Analysis of the data

The main study has followed on from the results of the pilot study and literature review: the former showed that there are strong features of Scots in daily use in the community, and this provides clearly identifiable linguistic variables with which to compare the social scores. What an investigator in this discipline needs to determine is whether there is a relationship between any of the social factors identified, such as age, sex and the various indices obtained from the answers to the questionnaire, and linguistic change in progress. The linguistic variables had been identified during the pilot study, and the picture lists and description tasks were designed to elicit these variables. As mentioned, informal narratives were encouraged during the interviews where possible.

The questionnaire drew up a social profile of the speaker with which the linguistic variables could be compared. It was at this stage that the life mode of the speaker was evaluated. Transcription of the recordings (which was done for the pilot study) was not necessary, as the variables chosen were clearly discernible. A quantitative method has been used to analyse the use of linguistic variables, comparing language use between individuals and between groups, and also to test for correlation with extra-linguistic variables. In this way, direct and accurate comparisons can be made between the language use of individuals in a particular age or sex group, between the means for one group and the others, and between the non-linguistic (independent variable) scores and the linguistic (dependent variable) scores within, and across groups. This process will be covered in more detail below.

3.5.1   Determining the social scores

The entire database was worked through at least twice, with some interviews being listened to three times. A score-sheet was filled in for each section of the interview for each speaker. Some of the social scores, such as MENURB, NATPRI and ATTDIA were arrived at during the interviews. The answers to the questionnaire, which were graded from 'strongly disagree' to 'strongly agree', were ticked off on score sheets during the interviews, and totalled up later. Others, such as SOCLAS and SOCNET, were simply captured verbally on the cassettes, and added up later, while the recordings were being played back. Such practice is normal for quantitative studies of this sort (Cheshire, Eckert 2000, Gillett, Kerswill and Williams 1994 and 1999, Labov 1966, Milroy 1980). There are problems with such indices, however. For the index to be trusted, the fieldworker must assume that each answer carries equal weighting. Two individuals who obtain scores of, say, 5/8 for networks may have quite different network structures and/or interaction characteristics, but it is assumed that the influence of the network on them is equivalent. There is no easy way to overcome this problem, and it is at least present in all such studies. This is a problem inherent in all quantitative work.

3.5.2   Subjects

The part of the valley studied consists of a rough triangle formed by the towns of Huntly and Insch, and the village of Kennethmont. The furthest of these are twelve miles apart. The 1996 population figures are as follows:

Huntly: 4,336
Insch: 1,644
Kennethmont: 174[36]

The sample has been stratified according to age and sex, and contains sixty-nine interviews, of which five have been excluded, due to the unsuitability of the speakers.[37] That is to say, males and females are equally represented, and the following age groups were sampled: 8 to 12, 14 to 17, 25 to 40, and over 60. These groups were chosen to fit in with the writer's existing networks, and also to be representative of the community. After a discussion in the sociolinguistics research group at the University of Reading, it was decided to include two child age groups. The youngest group was included because speakers are already at school-going age, but not yet old enough to be subject to the peer pressure involved in teenage groups, which have been shown to lead language change (Kerswill 1996). The writer also has family ties with children in this age group, which have been exploited as network contacts in the community. The teenage group was included because this group leads language change, and also because the writer has family ties with children in this age group in the community. A minimum of eight speakers per cell was aimed for. This reduces the likelihood of skewed results caused by sampling error, and increases the likelihood of capturing genuinely significant correlations and differences.

The schoolchildren are mostly from the Huntly Academy, a state non-selective secondary school. The selection was made as follows: all the children falling into the two age groups were given letters by the teachers, asking if they would participate, and those who agreed, and who obtained permission from their parents, were interviewed. The adult informants were accessed via network connections. This method makes use of the *benefits of association* provided by network contacts (Milroy: 1988). In Blom and Gumperz's (1972) study, self-recruited groups were used, as the participants have pre-existing obligations towards each other which they will uphold despite the presence of strangers, and the interviewers aimed to mobilise these obligations by engaging members in discussions among themselves (p. 430).

One possible source of skewing in the sample is of course the fact that the adult subjects were mostly accessed via network connections, and may therefore represent a certain type of speaker with a certain type of social network, excluding others with perhaps different networks. The adult sample is therefore not as 'random' as the child sample, which consists mostly of recordings made at the local school, where I had no control over the choice of subject. Another possible source is the size of each cell. Due to time and funding constraints, a total of sixty-four subjects is already rather large, and to add another social variable to the structure of the sample, such as location (urban/rural), or social class would have meant a large increase in the number of subjects. While this would have proved to be beyond the scope of this study, it was nevertheless felt that social class might prove to be important, and it was provided for in the ethnographic interviews. It has proved to be a powerful predictor of language use in the study, despite earlier misgivings about its possible application to rural communities.

The respondents were not *chosen* as Macaulay did in his 1991 Ayr study, where they had to meet certain requirements, such as occupational status, gender, age and religion. According to Macaulay, random sampling is not really a good method, as it presupposes that one can obtain comparable samples of speech from each of the respondents (Macaulay 1991: 22). Conversely, his specific selection of informants can be criticised for being non-random, and not reflecting the speech of the whole community, but then neither is Pedersen's. She chose speakers from the community based on their ages, educational backgrounds, and varying degrees of local orientation.

In this chapter I specified the research question, detailed the pilot study, and gave an overview of the descriptive material. I then detailed the linguistic and social variables selected for the study, with explanations of how they were elicited. I then gave details of the methodology used, and how the indices were calculated. Lastly, I discussed the individual informants recorded for the study. I now move on to an examination of age as a factor in observable dialect use in the Huntly community. Each linguistic variable will be checked for correlations with age. This will build an impression of how clear the patterns are between the various linguistic variables and age, before I go on to check for correlations between age and the composite dialect indices, which will be built up from all the individual indices for each speaker.

Notes

1. Permission had already been granted by the Director of Local Education for the Grampian Region, the head teacher, children and parents. The sampling method is acceptably 'random', as the interviewer had no influence on which parents would give permission and on who was selected, though there may consequently be a built-in bias.
2. See also chapter 7 for a discussion of Macaulay's (1997) views on the use of the term 'vernacular'.
3. These are discussed in 3.4.1.
4. Wallace, iii. 272. MS, from Jamieson (1861: 352).
5. These are discussed in more detail below.
6. More on this below.
7. Old Scots sar, sair, sare, Old English sār, Old Frisian, Old Saxon sêr. Sum deyd in cald and hungyr sare. Wyntown, vii. 2. 18, in Jamieson (1861: 190).
8. This is only used by very few older speakers now.
9. 'Do' is pronounced [dɪv] in interrogatives.
10. Instead of the expected [faɪ], this is simply 'what way' in the Doric pronunciation.
11. See below, under 'Morphological Features'.
12. From Old Scots cuit derived from Middle Dutch cote 'ankle' (Macafee 1997: 205).
13. From the Old Norse verb.
14. From Middle Scots avou, awou, Old French avouer 'to make a vow, declare openly'.
15. From late (northern) Middle English loun, lown, 'worthless young man/boy', often used fondly.
16. From Old English bearn 'child', 'offspring'.
17. From (northern) Early Middle English hap 'cover wrap, tuck'.

18. The origin is uncertain, perhaps from Old Scots <u>blad</u> 'a bodily injury'.
19. From Old Scots, (northern) Old English <u>dwalm</u>, <u>dwaum</u>, <u>dwam</u> 'a faint', 'a swoon'.
20. From Old Scots, (northern) Old English <u>holk</u> 'dig, dig out'.
21. From Old Scots <u>clart</u> 'sticky mud'.
22. From Old Scots, (northern) Old English <u>stur</u>, <u>stour</u>, <u>stowr</u> 'conflict, flying dust raised by people or wind'.
23. From Old Scots, Old English <u>ilkie</u>, <u>ilky</u>, <u>ilka</u> 'every'.
24. From Old Scots and Northern dialectal <u>puckle</u>, Old English <u>pickle</u> 'a few, an indefinite amount'.
25. A proto-form resulted in Latin <u>sēcūrus</u>, Italian <u>sicura</u>, German <u>sicher</u>, Dutch <u>zeker</u>, and French <u>sure</u> (the last has lost its medial consonant).
26. *OED* vol. xvii, p. 281.
27. Sir G. Haye, Law Arms (S.T.S.) (1456) p. 64, cited from *OED*.
28. The word 'every' is not used much in the Doric, and when it is, it is pronounced [ɪvrɪ]. Instead there is ɪlkɪ.
29. See chapter 7 for a discussion of levelled urban Scottish English.
30. See, for example, Chirrey (1999: 228), and Romaine (1978: 146) for a description of this phoneme in Edinburgh usage.
31. More on this below.
32. Or 4 down to 0, depending on whether the question related positively or negatively to the particular category. This was done in order to avoid a cumulative effect of consistent positive questioning about one view or the other.
33. A local mountain range.
34. Informal secondary recordings were, however, made for some informants.
35. I would like to thank Annie Williams for her assistance with the artwork.
36. Source: the Grampian Regional Population Census Board.
37. These speakers are not 'locals', having moved to the area from other parts of the UK.

4

Correlations Between Age and the Individual Phonological Variables

In this chapter I compare each individual linguistic score against age, in order to build up an idea of correlations which may exist at this level. As described in chapter 3, PHOVAR and SSSCOR are composite index scores, made up of the combined results for the individual phonological and morpho-phonological variables for each individual respondent. Before examining these composite indices against the various sociological variables, it will be useful to build up an idea of how each of the individual phonological scores pattern with AGE, in order to see if they are all in a sense 'measuring the same thing'. The following are the individual scores which make up PHOVAR.

4.1 The denti-labial fricative

The graphs of the individual phonological variables all show a strong age effect. The first variable is (f~hw), the characteristic north-east feature, found in initial position in wh-questions. The graph of the means for the groups (figure 6) shows the age and sex differentiation for this variable. The graph shows that the pattern of loss is quite even for the females, but that this is not so for the males. The youngest males use the dialect variant far more than the adolescent males. In fact, for this variable, they come close to matching the score of the 25 to 40 females. This pattern will reveal itself throughout the data, with some interesting exceptions. One must view group means with caution, of course, as they can often conceal large within-group individual variation. This can be checked by showing ndividual scores by means of a scatterplot, as shown in figure 7. We can see that the characteristic denti-labial variant of the onset in 'wh-questions' iis being lost. In each age group, it is the

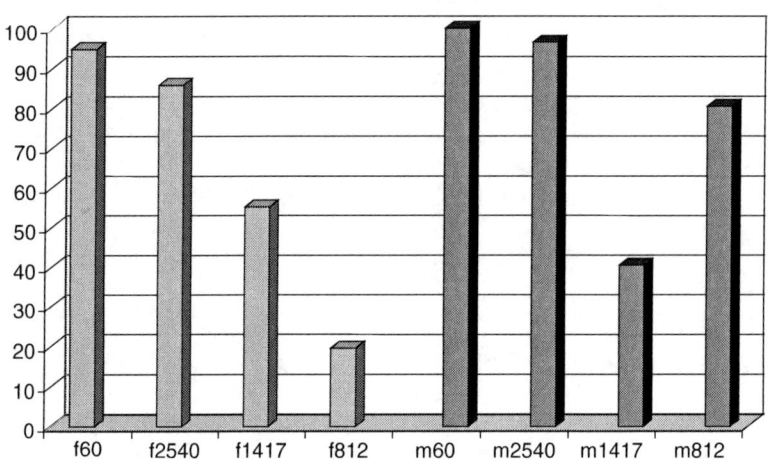

Figure 6 Means for the denti-labial fricative
Key: f60, m60 = females, males over 60.
f2540, m2540 = females, males between 25 and 40.
f1417, m1417 = females, males between 14 and 17.
f812, m812 = females, males between 8 and 12.

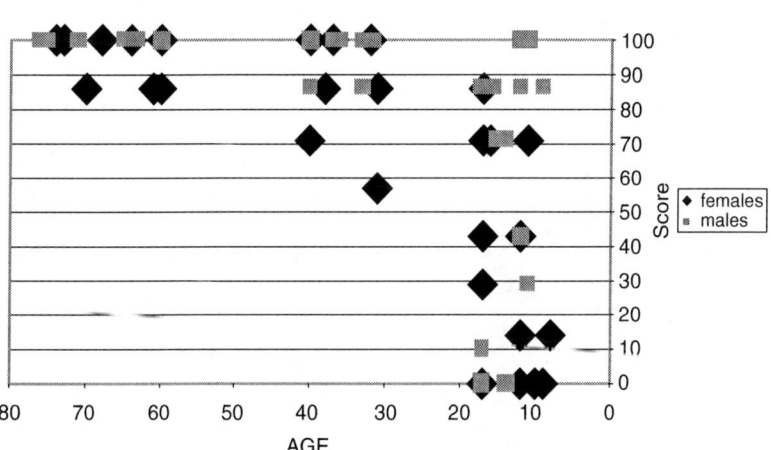

Figure 7 Individual scores for the denti-labial fricative

females who lead the change towards the supralocal form [м]. This sex effect is not strongly manifest in the adolescent group, where some males use the standard form 100% of the time. The intra-group variability in the two younger groups would seem to indicate instability, and a move towards loss of the dialect variant, if we are to accept that an apparent time study is a relatively good reflection of change in real time. Talking to some of the older informants after the interviews, it was quite clear to me that they had never used [м] at any time in their lives, except when forced to do so in school. It seems unlikely that the younger informants will replace [м] with [f] later in life, though this is not impossible.

4.2   The mid-high front vowel

Figure 8 shows the means for this variable, while figure 9 is a scatterplot showing a similar distribution of individual scores. The oldest group uses the variant 100% of the time, as does the second-oldest group, except for two females, showing again the females to be leaders of changes towards supralocal forms. There is great variability across the two younger groups, and such irregularity normally indicates a change in progress. Again, the youngest group shows the males to be holding on longer to dialect forms. This variable has two clearly distinct variants: the

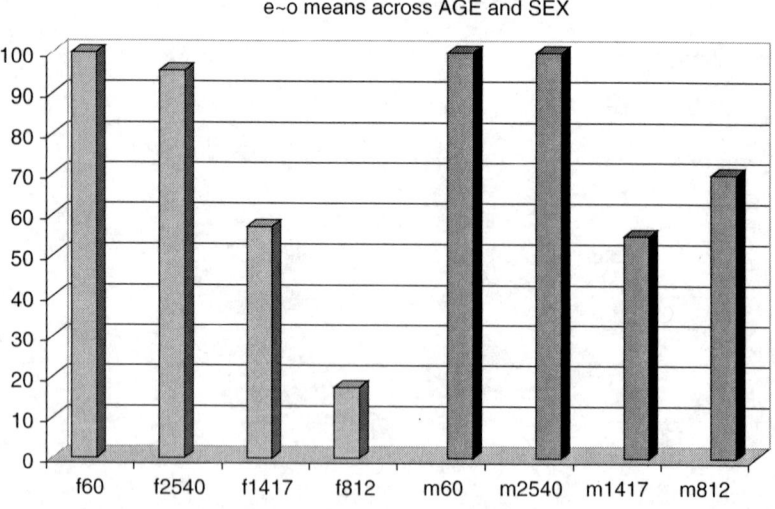

Figure 8   Means for the mid-high front vowel

e~o across AGE and SEX

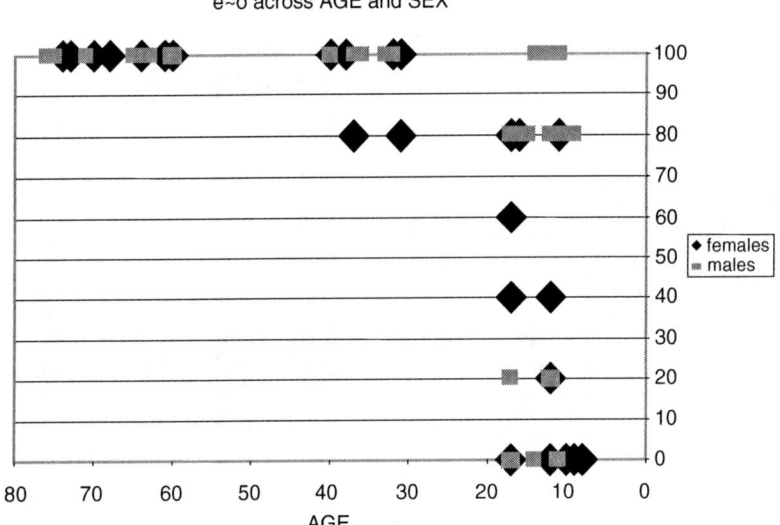

Figure 9 Individual scores for the mid-high front vowel

vernacular form is [e], while the Scottish Standard English form is [o]. The phonetic distance between the two is rather great, and there are no intermediate, or 'fudged' forms, such as *[œ]. The Scottish Standard English (supralocal) form [o] is overtly taught in school, used in the media, and easily distinguished.

The pattern of loss demonstrated for the denti-labial fricative in 4.1 is remarkably closely replicated here, showing that these two variables are both clear tests of dialect maintenance in this community. As will be seen, most of the variables chosen pattern in remarkably similar ways, though the exceptions are interesting in their own right.

4.3 /t/ Glottalling

As this variable shows different patterning from the rest, and as it is not in the same binary standard non-standard relationship, it will be discussed in more detail here and in chapter 7. The scores for this variable in the present study show a *categorical* use of the alveolar variant [t] by the oldest age group, and a near-categorical use by the 25 to 40 group. The two younger groups use the alveolar plosive much less, with the exception of the females aged 8 to 12, as figure 10 shows. This pattern

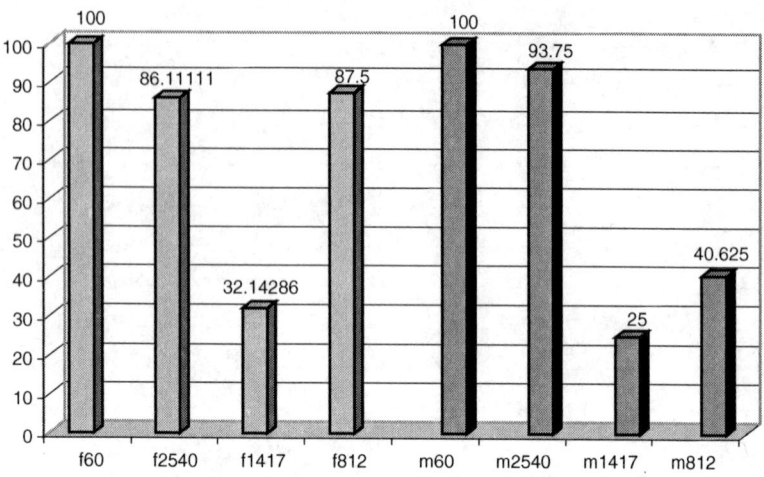

Figure 10 Use of the alveolar variant of /t/

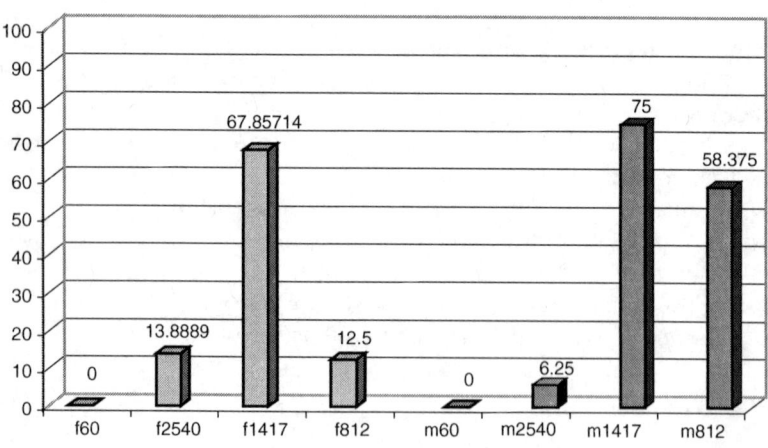

Figure 11 Use of the glottal variant of /t/

can be compared to the normal pattern for dialect variables in the Huntly data, as seen above in Figure 8. In order to compare these results with those of other studies, it is helpful to invert the scores, showing them as a percentage use of [ʔ], as in figure 11.

/t/ glottalling in Glasgow

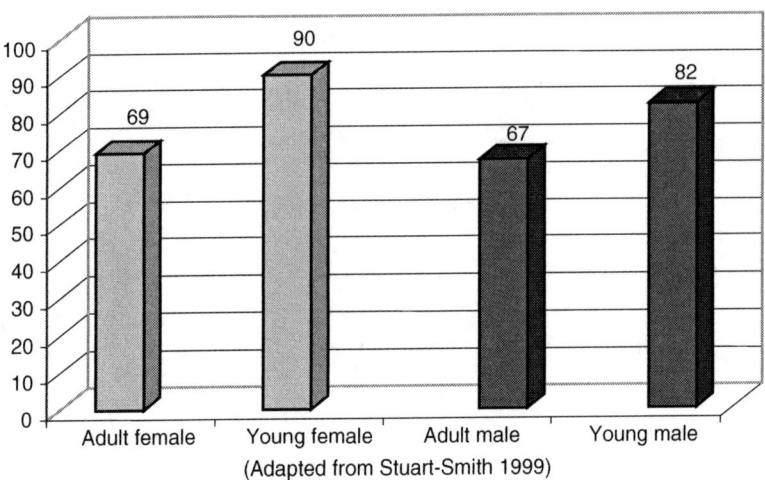

(Adapted from Stuart-Smith 1999)

Figure 12　Use of the glottal variant of /t/ in Glasgow
Key: Adult = over 40, Young = 13 to 14 years old.

There are two important points which immediately become apparent. First, if /t/ glottalling had been in use in the area for any length of time, it would presumably show in the speech of the oldest group, as is the case with Stuart-Smith's Glasgow data in figure 12 (taken from data on conversational speech). The age groups in the Glasgow study do not neatly coincide with those in the Huntly study, which reduces the validity of the comparison slightly. The adult group consists of speakers over 40, and shows a considerable use of the glottal stop. The adolescent group consists of speakers aged 13 and 14, placing them between the two younger Huntly groups. What is nevertheless clear from the Glasgow data, is a slight increase in the use of the glottal stop in the younger group over that of the older group. This may indicate age grading due to the life stage of the adolescents, rather than change in progress. The patterning of AGE and /t/ in Huntly is clear from figure 11, and elsewhere in this paper. The value of age as a predictor variable of /t/ glottalling in Huntly is highly significant (regression p < 0.000)

What we see in Huntly, therefore, is zero use of the glottal stop in the oldest group for both males and females. The rural areas of Buchan and Gordon, the sampling areas for this study, are regarded by most as the heartland of Scots (Hendry 1997), and so we can assume that [t] is, in

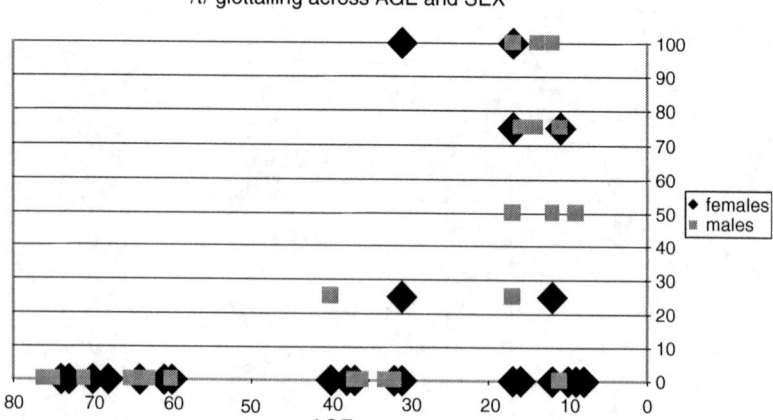

Figure 13   Use of [ʔ] across age and sex

fact, the rural vernacular form.[1] By contrast, Glasgow shows its recorded use in this variety of urban Scots from at least 1892, as is shown in 7.1 below.

The second point is that there is an irregularity in the 8 to 12 female scores. Instead of the expected pattern shown in figure 9, speakers in this group seem to be resisting /t/ glottalling. figure 13 shows the individual scores for this variable, confirming this deviation. Except for two individuals, the 8 to 12 females show zero use of the glottal stop. The failure to adopt the incoming feature by the 8- to 12-year-old females is striking. It could be due to the fact that the sociolinguistic status of this feature is *neither* traditional dialect *nor* incoming standard in the north-eastern area sampled, an important consideration, in the light of the fact that this is an area of exocentric innovation. This point will be developed in chapter 7.

4.4   The velar fricative

As expected, the phoneme /x/ is suffering attrition very rapidly now, and is expected to follow the pattern of loss it has in the rest of Scotland, surviving only as a fossil in certain lexical items, which may be more prominent in the levels of consciousness of speakers. The word 'loch', certain surnames, and the exclamation 'och' are probably the only places where it can be found elsewhere.[2] Figure 14 shows apparent categorical loss in the female population. The same pattern of loss

x~0 across AGE and SEX

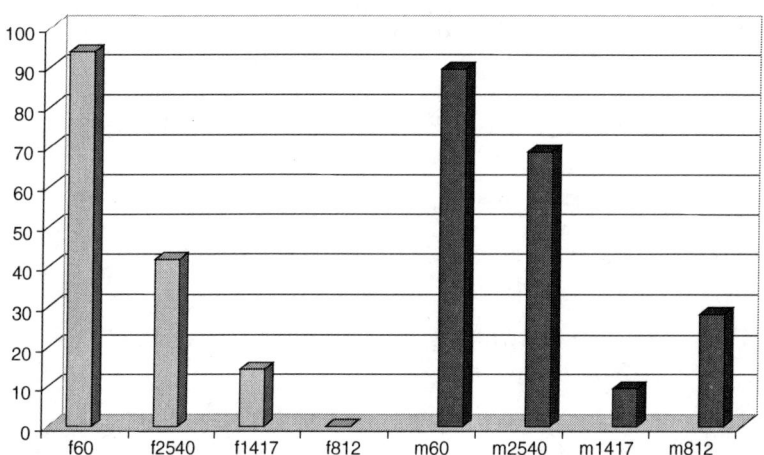

Figure 14 Means for the velar fricative

x~0 across AGE and SEX

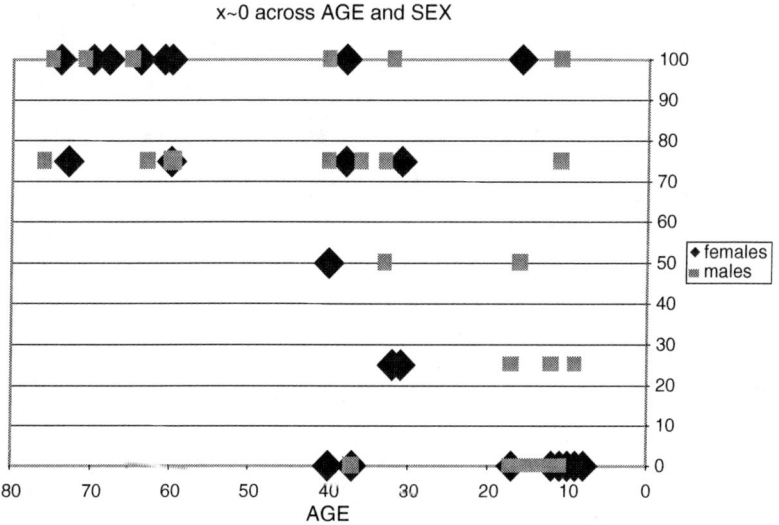

Figure 15 Individual scores for the velar fricative

present in the male population for the other variables is found again, though the scores for this variable are very low in the youngest two groups. A scatterplot of the individual scores (figure 15) reveals some different patterns of loss for this variable as compared to the others.

As expected, the oldest group scores the highest, but there is significant loss even there, and the males and females seem to be losing the dialect variant evenly. In the 25 to 40 group, there is far greater variability in the scores than for the other variables. And, apart from a single 14 to 17 female speaker, who uses it categorically, it has been completely lost by all the females in the youngest two groups.

4.5　Consonant-cluster reduction

The graph of the means reflects the following patterns:

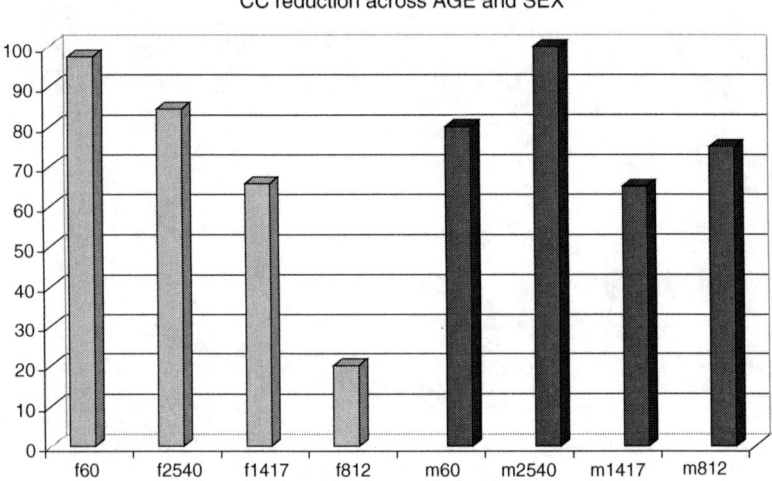

Figure 16　Means for consonant-cluster reduction

The trend for the other variables is continued here, with an even, though less striking, loss in the females. The male pattern is slightly different, however. The oldest males do not use the dialect variant as much as would be expected, scoring less than the 25 to 40 males and the two older female groups. The two adolescent groups show good maintenance of the dialect variant. Figure 17 shows the individual scores. The unusually low mean score for the 60 plus males is largely due to a score of 20% for one individual, 'AI'. Going back to the records shows that he was born and raised in the area, as were his parents. He scores a maximum network score of 8/8, and a low social class score of 2/8. His MENURB

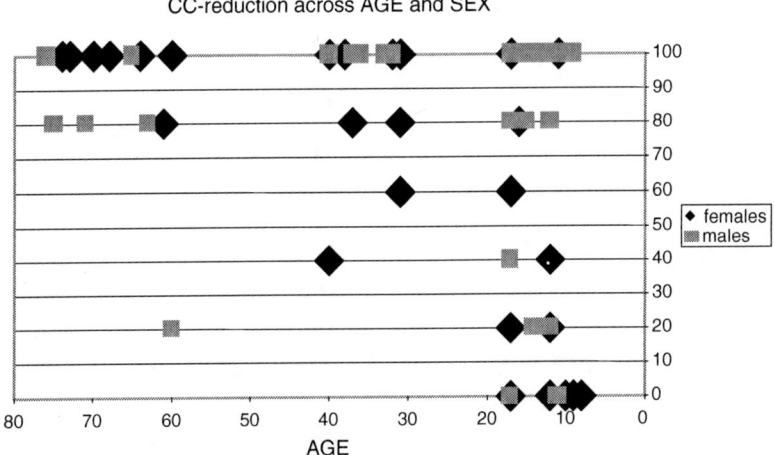

Figure 17 Individual scores for consonant-cluster reduction

score of 35/40 is average for the group. It is difficult to see why his dialect score for this variable is so low, given that his scores for the other variables are average for the group. In the 25 to 40 group, the females again lead the change away from the dialect norms. Sex differentiation is again not shown in the adolescent group, but is in the youngest group, with males using the non-standard variant far more than females.

4.6 /v/-deletion

Figure 18 shows that pattern of loss in the female population is rather more marked for /v/ deletion than for the other variables, though not as much as for /x/. The 25 to 40 males outscore the over-60s, as they do for about half of the variables. The youngest males again show higher use of the dialect variant than the adolescent males. The individual scores are shown in figure 19.

Even with only three occurrences, this variable shows the same pattern as the rest. The loss in the oldest age group is even between the two sexes, as it is in the adolescent group. In the 25 to 40 group, females again lead the change, as they do in the youngest group. The only individuals with categorical use of the dialect variant in the youngest group are all males, while many females have categorical use of the standard variant, except for two individuals.

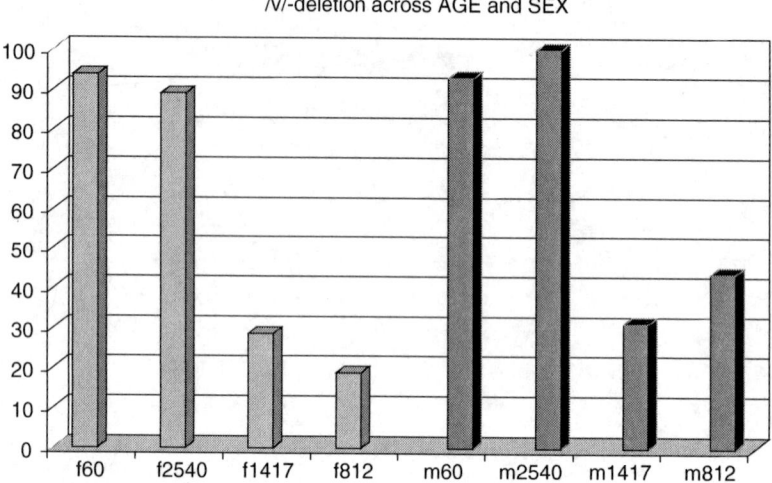

Figure 18   Means for /v/ deletion

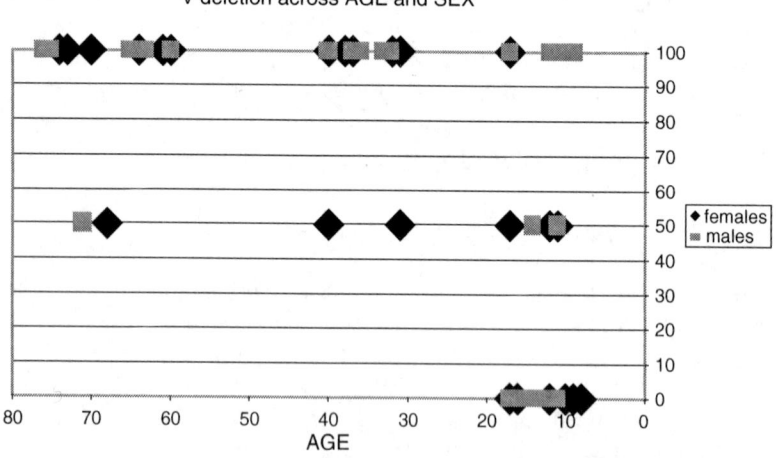

Figure 19   Individual scores for /v/ deletion

4.7   Pre-consonantal /r/

The next variable is pre-consonantal (including pre-pausal) /r/. While all Scots varieties have traditionally been rhotic, Romaine (1989) has shown some non-rhotic individuals in Edinburgh. In the north-east,

r --> [r] _ C across AGE and SEX

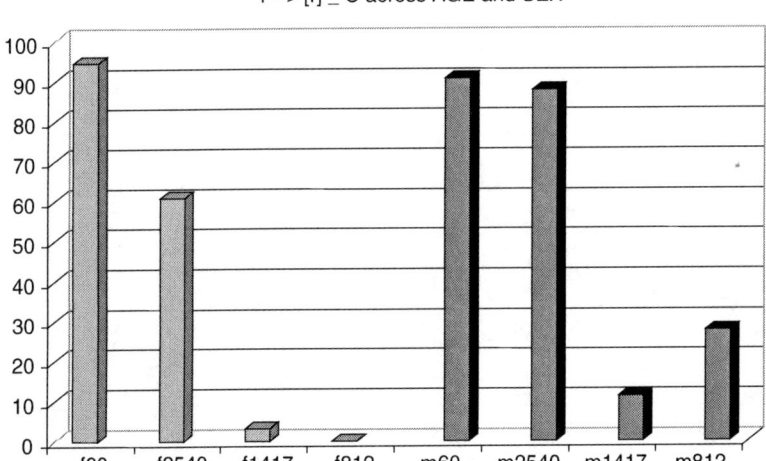

Figure 20 Means for pre-consonantal /r/.

however, all speakers are rhotic, with the variants of /r/ being [r] and [ɹ]. The use of the latter is being spread by overt social influence from prestige groups, as it is associated with middle class female speech in Scotland (Romaine 1989: 202). The trill has been regarded as the dialect variant for this study. Figure 20 shows the means. In pre-consonantal and pre-pausal position, where this sound is likely to be threatened, the graph shows a very steep decline in the females, to the extent that there has been categorical loss in the youngest group, and almost categorical loss in the adolescent group, meaning the Scottish Standard English variant [ɹ] is gaining ground. The usual pattern for the males is present, though the two scores for the two youngest groups are lower than with the other variables. What is clear here is a very marked loss of the trilled variant of /r/ in the two youngest age groups in pre-consonantal position. This could mean that Scottish English is moving towards being non-rhotic, as the change implies a weakening of articulation in this position:

Trill ⟶ approximant ⟶ loss in pre-consonantal position.

Figure 21 shows the combined means for the age groups, while figure 22 shows the individual scores for this variable. Interestingly, the females in the oldest group outscore the males for this variable, except for one

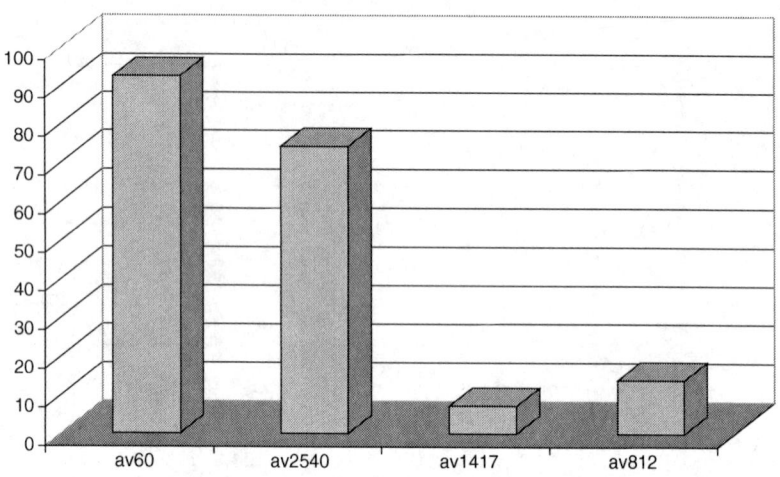

Figure 21 Combined means for pre-consonantal /r/

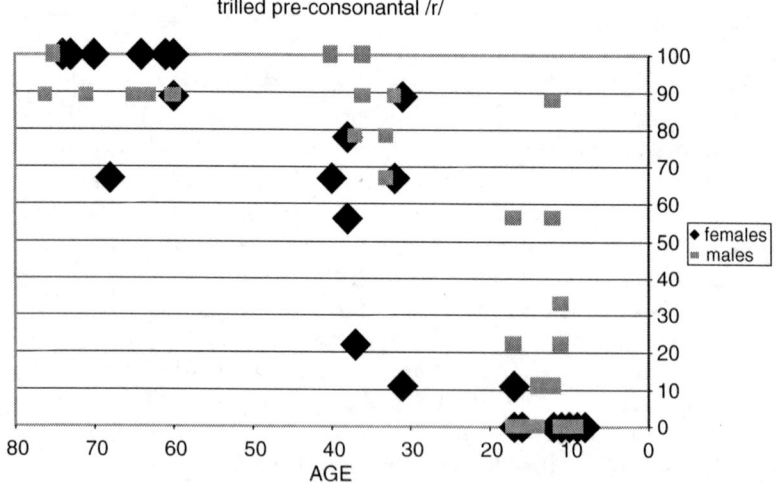

Figure 22 Individual scores for pre-consonantal /r/

individual. This may be because the variant [ɹ] was not available or popular when they were young and acquiring phonological skills. In the 25 to 40 group, the females again lead the change, but what is interesting here is the degree of intra-group variability. The absence of sex differentiation in the adolescent group for the other variables is not mirrored for this variable, though the differentiation found is rather weak, with the males using the trill slightly more. The youngest group shows clear sex differentiation, even more so than for the other variables. There is categorical loss of the dialect variant in the female population in this age group. So for each age group except the over-60s the females use the dialect form less than the males, showing support for Romaine's claim that the approximant variant (here scored as 0) is associated with (middle-class) female speech. The next set of scores is for the same variant, but in pre- and intervocalic position.

4.8 Pre- and intervocalic /r/

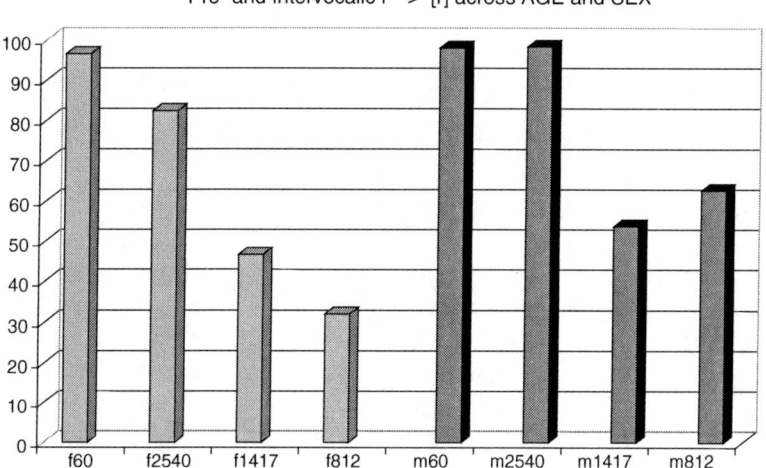

Pre- and Intervocalic r --> [r] across AGE and SEX

Figure 23 Means for pre- and intervocalic /r/

As expected, the trilled variant is used more in this phonetic environment. The pattern of loss here mirrors the normal pattern for the dataset as a whole: a strong, even loss in the females, and a by now familiar pattern for the males. Figure 24 shows the individual scores. These are distributed as for the other variables. The two groups which show the

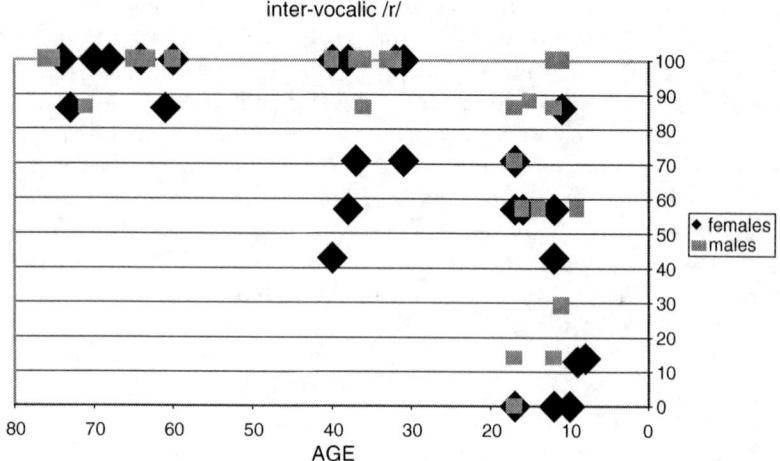

Figure 24   Individual scores for pre- and intervocalic /ɹ/

most sex differentiation are again the 25 to 40 and 8 to 12 groups, where the females once again lead the change.

4.9   Lowered Middle English /ʊ/

As mentioned in chapter 3, the lowering of OE, Middle English [ʊ] to [ʌ] swept through the lexicon in the north-east, leaving no fossils, as we find in Standard English. The pattern of dialect loss manifests again in figure 25. The remarkable similarity in age differentiation across the different variables would seem to indicate that they have been well chosen as indicators of dialect use. Except for /t/ glottalling, where the youngest females are resisting the change, most of the variables show near-identical patterning. However, as the individual scores below reveal, this particular variable is an example of mean scores concealing considerable intra-group variation. This may be partly due to the low number of observations (3) for this variable. This variable shows far more intra-group variation than any other. There is no clear sex differentiation, except in the 25 to 40 group.

However, there is no doubt that the dialect variant is being lost, as the 60 plus group has many individuals who use it categorically, while the youngest group has quite a number who use the standard variant categorically.

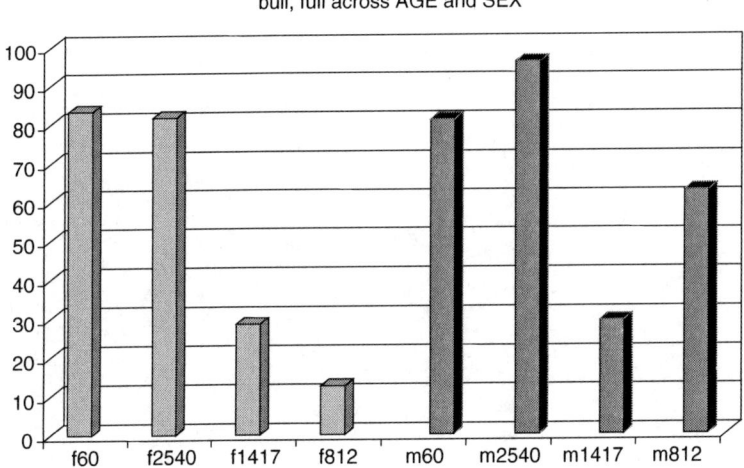

Figure 25 Means for lowered Middle English /ʊ/

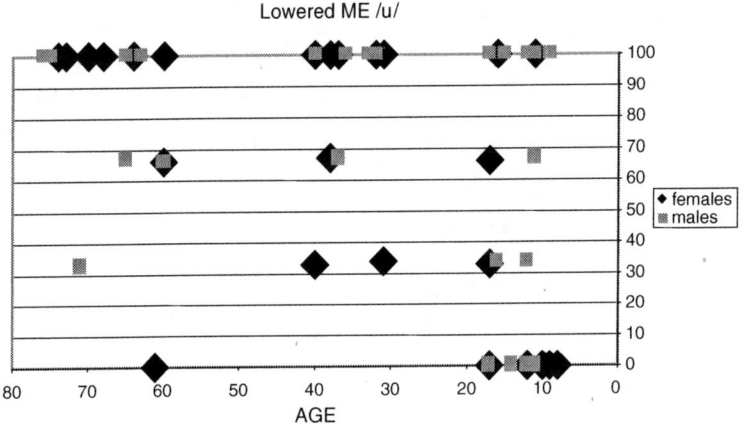

Figure 26 Individual scores for lowered Middle English /ʊ/

4.10 The low central vowel

The variable /a/ has the variants [æ] (SSE) and [a] (Doric). The dialect variant, which is a strikingly back vowel, is surviving rather better than the rest in the data. The pattern which has established itself in the data is again shown, but the loss is not as marked for this variable. Urban Scots also seems to retain the back variant (Chirrey 1999: 225). The

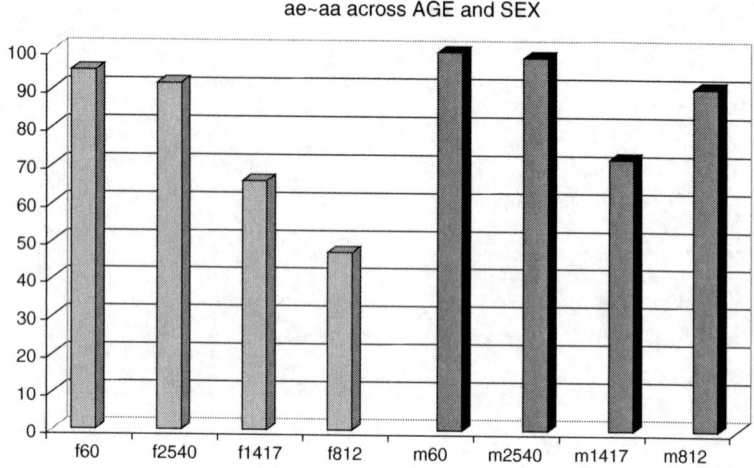

Figure 27 Means for the low central vowel

individual scores below show the normal pattern for the other variables, with little variation in the two older groups, and much variation
in the two younger groups. Sex differentiation is present throughout
the four groups, with the females again leading the move towards the
standard form. The 8 to 12 females show the most intra-group variability for this variable.

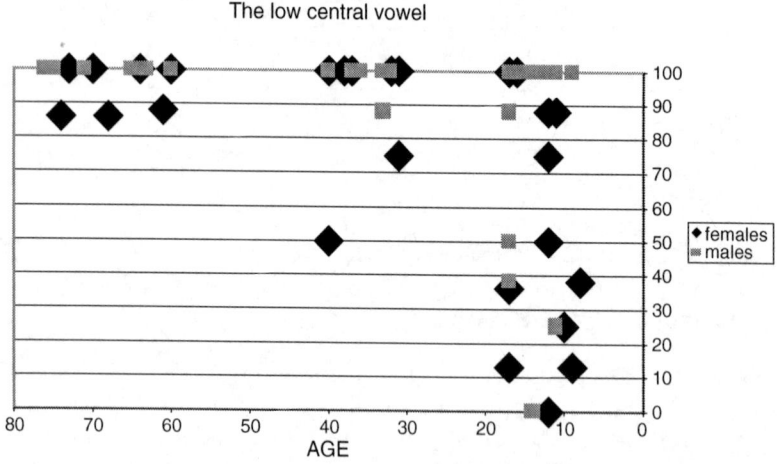

Figure 28 Individual scores for the low central vowel

4.11 Preterite endings

The next variable is morpho-phonemic: the preterite form of verbs. Some verbs which pattern according to the so-called 'strong verb paradigm' in Scottish Standard English follow the weak paradigm in the Doric, with no stem vowel change, yielding 'sell ~ sellt', 'tell ~ tellt'. Additionally, those weak verbs in Scottish Standard English with a phonetically reduced '-ed' suffix [t], have a fuller phonetic form in the Doric: [ɪt], yielding 'kick ~ kickit', 'pick ~ pickit'. The group means for this variable are shown in figure 29. As can be seen, the normal pattern is again evident, with an interesting difference. The male scores across the board are rather markedly lower than for the other variables. There is no obvious reason for this. The pattern of loss of this feature may have occurred at an earlier time than some of the other variables discussed here. This feature is not restricted to the north-east, as can be seen in the following citation:

> As far as official records are concerned, MacQueen (1967: 138) found that 'the older Scottish –*it* of the weak past participle (and past tense) has almost entirely anglicised by 1700'. These authors are, however, referring to the 'official' language, which ceases to be recognisably Scots by this time. As far as the spoken language and the Scots of literature is concerned, the picture is more complex. [...] Forms in –*it* do

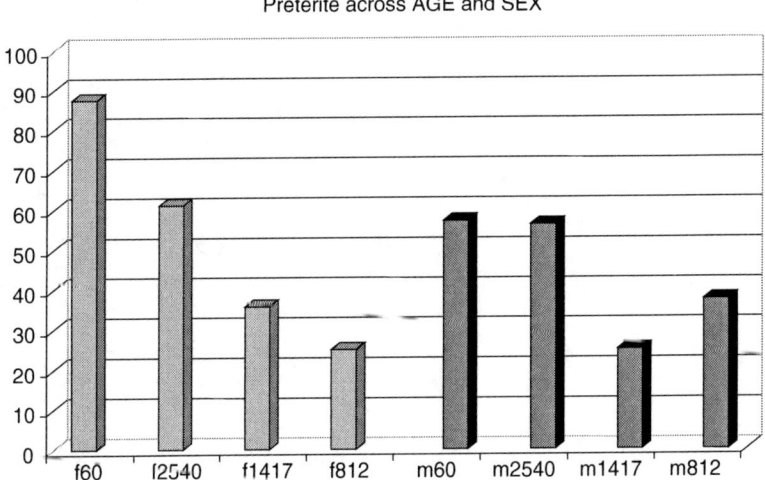

Preterite across AGE and SEX

Figure 29 Means for preterite endings

still occur in Scots: Macafee (1983: 49) tells us that in Glasgow, /ɪt/ is heard only after plosives, e.g. *landit* [...] /t/ is heard after /l/, /r/ and nasals, e.g. *killt, kent*. [...] McClure (1983: 6) notes that features such as 'the past tense ending of *dippit, helpit*...are general in Scots dialects' (Beal 1997: 352–353)

The individual scores in figure 30 confirm the sex differentiation shown in the means. The dialect variant is phonetically clearly distinct from the standard one. If it is a 'marker' in Labov's sense of the word, where it is above the level of consciousness of individuals, then it is not clear why the females consistently outscore the males (except for the 8 to 12 group, where the males score higher, though the difference is minimal). It is to be expected, following results from other research, and from this study, that females will use standard (supralocal) forms more than males, all other things being equal. This is not the case for this variable, as the females outscore the males at each level, except the youngest. Apart from this surprising sex differentiation, the effect of age is clear: the dialect variant is being lost.

Having examined in this chapter the patterning of the individual phonological variables, I look in the next chapter at large-scale correlations between the composite index scores and the sociological variables across the whole database. I will use correlations and plots as a first measure. This will allow us to form an idea of large-scale correlations

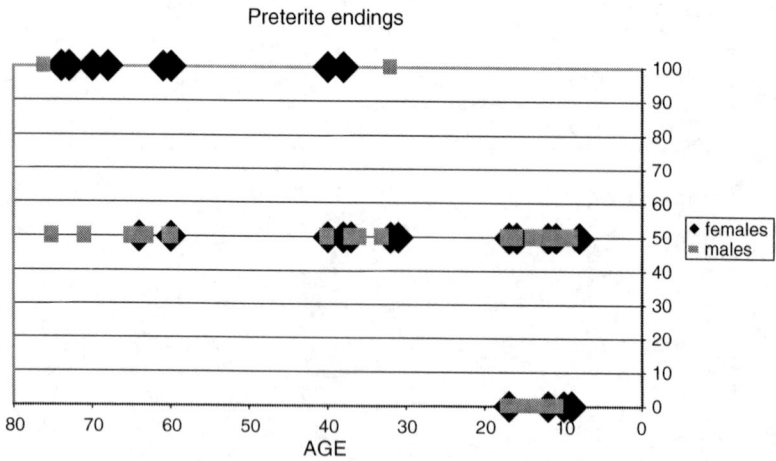

Figure 30   Individual scores for preterite endings

between the social and linguistic variables. Any correlations will be cautiously viewed at this point, as more rigorous statistical testing is required, before one can infer causality.

Notes

1. A personal communication from Jennifer Smith confirms this.
2. Because of this, these lexical items were avoided in the study.

5
Testing for Correlations Across the Entire Database

Statistical advice holds that the best way to build up an early impression of the distribution of the data is to generate correlations and scatterplots. This method has therefore been used in this chapter.

5.1   Correlations and plots

It was decided that, because the data is continuous, the only effective tests would be firstly correlations and then multiple (linear) regression, and these have been used throughout.[1] The aim of the data analysis is to see if any of the social variables are correlated with any of the linguistic ones (or in fact with any of the other social variables). This will help answer the research question related to the significance of mental urbanisation, social networks, age and sex as predictors of language change in rural areas.

As a first measure, Pearson's Correlation tests and plots were used to see which variables might be related to each other. Correlation shows whether two variables tend to vary together (positive correlation), or to vary in opposite directions (negative correlation). Showing such a correlation does not, however, mean that one variable is the *cause* of the variation in the other. The variation may be, at least partly, caused by other variables. A regression analysis is like the numerical representation of a scatter plot, and the regression line is a straight line through the middle of the data points, one which comes nearest to touching all of them. The measure of regression is then based on how much distance there is between the regression line and the actual points on the graph. Building a regression model involves successively entering the predictor variables into the equation, and the resultant output shows to what degree the predictor variables account for variation in the predicted variable. The reader will remember that the social variables are as follows:

1. MENURB: A measure of the speaker's degree of mental urbanisation.
2. SOCNET: Social Network. A measure of the social network of the speaker.
3. SOCLAS: Social Class. A measure of the social class of the speaker.
4. ATTDIA: Attitude to the Dialect. A measure of the way the speaker perceives the dialect in relation to the Scottish standard.
5. NATPRI: National Pride. A measure of the speaker's pride in Scotland.[2]

The linguistic variables are:

1. PHOVAR: Phonetic variables.[3] Elicited by means of sixty pictures, as it was felt that a wordlist written in the standard orthography of English would trigger a code-switch. The pictures were chosen after the phonetic markers of the Doric had been identified during the pilot study.
2. SSSCOR: Spontaneous speech score. Another phonetic score, this time observed during non-linguistic tasks, such as leading an age-mate or spouse to treasure on a map, or during a complex scene description. Calculated by dividing by the actual number of Doric variants observed by the total of all possible observations.
3. LEXREC: Lexical recognition. A list of fifty Doric lexical items was read to each speaker, whose task was to explain the meaning of the word, or to supply a suitable English equivalent.

Correlations are shown in the following manner: a perfect negative correlation will show as minus 1, and a perfect positive correlation as plus 1. Scores close to 0 will show no significant correlation. I bear in mind that these correlation tests are simply first measures, and any correlations shown are cautiously viewed. This variable may well contribute to the variance, but until one has tested for the contribution of other variables, as well as the interaction *between* such variables, one cannot say how great such a contribution is. The multiple regression analysis is better suited to that purpose. The question of how high a correlation score should be before one regards it as important is not one that statisticians will make any hard and fast rules about. The answer one usually receives is that it all depends upon the data and purpose of the study. Most agree, however, that a correlation coefficient of below −0.4, or above 0.4 can be regarded as important for any data, and warrants further, more rigorous testing. Therefore, any scores below or above these two will be regarded as important, at least as far as a correlation test can account for variance. Such scores have been printed in boldface. Table 8 shows the correlations for all the variables.

Table 8   Correlations for all the variables

	PHOVAR	SSSCOR	LEXREC	MENURB
AGE	**0.734**	**0.659**	**0.764**	**0.558**

	SOCNET	SOCLAS	ATTDIA	NATPRI
AGE	0.186	**−0.432**	0.334	−0.083

	AGE	SSSCOR	LEXREC	MENURB
PHOVAR	**0.734**	**0.886**	**0.794**	**0.782**

	SOCNET	SOCLAS	ATTDIA	NATPRI
PHOVAR	0.056	**−0.541**	0.356	−0.041

	PHOVAR	SSSCOR	LEXREC	AGE
MENURB	**0.782**	**0.767**	**0.704**	**0.558**

	SOCNET	SOCLAS	ATTDIA	NATPRI
MENURB	0.186	**−0.553**	**0.468**	0.242

	PHOVAR	SSSCOR	LEXREC	MENURB
SOCNET	0.056	0.040	0.197	0.186

	AGE	SOCLAS	ATTDIA	NATPRI
SOCNET	0.186	−0.140	−0.116	−0.132

	PHOVAR	SSSCOR	LEXREC	MENURB
SOCLAS	**−0.541**	**−0.440**	**−0.498**	**−0.553**

	SOCNET	AGE	ATTDIA	NATPRI
SOCLAS	−0.140	**−0.432**	−0.164	0.154

	PHOVAR	SSSCOR	LEXREC	MENURB
ATTDIA	0.356	**0.478**	0.306	**0.468**

	SOCNET	SOCLAS	AGE	NATPRI
ATTDIA	−0.116	−0.164	0.334	**0.581**

	PHOVAR	SSSCOR	LEXREC	MENURB
NATPRI	–0.041	0.031	–0.072	0.242

	SOCNET	SOCLAS	ATTDIA	AGE
NATPRI	–0.132	0.154	0.581	–0.083

5.1.1 Age

The individual tables will be reproduced for ease of reference.

Table 9 Correlations with AGE

	PHOVAR	SSSCOR	LEXREC	MENURB
AGE	0.734	0.659	0.764	0.558

	SOCNET	SOCLAS	ATTDIA	NATPRI
AGE	0.186	–0.432	0.334	–0.083

From these correlation coefficients we can see that AGE is positively correlated with (1) PHOVAR, (2) SSSCOR, (3) LEXREC, (4) MENURB, and negatively with (5) SOCLAS.

The correlation between age and the linguistic scores is expected: the dialect is being lost, and younger speakers do not have access to the range of dialect features that the older ones do. This corresponds with the finding of Kerswill (1987) in Durham. The graphs in chapter 4 showing the correlation between AGE and the individual linguistic variables showed a great deal of similarity, except for two, and so the composite score PHOVAR is expected to show the same pattern. As age is highly correlated with many variables, and as it is not included in the hypothesis, its effects will be statistically removed during the model-building process in the regression analysis. Age also correlates highly with MENURB. This shows that older people are less mentally urbanised than younger ones generally. Once the effect of age has been removed, correlations between MENURB alone and the linguistic scores can be more rigorously tested. From the table above, we see that age correlates negatively with social class. This shows that younger speakers are not only more educated, but also read more national newspapers, and have greater career aspirations, for example.

Next, each correlation was looked at individually, together with scatterplots. As the first two age groups are almost contiguous, the reader is reminded that there is in fact a small break between the 8 to 12 and the

14 to 17 groups. The reasons for including these two similar age groups are covered in 3.5.2.

5.1.1.a   AGE across PHOVAR

	PHOVAR
AGE	0.734

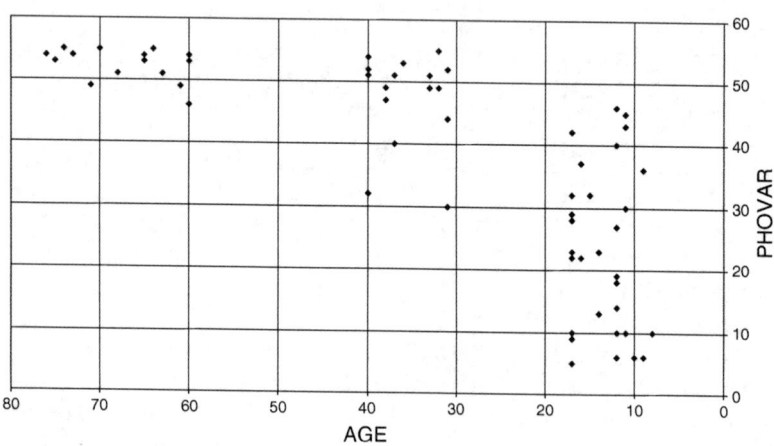

Figure 31   AGE across individual PHOVAR scores

The positive correlation of 0.734 means that a higher age correlates with a higher PHOVAR score. The values along the X axis (AGE) have simply been arranged in descending order, so that the changes in apparent time can be appreciated. The scatterplot shows a definite age effect in the data. The 8 to 12 group has slightly higher dialect scores than the 14 to 17 group, and the 25 to 40 group slightly lower scores than the over-60 group. This is to be expected, given the results of other research. Adolescents lead language change, whether it be *away* from the standard, as in urban areas (see Eckert 2000, discussed in section 2.2), or *towards* the standard, as in rural areas (see Røyneland 2000, discussed in section 2.3). Age is one of the strongest predictors of language use in the data, as figure 32, which presents means for the age and sex groups shows.

Male and female PHOVAR

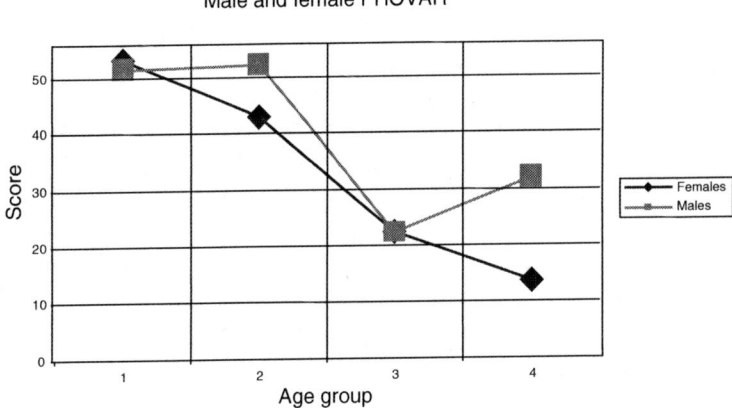

Figure 32   AGE across mean PHOVAR scores

The mean age group scores confirm the trend: AGE most certainly is correlated highly with PHOVAR. The abnormally high score of 32.125 in the 8 to 12 male group seen in the scatterplot mirrors the results of other studies, which show that males use more non-standard forms than females. In addition, there are two males in this group who show exceptional fluency in the dialect. This may be due to the fact that they live just outside the town, in a village called Kennethmont, a point which will be taken up in chapter 7. Statistical modelling will later be used to test what percentage of the variation in the linguistic variables is accounted for by AGE, and what percentage by the other social variables.

5.1.1.b   AGE across SSSCOR

We now plot AGE against SSSCOR – the spontaneous speech score.

	SSSCOR
AGE	0.659

The age effect is once again strongly present. The result closely resembles the result for AGE across PHOVAR. This shows that the two linguistic tests were well designed and accurately tested what they aimed to test: dialect phonological features in elicited linguistic tasks and in non-linguistic tasks. The oldest group shows the least variation, followed by the 25 to 40 group. There is great intra-group variation in

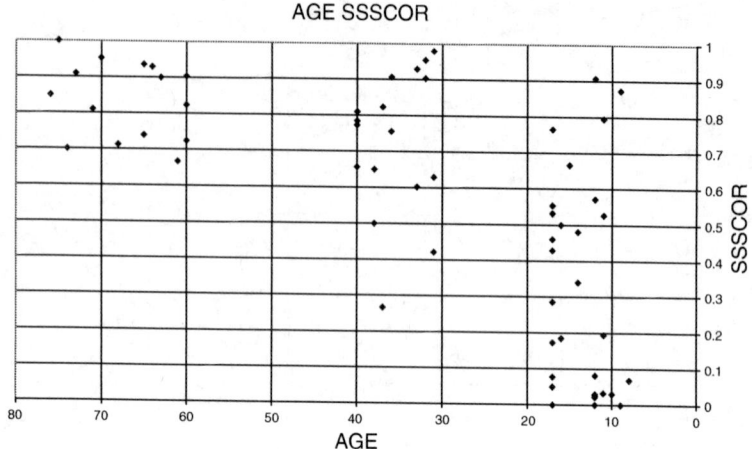

Figure 33 AGE across SSSCOR

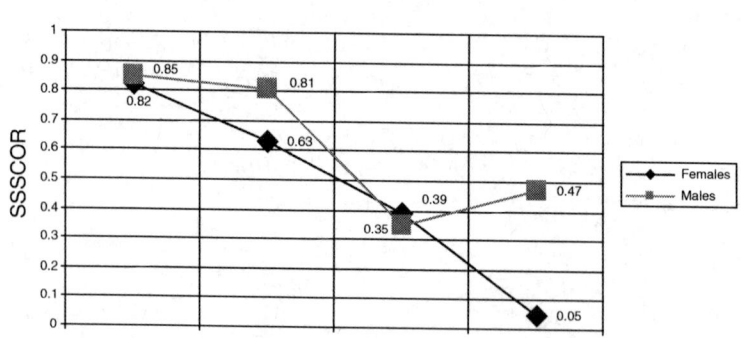

Figure 34 AGE across mean SSSCOR results

the two youngest groups, as was seen in the individual graphs above. As mentioned, such irregularity of patterning across age and sex often indicates the kind of instability associated with a process of ongoing change. The group means are again very similar to those for AGE across PHOVAR.

5.1.1.c AGE across LEXREC

Next, I examine AGE across LEXREC – the lexical recognition score.

	LEXREC
AGE	0.764

Lexical items often pattern differently from phonological ones. They seem to survive longer than phonological features during dialect loss,

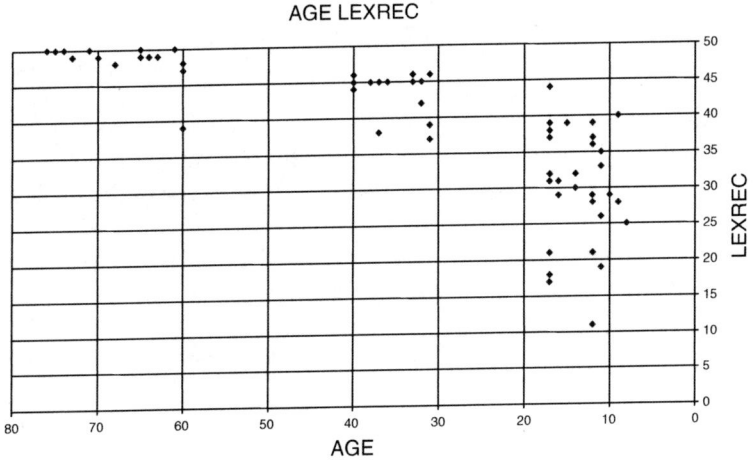

Figure 35   AGE across LEXREC

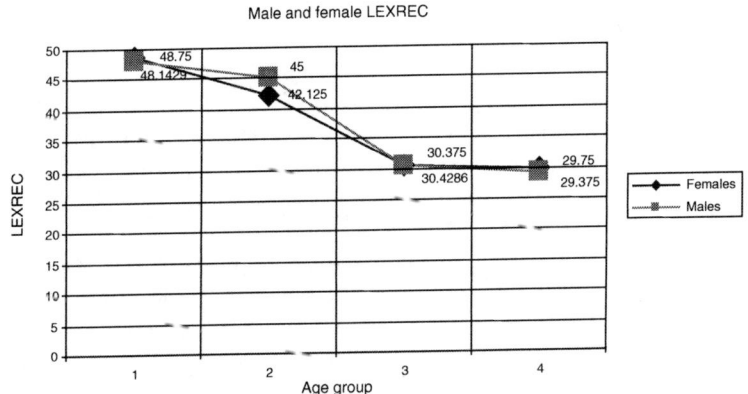

Figure 36   AGE across mean LEXREC scores

especially when they are connected with a group's cultural identity. Many a non-local can recall being told that the local word for 'dust' is 'stuur', but not many will have been told that the fricative is still pronounced in 'right'. This may not mean that lexical attrition lags behind phonetic change, though. A speaker may recognise a lexical item from its use in the community by, say, older people, and be able to give a standard equivalent, but this may not mean that the person normally and unselfconsciously uses the word in daily activities. The Huntly LEXREC scores display two things clearly:

1. They show a definite age effect. Thus lexical erosion is taking place across the generations, and the survival of lexical items does not seem to be any better than that of phonological features of the dialect.
2. Perhaps even more importantly, they pattern closely on the scores for the other two linguistic tests. As such it would seem that what was being tested in all three was similar: the speaker's use of the dialect.

The mean group scores show a definite age effect, with very little sex differentiation. Lexical erosion is marked between the older two and the younger two age groups. In sum then, AGE is a strong predictor of each of the three linguistic scores. It remains to be seen whether AGE is a predictor of the sociological scores.

5.1.1.d   AGE across MENURB

We now plot AGE across MENURB – the mental urbanisation index.

	MENURB
AGE	0.558

This scatterplot shows how AGE is a reasonable predictor of MENURB. The scores for the two oldest age groups are not vastly different from each other, but the 14 to 17 group has the lowest scores for this indicator of 'local team values'. For the most part, their sense of solidarity with the local rural community is lower than any other group. They are the ones who would more readily accept a city way of life than any others in the sample, and their use of local language forms shows this orientation: they are losing the dialect faster than the other groups. Members of this age group are at the stage in their lives when upward mobility is important, and staying on in the farming area means less choice when it comes to careers. A farmer with a farm and three children will normally leave it to one of them: the others will need to move on.

AGE across MENURB

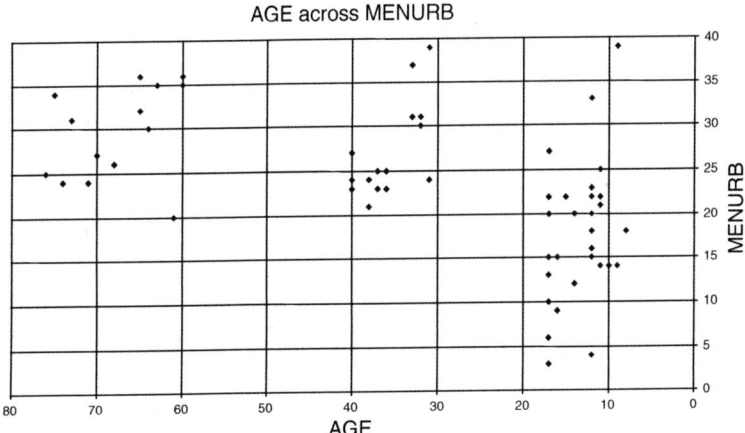

Figure 37   AGE across MENURB

The world of the city also offers many exciting attractions to those in this group, such as nightlife and entertainment. This point will be followed up in chapter 7. Figure 38, which shows the group means, reaffirms the individual scores. The youngest age group has higher scores than the 14 to 17 group and as has already been seen, their dialect scores are higher. This relationship between MENURB and dialect scores will be explored in more rigorous detail below.

The potential danger here is that there may simply be a correlation between AGE, as the predictor variable on the one hand, and MENURB

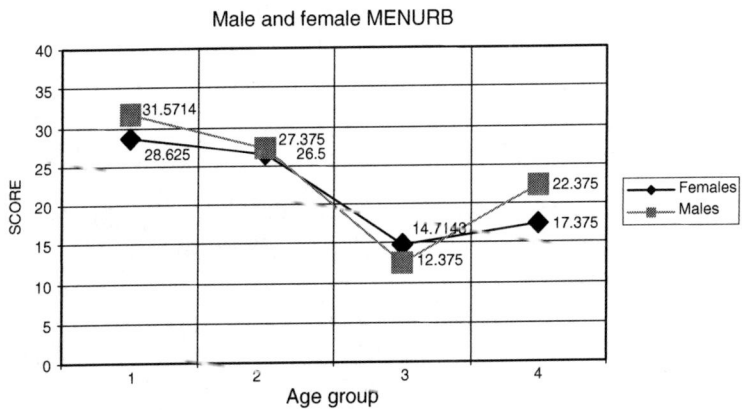

Figure 38   AGE across mean MENURB scores

and the linguistic scores on the other. In other words, one cannot simply assume that MENURB is a predictor of dialect maintenance. It could be the case that more teenagers have urban-oriented composite life modes *and* use less dialect than the other speakers, simply because that is what they choose to do at that age. The multiple linear regression analysis will show a more detailed result.

5.1.1.e AGE across SOCNET

AGE will now be plotted across SOCNET – the index of the individual's social network.

	SOCNET
AGE	0.186

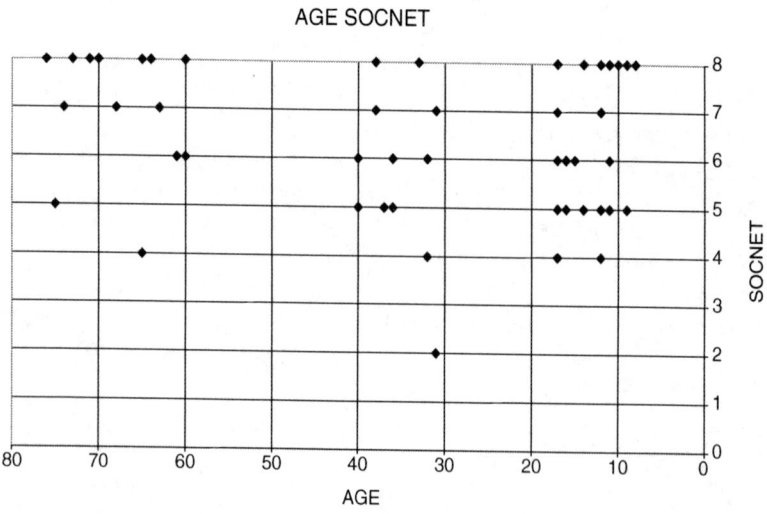

Figure 39 AGE across SOCNET

The scatterplot below reflects the non-significant correlation score 0.186. There is no visible tendency in the data points. There is no sign that age is correlated with social network strength. Old and young alike seem to have different degrees of integration into local social networks. Except for a single outlier in the 25 to 40 group, the scores for all the groups are between 4 and 8. The group means in table 10 show a slight trend, with slightly higher scores for the over 60 groups, though the statistical tests below will show these to be insignificant:

Table 10 Mean age across mean SOCNET

Group	Mean age	Mean SOCNET
f60	66.25	7.25
m60	67.86	6.86
f2540	34.75	5.88
m2540	35.88	5.88
f1417	16.86	5.86
m1417	15.88	6.25
f812	10.75	6.88
m812	11.25	6

In sum then, the individuals in this study are not integrated in local social networks in any way which can be said to depend upon their age.

5.1.1.f   AGE across SOCLAS
We now plot AGE across SOCLAS – the social class index.

	SOCLAS
AGE	–0.432

As the negative correlation above shows, the older two groups have slightly lower scores for social class. This is due to the fact that younger

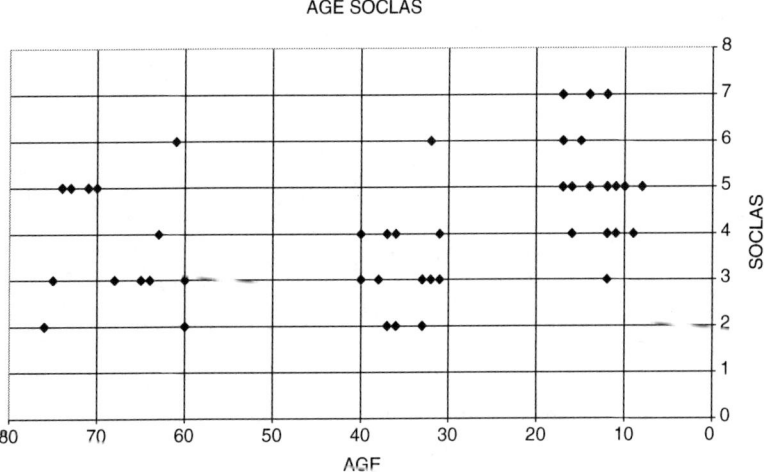

AGE SOCLAS

Figure 40   AGE across SOCLAS

speakers, especially the 14- to 17-year-olds, are staying at school longer, reading more national newspapers, and aspiring to more professional careers than the older folk did. Table 11 illustrates the combined-sex SOCLAS means for the age groups.

Table 11   Mean age across mean SOCLAS

Group	Mean age	Mean SOCLAS
f60	66.25	4.13
m60	67.86	3.14
f2540	34.75	3.25
m2540	35.88	3.25
f1417	16.86	5.71
m1417	15.88	5.88
f812	10.75	5.13
m812	11.25	4.25

The high SOCLAS scores of the adolescents are noteworthy, especially when considered with respect to their low dialect scores, as seen, for example, in 5.1.1.a. This relationship will be investigated below.

5.1.1.g   AGE across ATTDIA

Next I consider AGE across ATTDIA – the score for attitude to the dialect. There is not much age differentiation in the data on attitudes to the dialect.

	ATTDIA
AGE	0.334

There is no clear pattern in the data, except for some exceptionally low scores in the pre-adolescent group. Though the oldest group has no individual scores under 26 (range 0–40), the graph shows that most people sampled report very positive attitudes to the dialect, irrespective of age. This supports Macafee and McGarrity's (1999) results on attitudes. However, such reported attitudes may not be clear measures of actual attitudes. Some informants may be inclined to over-report such attitudes, especially where they are felt to signal in-group solidarity. As will be seen below, there is also no significant correlation between reported attitudes to the dialect and actual use of the dialect. The mean group scores do show a slight age effect, though this is not statistically significant.[4]

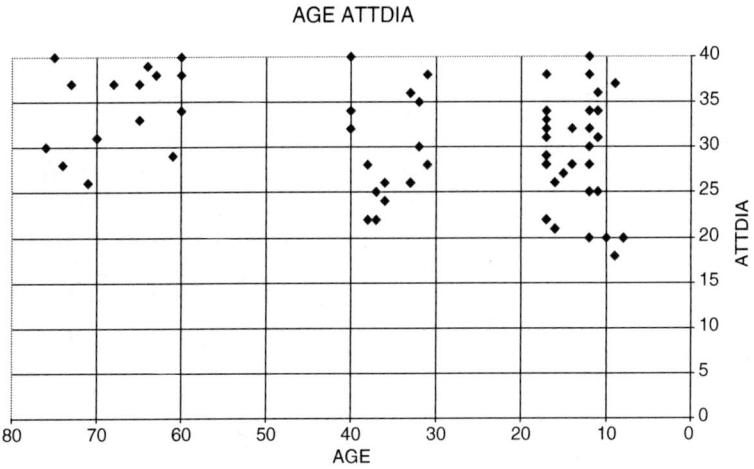

Figure 41 AGE across ATTDIA

Table 12 Mean age across mean ATTDIA

Group	Mean Age	Mean ATTDIA
f60	66.25	34.88
m60	67.86	34
f2540	34.75	30.13
m2540	35.88	29.38
f1417	16.86	28.29
m1417	15.88	29.88
f812	10.75	28
m812	11.25	30.5

5.1.1.h   Age across NATPRI

Next I consider AGE across. NATPRI – the index of national pride

	NATPRI
AGE	–0.083

Table 13   Mean age across mean NATPRI

Group	Mean age	Mean NATPRI
f60	66.25	31.5
m60	67.86	30.7
f2540	34.75	29.63
m2540	35.88	28.25
f1417	16.86	30.7
m1417	15.88	30.25
f812	10.75	32.38
m812	11.25	33.5

There is no clear correlation between AGE and NATPRI, though there are a few individuals in the adolescent and pre-adolescent groups who report maximal national pride of 40/40. The means in table 13 show no noticeable correlation.

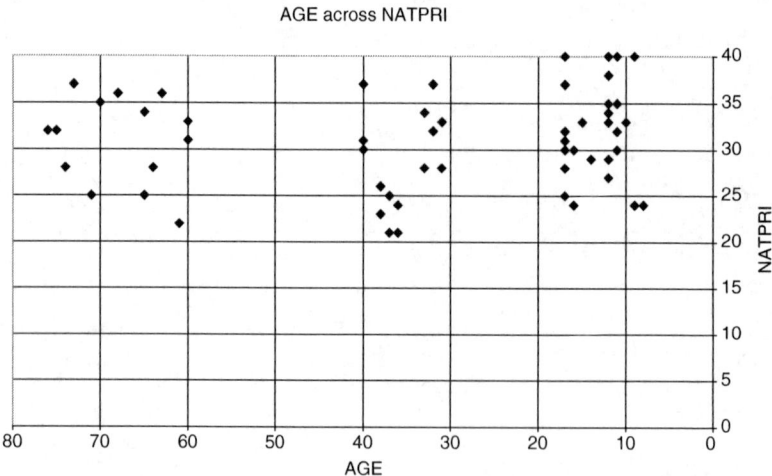

Figure 42   AGE across NATPRI

5.1.2   MENURB

Next the correlations between MENURB – the index of mental urbanisation – and the other variables will be considered. The section of the table is reproduced here for ease of reference:

Table 14   Correlations with MENURB

	PHOVAR	SSSCOR	LEXREC	AGE
MENURB	0.782	0.767	0.704	0.558

	SOCNET	SOCLAS	ATTDIA	NATPRI
MENURB	0.186	−0.553	0.468	0.242

From this we can see that MENURB is strongly positively correlated with PHOVAR, SSSCOR and LEXREC, less strongly with AGE and ATTDIA, and negatively with SOCLAS. This result is potentially indicative of a significant correlation between MENURB and the three linguistic variables, subject to statistical testing. This seems to show that, at this stage of the analysis at least, MENURB is a strong predictor of dialect use, and is also linked to some of the other social variables. The correlations of MENURB against the linguistic variables EXCEED even those of AGE against the two phonological variables PHOVAR and SSSCOR, and almost match even LEXREC, which is expected to be strongly correlated with age:

Table 15   AGE and MENURB across the linguistic variables

	PHOVAR	SSSCOR	LEXREC
AGE	0.734	0.659	0.764
MENURB	0.782	0.767	0.704

The implications of this will be discussed in chapter 7.

5.1.2.a   MENURB across PHOVAR

The scatterplot of the individual MENURB scores plotted against the individual PHOVAR scores supports the impression gained from the Pearson's Correlation of 0.782. The absence of any points in the first and fourth quadrants of the graph means that no individuals had high scores for one variable, and low scores for the other. The trend seems clear: the more strongly attached to the local group an individual is, the more dialect forms that person will use. This correlation will be tested further in chapter 6, and discussed in chapter 7.

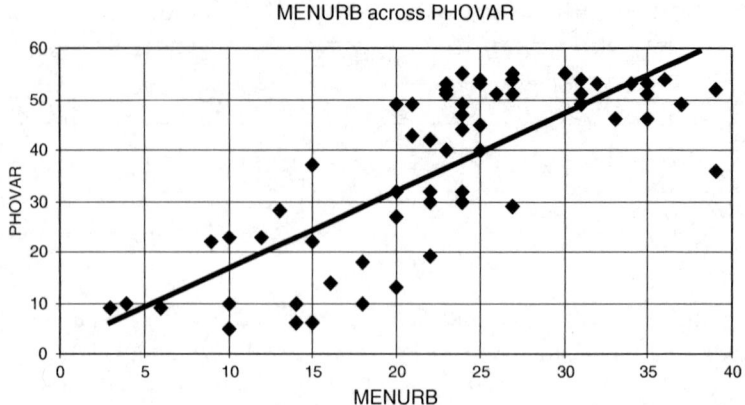

Figure 43   MENURB across PHOVAR

5.1.2.b   MENURB across SSSCOR

Next I examine the relationship between MENURB and the second linguistic variable, SSSCOR – the spontaneous speech score, measured during the scene description and treasure hunt tasks, which involved a partner, rather than the interviewer.

	SSSCOR
MENURB	0.767

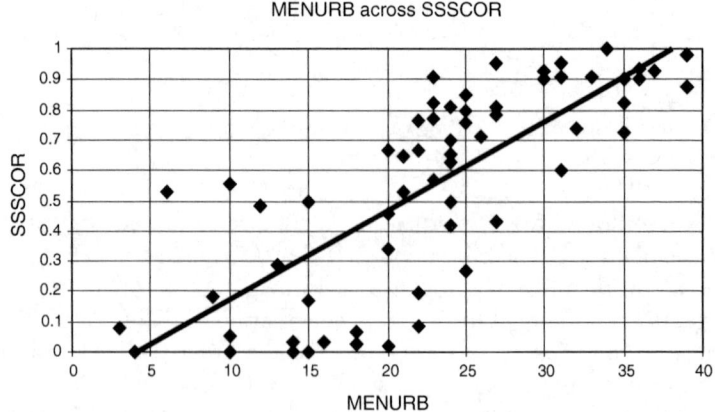

Figure 44   MENURB across SSSCOR

This result for MENURB across SSSCOR is very similar to the one for MENURB across PHOVAR, and serves to reinforce the initial impression of the apparent value of MENURB as a predictor of dialect use. The speech used by the individuals during the SSSCOR tasks, which involved less attention to speech, can be presumed to be closer to their speech in a non-interview setting. Their answers to the MENURB questions, regarding their feelings of integration into the local rural group, correlate highly with their use of phonological and morphological features of the local dialect in this section of the interview as well.

5.1.2.c MENURB across LEXREC

The correlation between MENURB and LEXREC will now be plotted.

	LEXREC
MENURB	0.704

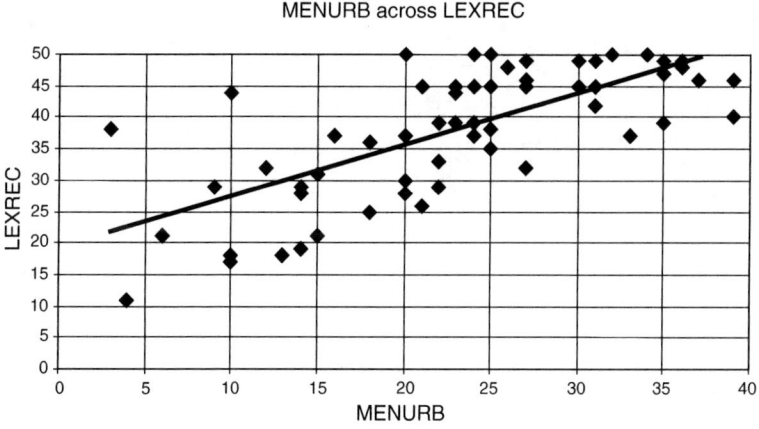

Figure 45 MENURB across LEXREC

The reliability of a lexical test as a test of dialect maintenance was initially in some question, due to factors mentioned above. Nevertheless, not only are all three linguistic scores highly correlated with each other, but also with MENURB. This would seem to indicate that lexical tests are in fact valid indicators of dialect maintenance. This will be discussed in chapter 7.

5.1.2.d   MENURB across SOCNET

As a matter of course, the social variables have also been checked against each other for correlation. This is useful in safeguarding against differently intended questions ending up measuring what is essentially the same thing. The scores for MENURB will now be plotted against those for SOCNET – the index of social network interaction.

	SOCNET
MENURB	0.186

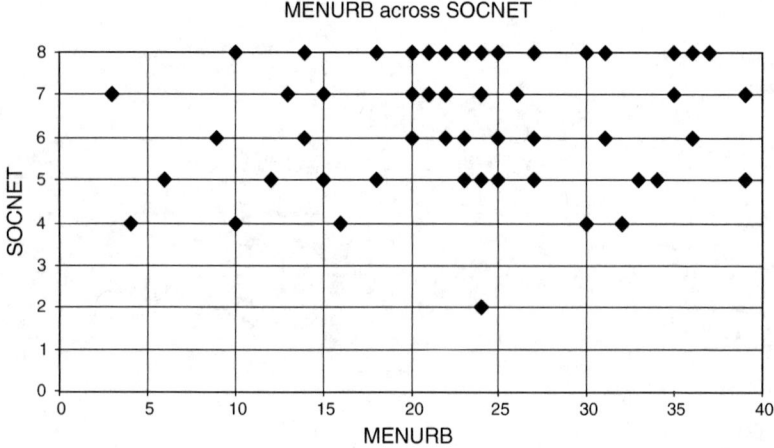

Figure 46   MENURB across SOCNET

This may be an important result. The Pearson's Correlation and scatter-plot show that a person's social network integration is not correlated with that person's degree of solidarity with the local group. It would seem intuitive to expect the opposite: that a person with a high degree of local solidarity would be involved rather fully in local social net-works. The review of networks presented in chapter 3, and discussed in chapter 7, foregrounds individual choice in such matters. The question of how free an individual is to integrate into social networks at what-ever level he or she prefers is worth examining in more detail.

5.1.2.e MENURB across SOCLAS

The question of whether an individual's socio-economic background will have an effect on his or her degree of solidarity with the local group is rather important, given the results of other studies. Milroy (1980: 162) writes about working-class speakers being less socially and geographically mobile, and more tied to the local group. If belonging to a higher socio-economic grouping implies being more open to supra-local contacts and mobility, we may expect a negative correlation between MENURB and SOCLAS.

	SOCLAS
MENURB	0.553

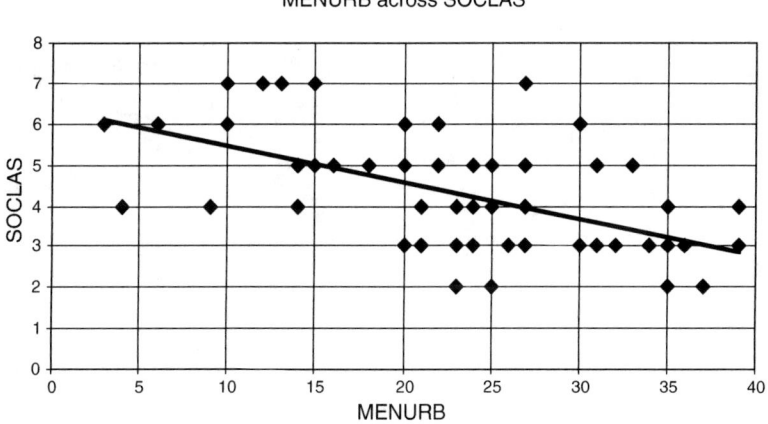

MENURB across SOCLAS

Figure 47 MENURB across SOCLAS

The negative correlation here indicates that, the higher the person's social class index, the lower such a person's local group solidarity. It is natural that those speakers who have been exposed to more education and national newspapers will be more open to adopting, in Pedersen's (1994) terms, urban-oriented composite life modes, as discussed in section 2.3. In terms of the Huntly study, this equates with lower levels of local solidarity, and lower MENURB scores.

5.1.2.f   MENURB across ATTDIA

We now consider the MENURB scores against those for ATTDIA – the speaker's reported attitude to the dialect.

	ATTDIA
MENURB	**0.468**

Both of these indices represent attitudes, and there is a positive correlation, though weak. As will be seen below, ATTDIA is generally not correlated with the three linguistic scores (the exception being SSSCOR, though the correlation is weak). It could be argued that the above correlation indicates that what is being measured by ATTDIA and MENURB is similar. Such a view seems logical, given that a dialect is a symbol of a local group, and positive views of one will correlate with positive views of the other.

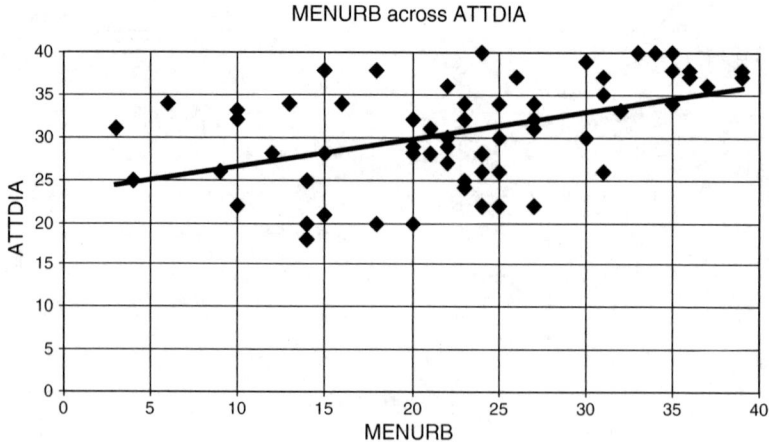

Figure 48   MENURB across ATTDIA

As was argued above, individuals may report, and even genuinely have, strong positive attitudes to a local language variety, but decide not to use it, for reasons of social advancement, for example. The fact that MENURB is highly correlated with dialect use, and ATTDIA is not, would support this view, and it seems reasonable to assume that these two sociological indices in fact measure different things.

5.1.2.g MENURB across NATPRI

We now turn to the relationship between MENURB and NATPRI – the reported degree of national pride.

	NATPRI
MENURB	0.242

There is no clear correlation between MENURB and NATPRI, as the graph above shows. This lack of correlation is more difficult to explain than the lack of correlation between MENURB and ATTDIA, as what we are dealing with are essentially two measures of solidarity with 'local' versus 'non-local' groups, simply at community versus national level. However, included in feelings of national pride for Scotland are elements that are not present in feelings for the rural farming community in the Strathbogie Valley. Scotland as a political unit includes many different areas, with differing histories, and many large urban centres. It has a history that captures the imagination of people around the world, and gives Scots pride. But such attitudes are still supra-local in the restricted sense, and are not about micro-level factors. In fact, some speakers responded with caution to questions about the 'yes' vote for the Scottish Parliament, citing fears of 'another Northern Ireland'. The same speakers responded enthusiastically to questions about the local area versus the city. This may explain the results of the Pearson's correlation above.

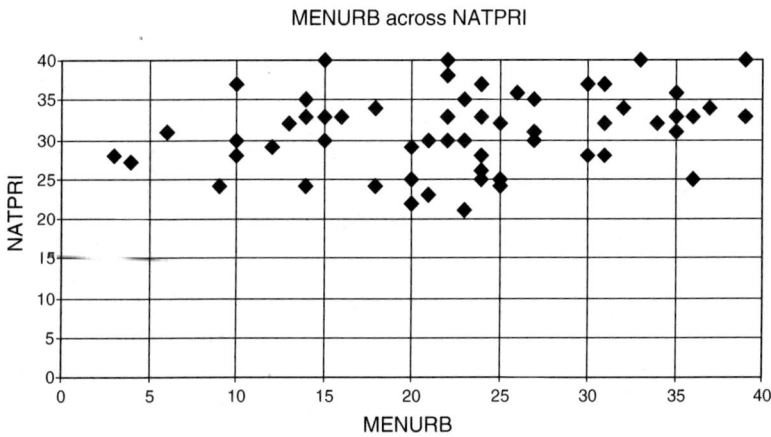

Figure 49 MENURB across NATPRI

5.1.3 SOCNET

Next, the correlations for SOCNET were considered:

Table 16 Correlations with SOCNET

	PHOVAR	SSSCOR	LEXREC	MENURB
SOCNET	0.056	0.040	0.197	0.186

	AGE	SOCLAS	ATTDIA	NATPRI
SOCNET	0.186	−0.140	−0.116	−0.132

It is immediately obvious that SOCNET is not correlated with any other variable. This lack of correlation would indicate, at this stage of the analysis, that SOCNET is not a good predictor of dialect use, or in Milroy's words, vernacular norm enforcement. In fact, the correlations between this variable and the dialect scores are more neutral than any other correlations tested here. This means that correlations between SOCNET scores and the dialect scores are closer to random (neither positive nor negative correlation) than any of the other scores. The scatterplots are no more illuminating, and only the first one has been included, as there are two points worth noting:

5.1.3.a SOCNET across PHOVAR

One individual (marked) has an exceptionally low SOCNET score of 2/8, yet achieved a score of 44/56 for PHOVAR. By comparison, there are many speakers who have SOCNET scores of 8/8, and who achieved less than 15/56 for PHOVAR. The same is true for the scatterplots of SOCNET across the other two linguistic variables. The absence of correlation between SOCNET and any of the linguistic variables is striking, and requires explanation. The concept that the nature of an individual's social network may have an effect on that person's behaviour seems logical, and it is for this reason that the section on social networks was included in the experimental design as one of the most important sociological variables. The results shown here, however, call into question the 'vernacular norm-enforcement' effect of dense, multiplex networks. In fact, upon closer inspection of Milroy's (1980) data, network scores were not correlated very highly with vernacular maintenance. Out of nine variables, only two were correlated significantly in Ballymacarrett, one in Clonard, and two in Hammer, a point which will be developed in chapter 7. When considering the whole Belfast database, consisting of all three areas and all nine variables, the correlation between dense, multiplex social networks and vernacular norm maintenance must be rather less marked. This point will be developed in chapter 7. The relationship between AGE and SOCNET, and between MENURB and SOCNET was discussed in sections 5.1.1.e iand 5.1.2.d, and so I now move on to SOCNET across SOCLAS.

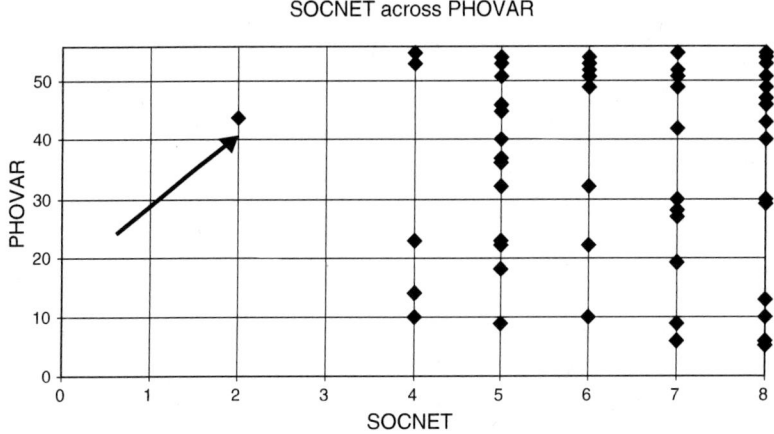

Figure 50 SOCNET across PHOVAR

5.1.3.b   SOCNET across SOCLAS

	SOCLAS
SOCNET	−0.140

According to Milroy, working class individuals are more likely to be integrated into local social networks than the socially and geographically mobile middle-class individuals. The Huntly SOCLAS score does not place individuals in large-scale categories such as 'working class' or 'middle class', but is a finely graded scalar index of socio-economic background. As such it is a more suitable measure for statistical testing. The prediction of the social network framework is that there should be a strong negative correlation between these two indices. There clearly is no such correlation here. This would indicate that individuals with differing socio-economic indicators may be integrated in social networks in similar ways, and also that individuals with the same socio-economic indicators may be integrated in different ways. This only serves to

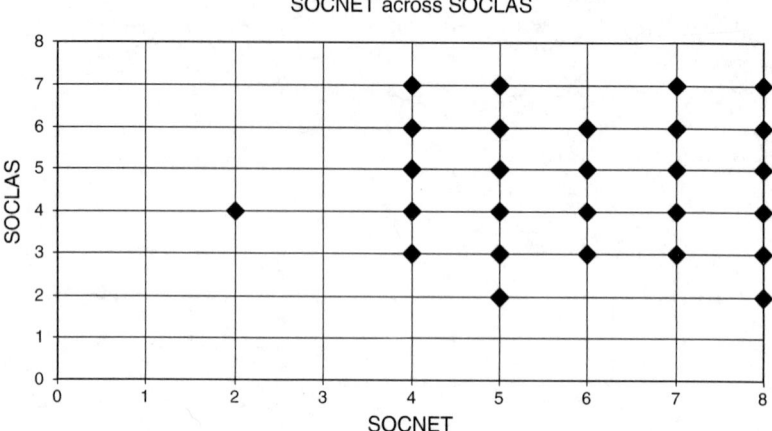

Figure 51   SOCNET across SOCLAS

high-light the possibility of other possible factors operating, for example, the freedom of choice of the individual, when it comes to such things as level of integration in local social networks, use of local language forms, dress, and other patterns of behaviour. Any norm-enforcement mechanism of the network does not seem to have operated on the individuals in the Huntly study.

5.1.3.c   SOCNET across ATTDIA

Based on the predicted ability of close-knit social networks to enforce vernacular norms, we would expect such networks to also reinforce positive *attitudes* to the local vernacular, and therefore yield a strong positive correlation between SOCNET and ATTDIA in the Huntly data. It is unlikely that norms can be enforced upon unwilling individuals.

	ATTIDA
SOCNET	0.116

Individuals are clearly integrating themselves at different levels into local social networks, regardless of any pre-existing attitudes to the local language variety. Put another way, an individual's level of integration into local social networks does not seem to influence his or her attitude to the local vernacular.

5.1.4 SOCLAS

Next, I consider the correlations for SOCLAS.

Table 17 Correlations with SOCLAS

	PHOVAR	SSSCOR	LEXREC	AGE
SOCLAS	−0.541	−0.440	−0.498	−0.432

	MENURB	SOCNET	ATTDIA	NATPRI
SOCLAS	−0.553	−0.140	−0.164	0.154

SOCLAS is negatively correlated with PHOVAR, SSSCOR, LEXREC, AGE and MENURB, though not strongly with any of them. This is a sign that, contrary to earlier expectations for this study, social class may be (a) measurable in a rural community, and (b) significant as a predictor of language use in such areas.

5.1.4.a SOCLAS across PHOVAR

	PHOVAR
SOCLAS	0.541

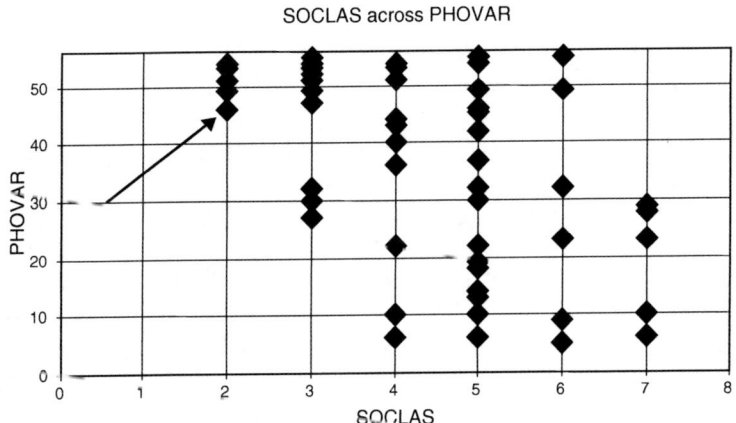

Figure 52 SOCLAS across PHOVAR

Though there is a negative correlation between SOCLAS and PHOVAR, the correlation is not as strong as the one between MENURB and the three linguistic scores. Nevertheless, there is a cluster of speakers who have the lowest scores obtained for SOCLAS (2/8), and who all have dialect scores higher than 46/56 (shown with an arrow). This particular group would in fact make an interesting case study on their own. A very similar cluster is found in the group which scored 3/8 for SOCLAS, though there are a few in this group who have lower PHOVAR scores. There is then a complete lack of trend in the three middle groups, who scored 4, 5 and 6 out of 8 for SOCLAS. The top end of the socio-economic scale, those who scored 7/8, all have low PHOVAR scores, between 5 and 28 out of 56. So, at least as far as the top and bottom ends of the scale go, socio-economic indices definitely correlate with dialect use, as has been found time and again in other, especially urban, studies. As social class is not part of the research hypothesis, this relationship will not be investigated in any great depth, though its significance will be tested statistically. The correlations between SOCLAS and the remaining two linguistic variables, SSSCOR and LEXREC are very similar to this result, and will not be discussed any further here.

5.1.4.b   SOCLAS across ATTDIA

Given the results of other studies, which show strong correlations between social class and language use (Labov 1966, Kerswill and Williams 1994, Cheshire 1982), we may expect middle-class people not only to use less vernacular, but also to have less favourable attitudes towards the vernacular han working-class people.

	ATTDIA
SOCLAS	0.164

There is only a very weak negative correlation between SOCLAS and ATTDIA. The scatterplot does, however, show a trend: the lack of any low scores for ATTDIA. Individuals situated at all points along the socio-economic scale report very positive attitudes to the dialect. This supports what has been found in the north-east by other studies (Macafee and McGarrity 1999), and is unusual, if compared to other areas, even in Glasgow (Macaulay 1991). People, especially middle-class people, are likely to report negative attitudes to non-standard varieties. The special situation in Scotland does cause more positive attitudes to be found, though Macaulay found these only came to the fore after more questioning. This point will be developed in chapter 7.

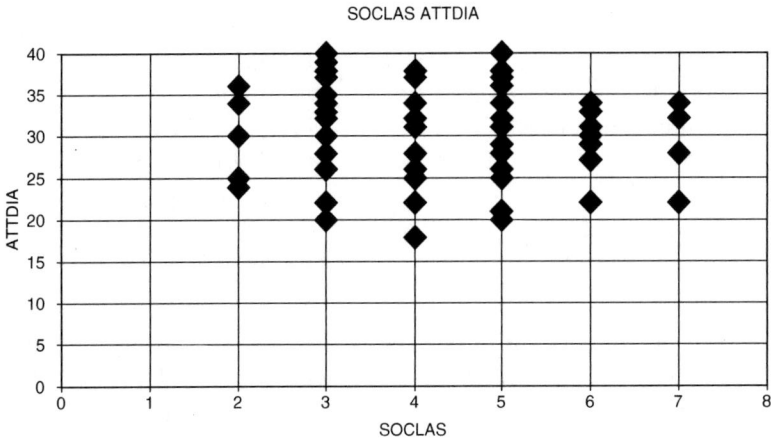

Figure 53 SOCLAS across ATTDIA

5.1.4.c SOCLAS across NATPRI

Plotting SOCLAS across the last social variable, NATPRI, does not reveal any striking correlation.

	NATPRI
SOCLAS	0.154

This result shows that speakers with differing socio-economic indices report similarly high levels of national pride. Socio-economic factors do not seem to have an effect on feelings of patriotism in this database.

5.1.5 ATTDIA

We now turn to the correlations between ATTDIA and the other variables.

Table 18 Correlations with ATTDIA

	PHOVAR	**SSSCOR**	LEXREC	SOCLAS
ATTDIA	0.356	**0.478**	0.306	−0.164

	MENURB	SOCNET	AGE	**NATPRI**
ATTDIA	**0.468**	−0.116	0.334	**0.581**

ATTDIA is positively correlated with (1) SSSCOR, (2) MENURB and (3) NATPRI, though not strongly. The three social scores correlated here are all measures of some sort of attitude. It would seem that a positive attitude to the dialect correlates with a positive attitude to the local rural community and, on a wider scale, to Scotland. This table compares distinctively with table 16, which showed the results for SOCNET.

5.1.5.a ATTDIA across SSSCOR

The only correlation higher than 0.4 with any linguistic variable is with SSSCOR. This potentially promising result is offset somewhat by an unconvincing scatterplot, which shows that, while there is a cluster of data-points in the far top right hand quadrant, there are many individuals with high ATTDIA scores, who have low spontaneous speech scores, as can be seen in the bottom right-hand quadrant.

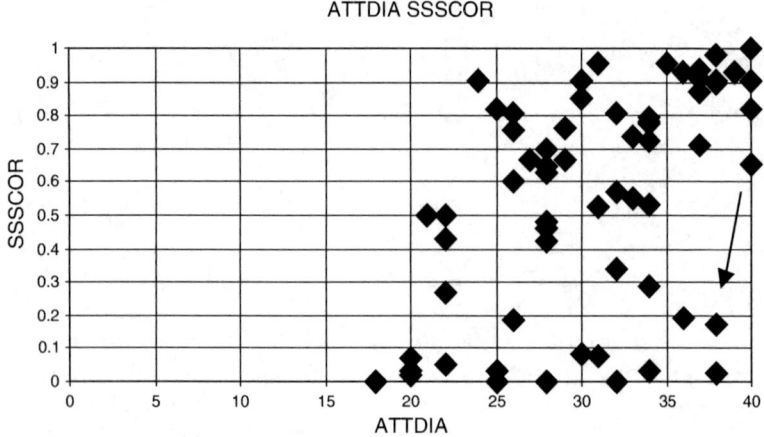

Figure 54 ATTDIA across SSSCOR

The correlation between ATTDIA and the other two linguistic variables is even weaker, and is therefore not discussed further.

5.1.5.b ATTDIA across MENURB

	MENURB
ATTDIA	0.468

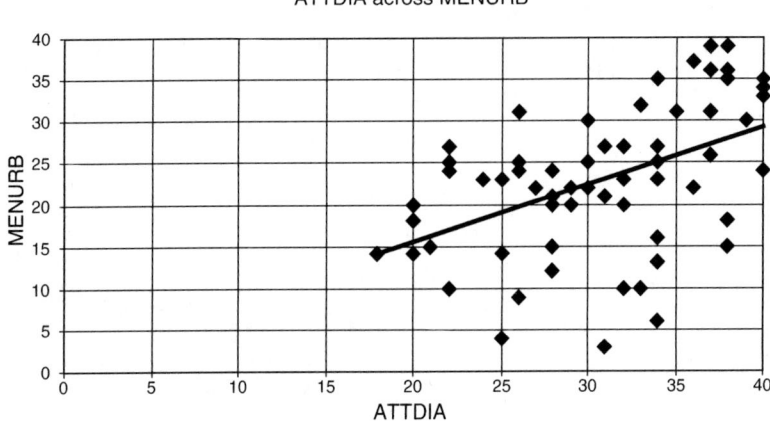

Figure 55 ATTDIA across MENURB

The correlation here is positive, even if not very strong. There is a rather dense cluster of data-points in the far top right hand quadrant, and an absence in the far bottom right hand quadrant. In a sense, similar attitudinal factors are being measured here, though, crucially, ATTDIA does not correlate highly with dialect scores, whereas MENURB does.

5.1.5.c   ATTDIA across NATPRI

	NATPRI
ATTDIA	0.581

This Pearson's Correlation shows a rather better result. ATTDIA is more highly correlated with NATPRI than with any other variable. These two lines of questioning must measure a similar attitudinal entity. This is not surprising, considering how, in Scotland, feelings about language and about nation are bound to be intricately linked. This link will be discussed further in chapter 7.

5.1.6   NATPRI

The next sociological variable to be checked is NATPRI. Because language is such a potent symbol in any speech community, and given the social history of Scotland, we may expect a positive correlation between NATPRI and language use. The only strong correlation is between NATPRI and ATTDIA. This shows a considerable interaction between an individual's attitudes towards Scotland and towards the Scots language. The absence of correlations with the linguistic scores may be due to high reported levels of national pride in the younger speakers, who do not generally have a good command of the Doric. However, the scatterplots reveal no strong correlation between NATPRI and the three variables, even for the older speakers. This point will be explored in chapter 7.

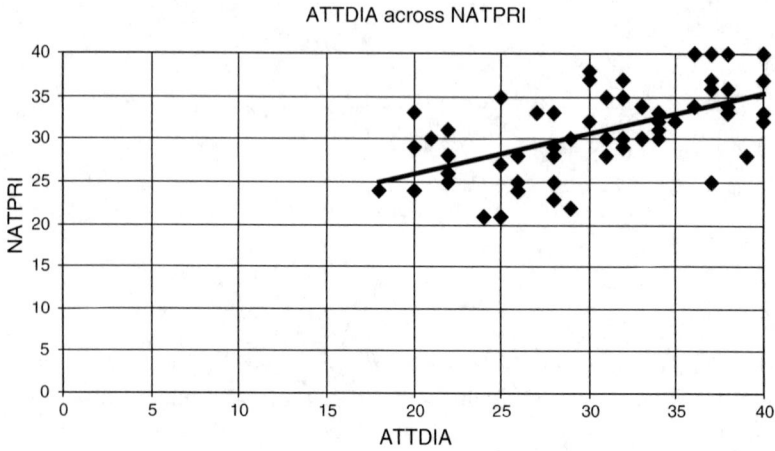

Figure 56   ATTDIA across NATPRI

Table 19   Correlations with NATPRI

	PHOVAR	SSSCOR	LEXREC	SOCNET
NATPRI	−0.041	0.031	−0.072	−0.132

	SOCLAS	ATTDIA	AGE	MENURB
NATPRI	0.154	0.581	−0.083	0.242

5.1.7   PHOVAR

Before continuing with the usual comparison across the other variables, I shall examine the dialect scores across the two phonological variables: PHOVAR and SSSCOR. As discussed in section 3.5, investigators often devise interview structures that begin with relaxed conversation, and then move on to a reading passage, a word list, and a minimal pair list. The notion behind this is that each stage will bring with it a higher level of linguistic awareness, and therefore closer self-monitoring of speech. In the Huntly study, no such elicitation aids were used, though it is reasonable to assume that PHOVAR, by its very nature, would bring more attention to speech than SSSCOR, as the latter firstly involved a partner, and not the interviewer, and secondly involved concentrating upon the task of describing, as well as possible, a complex scene and a treasure map to the partner.

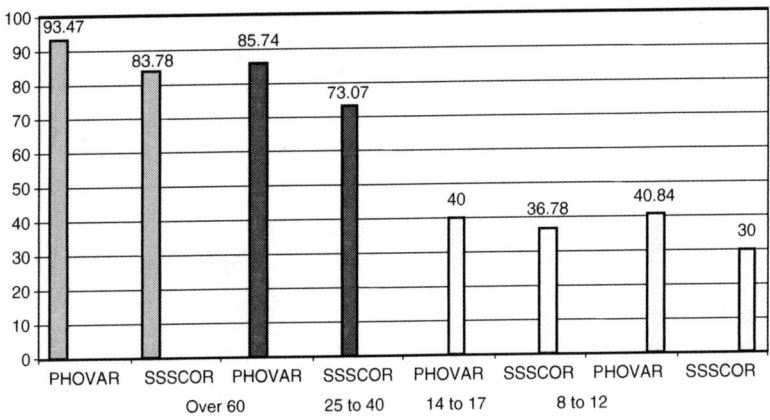

Comparing dialect use with level of formality

Figure 57 PHOVAR and SSSCOR means

For each age group, the dialect score is slightly higher in the case of PHOVAR than SSSCOR, the difference being significant at the level $p = 0.008$. This would seem to indicate a more relaxed speaker, less focused on pronunciation, in the picture list exercise which produced the PHOVAR scores, than in the process-based tasks involving a scene description and a treasure hunt. Though the two tests were not designed with differing levels of formality in mind, this result would seem counter-intuitive at first. The aim for both tests was simply to access the most natural speech of the respondent. The high scores for PHOVAR are an encouraging sign that the use of a picture list instead of a word list, especially when the variety being investigated is linguistically distant from the standard and its orthography, is a highly effective methodological device. Nevertheless, this result would not seem to call into question the notion of increased levels of formality bringing increased self-monitoring of speech. It is possible that the picture list simply elicited items that are more likely to be non-standard.

Comparing PHOVAR across the other variables

The correlations for PHOVAR across the other variables are as follows:

Table 20   Correlations with PHOVAR

	SSSCOR	LEXREC	SOCNET	SOCLAS
PHOVAR	0.886	0.794	0.056	−0.541

	ATTDIA	AGE	MENURB	NATPRI
PHOVAR	0.356	0.734	0.782	−0.041

PHOVAR is positively correlated with SSSCOR, LEXREC, AGE, and MENURB, and negatively with SOCLAS. I have already covered the correlations between each of the social variables and the three linguistic variables. Here it is the correlations with the other linguistic scores which are of interest. These correlations are the highest in the database. The value of 0.886 returned for PHOVAR across SSSCOR is to be expected, as they each measure phonological features of the speaker's linguistic performance in the dialect, albeit in different tasks, and a scatterplot reveals this.[5] The strong correlation between

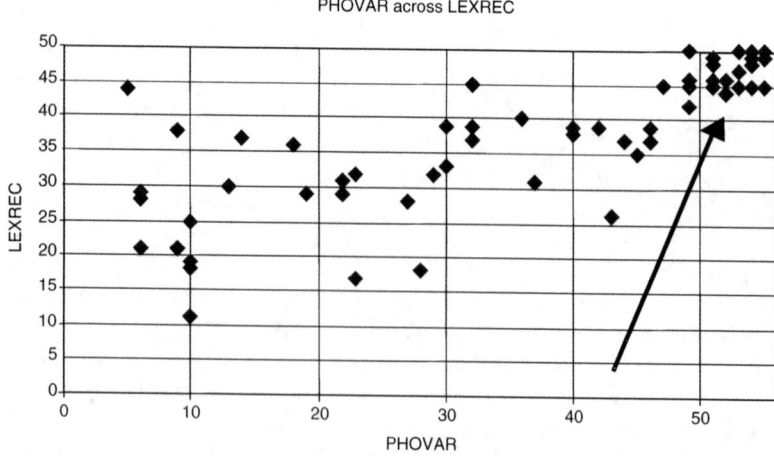

Figure 58   PHOVAR across LEXREC

PHOVAR and LEXREC would again seem to support the concept of using lexical tests as a measure of dialect maintenance. The scatterplot for this does reveal less of a strong trend throughout the data, although there is a strong trend at the upper end of the scores, as can be seen in figure 58.

The top scorers for dialect phonetic features consistently also show high degrees of dialect lexical knowledge. Those who have lower phonetic scores show great variability in their lexical knowledge.

5.1.8 SSSCOR

Table 21   Correlations with SSSCOR

	PHOVAR	LEXREC	SOCNET	SOCLAS
SSSCOR	0.886	0.735	0.040	–0.440

	ATTDIA	AGE	MENURB	NATPRI
SSSCOR	0.478	0.659	0.767	0.031

SSSCOR is positively correlated with PHOVAR, LEXREC, ATTDIA, AGE and MENURB, and negatively with SOCLAS. As most of these correlations have already been covered, I consider only two here. First, SSSCOR is strongly positively correlated with ATTDIA, whereas the other two linguistic scores were not. There is no clear reason for this, except that SSSCOR is thought to be a measure of the most vernacular speech available in the database, which may yield this correlation with attitudes towards the dialect. A speaker with a positive attitude to the dialect may still suppress dialect features in 'interview' speech, but not be able to do this effectively when concentrating on 'paralinguistic', or at least, less linguistically focused, tasks, such as those performed for SSSCOR. Second, SSSCOR is correlated positively with LEXREC, which again would seem to confirm that lexical maintenance is inseparably linked with phonological and morphological maintenance.

In order to confirm the impressions gained by the correlations and plots, in chapter 6 I subject the variables to more advanced statistical testing, in the form of multiple linear regression.

Notes

1. This was decided in consultation with the Applied Statistics Advisory Service at the University of Reading.

2. The questionnaires are given under 'Appendices'.
3. As mentioned, the term is used simply for convenience. As these phonetic forms are restricted to small lexical sets, it is more useful to see the variation as morpho-lexical.
4. See chapter 6 for statistical results.
5. The scatterplot has not been included, as the trend is strong and clear throughout the data.

6
Statistical Testing

The aim of this chapter is to test more effectively the relationships indicated by the Pearson's Correlations and scatterplots in chapter 5. In statistical terms one has an independent, or predictor, variable(s) and a dependent, or predicted variable(s). The first is normally the variable one believes affects the second. In the Huntly study, the independent variables are AGE, SEX, MENURB, SOCNET, SOCLAS, ATTDIA and NATPRI, as it was believed that these would have an effect on the language of the individuals interviewed, which was measured by the dependent variables PHOVAR, SSSCOR and LEXREC.

In conjunction with the Applied Statistics Advisory Service at the University of Reading, it was decided that the best test would be multiple linear regression. This is a statistical model which one builds by adding the independent variables one at a time across a single dependent variable. As each independent variable is entered, the output is checked. The r-squared value at each step of the way indicates what percentage of the variance in the dependent variable is accounted for by that particular independent variable. A p-value is also given, which indicates whether the correlation is significant, and at what level of significance. These two values are the most important in a multiple linear regression test, and I will refer to them at each stage of the testing. I have, according to convention, decided to accept any p-value of 0.05 or smaller as significant, and any value of 0.01 or smaller as highly significant. Before building the regression model, I show the summary statistics.

6.1 Summary statistics

Summary statistics have been produced only for AGE and SEX across the dependent variables, as these are the only two independent variables with groupings, such as FEMALE, MALE, AGE GROUP 1, etc. The other independent variables are scalar indices, and they are tested in more detail below.

AGE

The summary statistics confirm what the correlation tests showed: the effect of age on language use is marked, as can be seen by the decreasing means in the column in bold. The variable in column one is age group, and the mean scores are for the three linguistic scores, PHOVAR, SSSCOR, and LEXREC.

Table 22   AGE: PHOVAR

Age group	N	Mean
60+	15	52.400
25–40	17	47.76
14–17	15	22.40
8–12	16	22.88

Table 23   AGE: SSSCOR

Age group	N	Mean
60+	15	0.8369
25–40	17	0.7261
14–17	15	0.3666
8–12	16	0.2599

Table 24   AGE: LEXREC

Age group	N	Mean
60+	15	48.467
25–40	17	43.706
14–17	15	30.40
8–12	16	29.56

There is a marked difference in dialect use between the two older groups on the one hand, and the two younger groups on the other. This was expected after the pilot study showed a marked loss of the dialect in younger speakers. Also of interest are the large standard deviations in the two younger groups. Such intra-group variability would seem to indicate instability and change in progress. As age does not play a part in the research question, I will not consider this in any more detail, except to include age in the regression model.

SEX

The results of other sociolinguistic studies predict that males will use the vernacular to a higher degree than females, and this is indicated by the data for Huntly.

Table 25 SEX: PHOVAR

SEX	N	Mean
female	32	33.94
male	31	39.16

Table 26 SEX: SSSCOR

SEX	N	Mean
female	32	0.4872
male	31	0.6117

Table 27 SEX: LEXREC

SEX	N	Mean
female	32	38.25
male	31	37.90

The males have higher scores for PHOVAR and SSSCOR, whereas their scores for LEXREC are slightly lower than those of the females. This last difference, however, is not significant (p = 0.89). The results may be due to the prestige of phonological and morphological features of the dialect for males, whereas women generally seem to lead sound changes in that they abandon conservative linguistic features more readily than men. However, the females may have more etymological and lexical interest in the dialect. This interest was made clear during the field-work, where women talked of their involvement in writing vernacular poetry and in public readings of such poetry, for example at traditional Scots gatherings. Women were far more likely to voluntarily list local vernacular lexical items during free narratives, and to explain their meanings.

However, generalising about such changes based on sex, rather than the speaker's social values and network structures would be unwise (Milroy 1980: 113). The effect of sex is not part of the research question for this study either, and will be removed during model building. This will enable us to see whether the other social variables identified have a significant effect on their own.

6.2   Regression analyses: building regression models

As detailed above, a linear regression analysis involves building a model that adds first the predicted variable, and then the predictor variables into the equation one at a time (see for example Hatch and Lazaraton 1991). The output at each stage shows to what degree each predictor variable accounts for the variance in the predicted variable, expressed as a percentage. AGE and SEX will be entered first and second, as they clearly account for a great deal of the variance, and their effect will need to be removed from the output. After that, the relevant social variables will be added in order to test their significance as predictors of language use. The output below shows first the predicted variable and then the predictor variables in the order chosen.

The two results to take note of are:

1. The p-value (probability of the variation occurring by chance) – the lower this figure the more significant the result. The minimum accepted for most studies is 0.05, and the significant results are in bold below.
2. The r-squared value, a measure of how much of the variation in the dependent variable is accounted for by the independent variable(s), shown as a percentage.

6.2.1   Regression model for PHOVAR

The effects of AGE and SEX on the dependent variables is now determined.

AGE

Predictor	p-value
AGE	0.000
R-Squared (adjusted) 53.1%	

The p-value is highly significant, and the r-squared value is high. This shows us that AGE accounts for a substantial 53.1% of the variation in PHOVAR. It is unlikely that any other independent variable will exceed this value, but what we are interested in is whether the other sociological scores will prove to account for substantial percentages of the variation in the linguistic scores. Next, I add the variable SEX to the model.

AGE and SEX

Predictor	p-value
AGE	0.000
SEX	0.042
R-Squared (adjusted) 55.5%	

The p-value for SEX is significant, but only at the 0.05 level, and the r-squared value has risen only slightly, showing that the addition of the independent variable SEX has only improved the model by a small amount, accounting for a further 2.4% of the variation. This is interesting, in that research elsewhere has shown that females use significantly more standard (or supralocal) forms than males (Watt and Milroy 1999, Williams and Kerswill 1999, Trudgill 1983, Stuart-Smith 1999, Eckert 2000). The difference here, where the data is tested as a whole, is very small. This would seem to support Macafee's results, which showed the north-east to show the most positive attitudes to the local variety on the part of both males and females, and the local variety is therefore probably not evaluated so negatively by females as other more negatively evaluated varieties elsewhere are by their speakers.

AGE, SEX and AGE × SEX

The possibility exists that certain independent variables may also interact with each other, and so this potential interaction must also be entered as a predictor variable. The interaction column in the spreadsheet is created by indexing the two sexes, in this case 1 for females and 0 for males, and then multiplying the indices by the individual ages in the column for the variable AGE. The results are then entered into the regression model at this point.

Predictor	p-value
AGE	0.000
SEX	0.011
AGE × SEX	0.086
R-Squared (adjusted) 57.0%	

The interaction between AGE and SEX accounts for only 1.5% of the variation in PHOVAR, and the p-value is too high to be accepted as significant. This would indicate a lack of interaction between the two 'natural' social factors, AGE and SEX, in the data. I now add MENURB.

6.2.2 Adding MENURB to the model

Predictor	p-value
AGE	0.003
SEX	0.003
AGE×SEX	0.024
MENURB	0.000
R-Squared (adjusted) 76.1%	

The effect of the first of the 'non-natural' independent variables, MENURB, is highly significant at the level $p < 0.001$, and its inclusion has increased the r-squared value of the model by 19.1%. The increase shows that MENURB accounts for almost 20% of the variation in PHOVAR. The implications for this are important, and will be discussed in chapter 7. The same process will now be applied to the next independent variable, SSSCOR.

6.2.3 Regression model for SSSCOR

AGE

Age is entered again as the first independent variable across SSSCOR. The regression equation is:

Predictor	p-value
AGE	0.000
R-Squared (adjusted) 42.5%	

The effect of AGE on SSSCOR is highly significant ($p < 0.001$), and the r-squared value, while lower than for AGE across PHOVAR, shows that AGE is a powerful predictor variable, accounting for 42.5% of the variance in SSSCOR.

AGE and SEX

Predictor	p-value
AGE	0.000
SEX	0.030
R-Squared (adjusted) 46.0%	

The p-value for SEX is significant at the lower level of 0.05, but the r-squared value has risen only slightly, showing that SEX is statistically significant as a predictor at this stage, but accounts for only 3.5% of the variance in SSSCOR.

AGE, SEX and AGE×SEX

Predictor	p-value
AGE	0.000
SEX	0.030
AGE×SEX	0.196
R-Squared (adjusted) 46.6%	

The interaction between AGE and SEX is not statistically significant, and this interaction only accounts for 0.6% of the variance in SSSCOR.

6.2.4 Adding MENURB to the model

Predictor	p-value
AGE	0.044
SEX	0.012
AGE×SEX	0.097
MENURB	0.000
R-Squared (adjusted) 68.3%	

The p-value for SEX is still significant at the 0.05 level, and the interaction between AGE and SEX is still not significant. The p-value for MENURB, however, is highly significant. The r-squared value has risen by a full 21.7%, showing that the addition of MENURB accounts for almost 22% of the variance in SSSCOR. Again, the importance of these findings is discussed in chapter 7.

6.2.5 Regression model for LEXREC

Predictor	p-value
AGE	0.000
R-Squared (adjusted) 57.7%	

The p-value for AGE is highly significant ($p < 0.001$) and the r-squared value shows that AGE accounts for almost 58% of the variance in LEXREC.

AGE and SEX

Predictor	p-value
AGE	0.000
SEX	0.948
R-Squared(adjusted) 57.0%	

The p-value for SEX is not significant at all, and the r-squared value has actually dropped slightly, indicating that the inclusion of this variable has worsened the regression model.

AGE, SEX and AGE × SEX

Predictor	p-value
AGE	0.000
SEX	0.901
AGE×SEX	0.916
R-Squared (adjusted) 56.2%	

The interaction between AGE and SEX is not significant, and has lowered the r-squared value by a further 0.8%. The inclusion of this variable has again not improved the regression model.

6.2.6 Adding MENURB to the model

Predictor	p-value
AGE	0.000
SEX	0.871
AGE×SEX	0.909
MENURB	0.000
R-Squared (adjusted) 67.5%	

The p-values for SEX and for AGE × SEX are still not significant, whereas that for MENURB is highly so ($p < 0.001$). The r-squared value for the model has risen by 11.3%, showing that the inclusion of MENURB has improved it significantly. The same type of regression models will now be built for the other independent variables.

6.2.7 Adding SOCNET to the model for PHOVAR

The penultimate output for the model, before the inclusion of MENURB in section 6.2.2, was:

Predictor	p-value
AGE	0.000
SEX	0.011
AGE×SEX	0.086
R-Squared (adjusted) 57.0%	

Recall that the effects of AGE and SEX were shown to be significant, but the interaction between the two was not. I now add SOCNET to the model:

Predictor	p-value
AGE	0.000
SEX	0.012
AGE×SEX	0.084
SOCNET	0.398
R-Squared (adjusted) 56.8%	

The effect of SOCNET is not statistically significant at all, and including it lowers the r-squared value by 0.2%. This compares rather disfavourably with the results for MENURB. The social network framework has therefore failed to predict vernacular maintenance in Huntly. The importance of this finding will be elaborated upon in chapter 7.

6.2.8 Adding SOCNET to the model for SSSCOR

The penultimate output for the regression model for SSSCOR, before the inclusion of MENURB in 6.2.3, was:

Predictor	p-value
AGE	0.000
SEX	0.023
AGE×SEX	0.196
R-Squared (adjusted) 46.6%	

Next I add SOCNET, in order to test whether it will improve the model.

Predictor	p-value
AGE	0.000
SEX	0.025
AGE×SEX	0.193
SOCNET	0.449
R-Squared (adjusted) 46.2%	

Again, SOCNET is not statistically significant at all, and its inclusion lowers the r-squared value by 0.4%, a result followed up below.

6.2.9   Adding SOCNET to the model for LEXREC

The penultimate output from the regression model for LEXREC, before the inclusion of MENURB in 6.2.5, was:

Predictor	p-value
AGE	0.000
SEX	0.901
AGE×SEX	0.916
R-Squared (adjusted) 56.2%	

Next I Add SOCNET.

Predictor	p-value
AGE	0.000
SEX	0.887
AGE×SEX	0.925
SOCNET	0.512
R-Squared (adjusted) 55.8%	

Again, the effect of SOCNET is not statistically significant, and its inclusion lowers the r-squared value by 0.4%. At this stage I summarise the results of the regression analyses in table 28, with the r-squared values showing what percentage of the variation in the predicted variable is accounted for by the predictor variable:

Table 28   MENURB and SOCNET across the linguistic variables

Predictor	predicted	p-value	r-squared
AGE	PHOVAR	0.000	53.1%
SEX	PHOVAR	0.042	2.3%
AGE×SEX	PHOVAR	0.086	1.5%
MENURB	PHOVAR	0.000	19.1%
SOCNET	PHOVAR	0.398	−0.2%
AGE	SSSCOR	0.000	42.5%
SEX	SSSCOR	0.030	3.5%
AGE×SEX	SSSCOR	0.196	0.6%
MENURB	SSSCOR	0.000	21.7%
SOCNET	SSSCOR	0.449	−0.4%
AGE	LEXREC	0.000	57.7%
SEX	LEXREC	0.948	−0.7%
AGE×SEX	LEXREC	0.916	−0.8%
MENURB	LEXREC	0.000	11.3%
SOCNET	LEXREC	0.512	−0.4%

These vastly different results for the two main independent variables in the study would seem to indicate strongly that:

1. A rural person's maintenance of the local vernacular will to a large extent be tied to that person's low degree of mental urbanisation, or, put another way, a strong sense of local identity will be tied to use of the local vernacular.
2. A rural person's degree of integration in local social networks does not *necessarily* indicate that person's maintenance of local vernacular norms.

These points will be discussed in more detail in chapter 7. The rest of the independent variables were tested in the same way, but none of them produced a telling result, and the details are summarised in table 29.

Table 29 Regression output for SOCLAS, ATTDIA and NATPRI

Predictor	predicted	p-value	percentage
SOCLAS	PHOVAR	0.002	5.9%
ATTDIA	PHOVAR	0.272	0.2%
NATPRI	PHOVAR	0.849	0.7%
SOCLAS	SSSCOR	0.072	1.9%
ATTDIA	SSSCOR	0.006	5.8%
NATPRI	SSSCOR	0.364	0.1%
SOCLAS	LEXREC	0.022	3.1%
ATTDIA	LEXREC	0.534	0.4%
NATPRI	LEXREC	0.919	0.7%

The effect of SOCLAS on PHOVAR and on LEXREC is statistically significant, but accounts for only 5.9% and 3.1% respectively of the variance in these two dependent variables. The only other statistically significant result was for ATTDIA across SSSCOR, but again, this only accounted for 5.8% of the variance in the dependent variable.

6.3 Separating SOCNET by sex

Milroy's (1980) data shows marked gender differences, both in the linguistic and network scores. The network effect is greater for women than for men. Labov's (2001) Philadelphia data shows the same trend, with even stronger correlations (see chapter 7). I now examine the Huntly data on networks for women and men separately, in order to test for such a trend.

The scatterplots for the separate-sex individual scores for SOCNET across the three linguistic variables (not shown here) do not show any trends. SOCNET across LEXREC shows a slight grouping for the females, though no definite trend. The Pearson's Correlation tests reveal the following:

Table 30 Correlations: Female SOCNET across dependent variables
Females

		PHOVAR	SSSCOR	LEXREC
SOCNET	Pearson's Correlation	.052	.075	.230
	p-value	.776	.684	.204

Table 31 Correlations: Male SOCNET across dependent variables
Males

		PHOVAR	SSSCOR	LEXREC
SOCNET	Pearson's Correlation	.092	.035	.164
	p-value	.624	.854	.379

The lack of trend in the scatterplots is mirrored here. The correlation coefficients are all close to 0, and none of them are significant. The impression gained above is supported: the strongest of these weak correlations is female SOCNET across LEXREC at 0.230 and p = .204 – still far short of statistical significance. In sum, there are no significant gender differences by social network across the three linguistic scores.

6.4 Summary

The two 'natural' social variables, AGE and SEX, were expected to have a marked effect on the dependent variables. The results indicate that the effect of AGE especially, is marked, accounting for well over 50% of the variance in two of the three dependent variables. The effect of SEX is also present, at least for the two dependent variables which tested phonological and morphological variation. However, as the research question focuses on other social factors, it is the effects of those which interest us. From the results in tables 26 and 27, it is clear that the only variable, other than AGE, which has any significant effect upon the use of the vernacular, is MENURB, the index of a speaker's degree of mental urbanisation. For the two dependent variables which measure phonological and morphological variation, the effect of MENURB is not only maximally statistically significant, but also accounts for around 20% of the variance in these two variables. For the third, LEXREC, the effect of MENURB is again maximally significant, accounting for 11.3% of the variance. No other independent variable used in this study approaches these results. Having applied statistical tests of significance to all the data, I have obtained the output from the linear regression models. The results show little support for the idea that social network strength will have a vernacular norm enforcement effect on individuals. What is shown is strong support for the theory that positive attitudes to the local group will lead to use of local speech patterns. The wider implications of this will be discussed in chapter 7.

7
Discussion

In this chapter, I discuss first the abnormal patterning of /t/ in the Huntly data. I then go on to examine the outliers in the sample, discuss the geolinguistic model in more detail, compare the results of the Belfast study with those of the Huntly study, discuss other critiques of the social network framework. I then offer an outline for developing the life mode concept, compare the Huntly results with those of Labov in Martha's Vineyard, give an overview of other attitudinal studies, detail a language study conducted by a teacher in the area, and summarise a critique of Milroy's use of the term 'vernacular'.

Before discussing the large-scale regular patterns in the data, I examine the irregularities first. When an individual displays a large deviation from the group norm in a sociological or linguistic score, it is worth a closer examination. This is where the quantitative method is not particularly effective, and a more ethnographic approach is required. Similarly, a linguistic variable which shows different large-scale patterns from the rest attracts attention.

7.1   The abnormal patterning of /t/ in Huntly

In chapter 5 I considered the abnormal patterning of the data for /t/, when compared to the rest of the data. As this variable has turned out to be different from the others in important ways, it will be useful to discuss it in somewhat more depth.

The spread of the feature in British English has been well documented in the recent literature (Macafee 1994, Macaulay and Trevelyan 1973, Stuart-Smith 1999). It is spreading rapidly throughout Scotland in predictable patterns along the lines of social class, age and sex (Macaulay 1991, Stuart-Smith 1999, Romaine 1982a). In the rest of the data used in the Huntly study, the variants of the different variables chosen are in a binary 'standard–dialect' relationship, and the direction of change is towards the standard, as is characteristic of rural communities (Røyneland 2000). All of the variables show remarkable similarity of patterning across age, except for the /t/ glottalling. The reason for this has to do with its status as an incoming variant which is not a Scottish Standard English form, and the groups which resist it and those which adopt it are predictable from the results of sociolinguistic research elsewhere (e.g. Kerswill and Williams 1994).

Results of other studies in Scotland

Stuart-Smith's (1999) article covers her 1998 study of /t/ glottalling in Glasgow, the first since Macaulay and Trevelyan's 1973 study. The results show clear sociolinguistic stratification and sharp stylistic variation, as might be expected, and, despite methodological differences between the two studies, Stuart-Smith believes that the data may be comparable with the 1973 study. This would mean that a real-time comparison could be made. Macaulay and Trevelyan's study concentrated on the usual Labovian independent variables, such as age, social class and sex. However, Johnston (1983: 1) points out that

the range of variation in standard and vernacular varieties is not always organised along a linear continuum. Historically, the varieties of the middle and working classes in Glasgow are derived from two distinct, yet related sources. [...] Working-class speech continues urban Scots, which has shown T-glottalling for at least a century. Middle-class speech, typically Scottish Standard English, has no recorded history of T-glottalling beyond what is assumed for other standard varieties of English. However, given that Glasgow is a traditional dialect area, continuing two once distinct linguistic systems, it is not impossible that while appearing quantitatively continuous, T-glottalling may in fact be qualitatively discrete for speakers of working- and middle-class backgrounds respectively (cited from Stuart-Smith 1999: 185).

By 'qualitatively discrete' I presume the author means that the feature may have originated separately in urban Glasgow Scots and in Standard English. Whether this is the case in Huntly is a point to which I will return below.

Reid's (1978) Edinburgh study was restricted to eleven-year-olds, but shows that the use of a glottal stop as a variant of /t/ varies between 18% and 100%, depending on the individual and the phonetic environment. Reid shows the following ordering on the favouring of glottalisation:

Least favouring glottal	↕	word-medial (presumably intervocalic)
		word-final/with following vowel
		word-final/with following pause
Most favouring glottal		word-final/with following consonant

As this variable was only part of a much larger number of variables in the present study, it has only been considered in word-medial position. The situation described for Glasgow is that /t/ glottalling has been commented on for more than a century, though there is no quantitative data for this:

> Strangers hurl at us a sort of shibboleth such sentences as 'pass the wa'er bo'le, Mr Pa'erson' (a letter of 1892, in Macafee 1994: 27, cited from Stuart-Smith 1999: 183).

This does not seem to hold for the rural north-east of Scotland, which is also a traditional dialect area. The Huntly data shows that the feature is newer there.

The other point brought out by the Huntly data was that the pre-adolescent females seem to be avoiding the new glottal variant. This is remarkably similar to the results of Kerswill and Williams's 1994 data from Milton Keynes, where glottalling is not thought to be a new feature. I consider first their data from the interviews: note that this speaking style is more informal than the elicitation style on which most of the data for the Doric study is based. Table 32 shows the results of the Milton Keynes interview data, which are not split into sexes, as there were no significant differences. It is clear that a high proportion of glottal stops is in use.

Table 32 [ʔ] in Milton Keynes interviews (Kerswill and Williams 1994)

age 4	82.8%
age 8	79.3
age 12	91.4

Table 33 shows the Milton Keynes data for elicitation tasks, which were similar to those used for the Doric main data. Here, the pattern for the 12-year-olds closely matches that for the Huntly 8- to 12-year-olds, in that there is a sharp gender differentiation. Girls in this age group in both studies have a very low frequency for this feature at around 10 per cent, while the boys have considerably more (40–60 per cent). In this style, gender differentiation is also present for the 4- and 8-year-olds in Milton Keynes.

Table 33 [ʔ] in Milton Keynes elicitation (Kerswill and Williams 1994)

	girls	boys
age 4	50.8	83.7
age 8	61.5	79.5
age 12	10.1 (Huntly 12.5)	41.6 (Huntly 58.4)

Comparing Table 33 with Table 32, we can infer that, in elicitation tasks, the girls in all three age groups style-shift away from the use of the glottal stop. This tendency is very much stronger among the 12-year-old girls, at which age they are joined by the boys, who now begin to style shift. By the age of 12, it seems that these children are becoming increasingly sensitive to the stylistic difference between a task which requires relatively monitored speech and the less formal interview. The Milton Keynes data also shows that girls display greater, and earlier, sensitivity. We can probably legitimately apply the same interpretation of the data for the Huntly 8- to 12-year-olds. The girls, and to some extent the boys, interpret the feature as 'inappropriate' in this speech style, and avoid it. However, this does not explain the Huntly teenagers' scores, which are almost uniformly high. I turn to this question now.

The interpretation of the teenagers' scores is complicated by two factors; first, the lack of comparable elicitation data from other studies, and second, more importantly, the fact that /t/ glottalling is a recent innovation in the Doric (see figure 11). In two recent studies from outside the south-east of England, it has been shown that incoming full glottal replacement of /t/ is used more by younger women and by middle-class speakers. Thus, in Tyneside (Watt and Milroy 1999: 29–30) we find middle-class females introducing this variant, replacing the older glottally reinforced variant [tʔ]. A comparable situation pertains in Cardiff, where the same social group appears to be replacing the vernacular [t] word-finally (Mees and Collins 1999: 195). The consequences of these findings are complex for the Doric data, for the reason that these relate to urban, not rural communities. First, the rural community in Huntly shows little class stratification, with the majority of the population having a rural life mode, or rural-dominated composite life mode (Højrup 1983, Pedersen 1994).

Figure 59, which is a plot of the /t/ data against an 8-point social class scale,[1] shows that there is no class stratification of this feature at all, a situation clearly differentiating it from the same feature in the two urban communities. In fact, some speakers with the lowest social class indices (2/8) use the alveolar variant categorically, though there is probably an age effect here, too. There are sixty-four data points in the above graph, many laid one on top of the other. There are clearly many speakers who use the glottal variant categorically, and these have social class indices ranging from 3/8 to 7/8. The same is true for those who use the alveolar variant. Similarly, there is, for almost all the linguistic variables examined, little gender differentiation – and this is also true for (t), except of course for the young child group, as table 34 shows. Second, I have

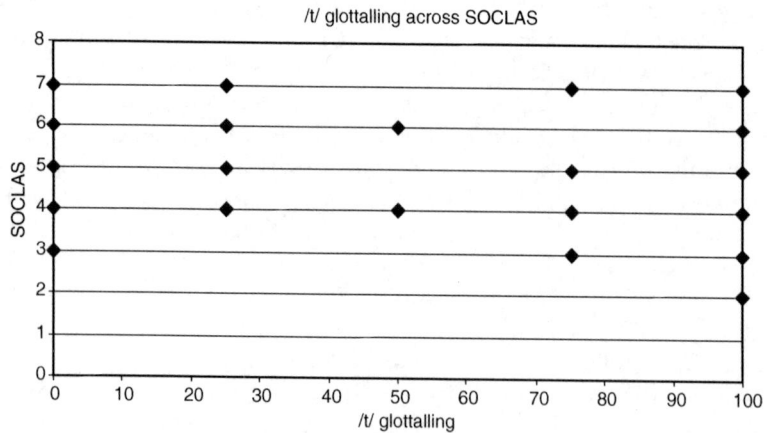

Figure 59 Correlation of /t/ and Social Class Index

Table 34 Differing use of (t) across sex in Huntly

Age group	p-value
60+	cannot compute (categorical zero use)
25 to 40	0.486
14 to 17	0.552
8 to 12	0.035 (significant at p < 0.05)

argued that innovation in the Huntly area is likely to be exocentric, and I have shown that practically all the new features there are indeed those already present in the urban Scots of Glasgow and Edinburgh. Admittedly Tyneside and Cardiff are affected by the diffusion of features from the south-east, particularly consonantal ones (see discussion of this point in relation to Hull in Williams and Kerswill 1999); however, the various vocalic changes reported for Tyneside are clearly endocentric, that is, generated from within the linguistic system rather than borrowed (see Watt and Milroy 1999 for examples of Tyneside vowel shifts).

We must now try to resolve the complex relationship between the rural character of this community and the sociolinguistic patterns I have uncovered so far for (t). I begin with the observation that linguistic innovation within a speech community is most likely to be found among adolescents (Aitchison 2001: 209–210; Kerswill 1996). It follows that the exocentricity found in Huntly will be most clearly visible in their speech. The data seems to be consistent with this observation. The incoming, clearly exocentric (arguably pan-British) norm is the use of [ʔ] for intervocalic and final /t/, and this is being enthusiastically taken up by the teenagers. The lack of both gender and class differentiation is likely to be a reflection of the rural life modes of most of the speakers. In sum then, the feature does pattern with age, the younger speakers generally using it more, though the youngest females greatly prefer the standard variant. This differs from the results of Stuart-Smith's Glasgow study, where use of the variable patterns with social class and age, but not sex.

Table 35 /t/ glottalling patterns with social category

Category	Glasgow	Huntly
Age	YES	YES
Social class	YES	NO
Sex	NO	NO (YES in 8 to 12s)

Use of /t/ across other social variables

We have argued that the use of the glottal stop as a variant of /t/ has not traditionally been a feature of rural north-east Scots, and its increased use in younger speakers there does not pattern according to the increased use of levelled urban Scottish English features. The adoption of this incoming glottal variant is not correlated with any of the other sociological scores either, including MENURB.

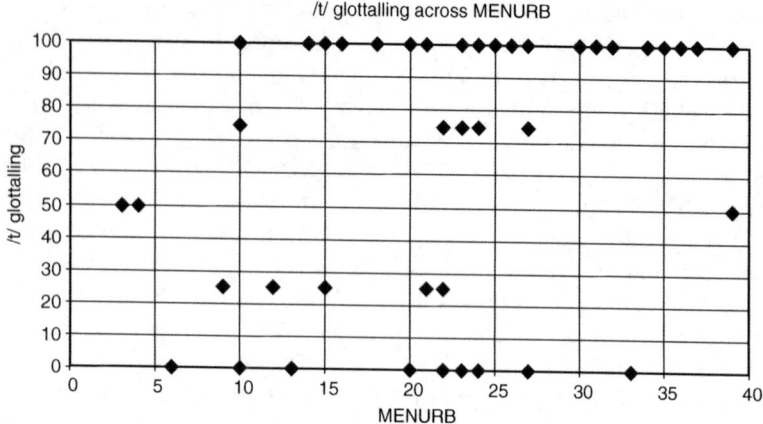

Figure 60 The variable (t) across MENURB in the Huntly data

Figure 13 in section 4.3 shows not only that the two younger groups use the glottal variant of (t) more than the two older groups, but also that the greatest variation is found in the two youngest groups. The use of [ʔ] is rapidly gaining acceptability among the adolescent speakers, especially the males. The ones who use [t] categorically in the two younger groups are all females, except for one male in the 8 to 12 group. In the youngest group, all except two of the females use the standard form categorically. So far the males in this database have shown that they are far more willing to use non-standard forms than females, as has been found in most studies in Western societies.

The apparent failure, at least in interview style, by the 8- to 12-year-old females, to adopt the incoming feature requires explanation. I argue that the reason for this lies in the fact that the status of this feature is neither traditional dialect nor incoming standard in the north-eastern area sampled, an important consideration, in the light of the fact that this is an area of exocentric innovation. This is supported by the 0 scores for both males and females in the over 60 group. The reason for the failure to adopt this variant on the part of the 8 to 12 females may lie in the fact that young females everywhere usually show greater sensitivity to style, a trend which is manifest in the rest of the Huntly data.

The adolescents' adoption of the new variant is striking. As an incoming non-dialect, non-standard feature, it has been taken up by both the female and male adolescents, who have been shown to be more suscep-tible to peer pressure than normative pressure from education and parents (Kerswill and Williams 1997). This feature has been adopted, even in this speech style, probably because it is associated with youth culture and city values. The perception of this variant by the adolescent group may therefore differ from that of the 8 to 12 group. This age group is not yet peer-oriented. As a low-prestige variant acquires connotations of being associated with youth and fun, it tends to acquire prestige over time. The group most likely to pick up on this first is the adolescent group, as they are more intensely aware of peer pressure than other groups.

The point made by Johnston (1983: 1) relating to separate geneses of the feature in the traditional dialect of Glasgow and in Scottish Standard English does not appear to hold for Huntly, as the data presented in figure 11 strongly suggests that the glottal variant of (t) is relatively new in the area. Given the exocentric focus of the area, it is highly likely that the feature is filtering in from mainstream Scottish English.

All the other variables in the Huntly study have a dialect-standard dichotomy, whereas with (t) the dialect form [t] is the same as the Scottish Standard English (supralocal) form. It does, however, have covert prestige, and possibly increasing overt prestige,[2] and as such the adolescents accept it as a symbol, whereas the youngest females resist it longer as a non-standard marker. The effect on the adolescent females of the overt stigma-tisation of this variant will be felt less now than when they were younger.

Unlike the results of studies in Newcastle and Cardiff, which show that the adoption of the glottal variant of /t/ is being led by young, middle-class females, the results presented here show correlations only with age, and not social class or (for the three oldest groups) sex. The youngest females do not use the glottal variant much, perhaps because they are still matching the older vernacular norm of their parents in the 25 to 40 age group. By the time they reach adolescence, they will have caught up with the boys. They are clearly differentiated from the boys in the same age group, a pattern which was exactly matched by 12-year-old girls and boys in Milton Keynes doing elicitation tasks. However, what we see here may be evidence of complex issues of child versus adolescent versus adult life stages, with differing perceptions of the status of the incoming glottal variant of /t/. The nearly identical variation exhibited in Glasgow, Milton Keynes and Reading is what Labov (2001: 417) calls 'stable variation'. The Doric shows a new, dynamic stage.

7.2 Individual outliers in the Huntly data

Large-scale comparisons across the data can enhance our understanding of the various mechanisms involved in language use in a particular community. There are always exceptions to the norm, however, and it is to these I now turn, in the hope of discovering facts that are equally helpful to that understanding.

The data presented in chapter 5 showed exceptionally high dialect scores in the 8 to 12 male group. Examination of the individual scores indicates that two of the speakers in this group have higher than average scores. Both have only recently started at Huntly Academy. Kennethmont, the village from which they come, is four miles up the valley. It may be that language use in Kennethmont is slightly more conservative than in Huntly, as it is smaller, and more rural. Even more telling, though, are their MENURB scores, which are higher than most in the group, as figure 61 shows. This reinforces the argument for mental orientation as a powerful predictor of language use. Even at the intra-group level like this, where only small-scale comparisons are possible, we see MENURB showing strong correlations with dialect maintenance. They are outliers in the data, and without their scores the gender bias is far less marked in this group. If in fact there were still a gender bias after removing their scores, one would be hard pressed to explain the absence of such a bias in the adolescent group (and, for that matter, in the older groups). Also, these pre-adolescent boys are unlikely to have acquired the socialised gender patterns that Watt and Milroy (1999) found in Newcastle men.

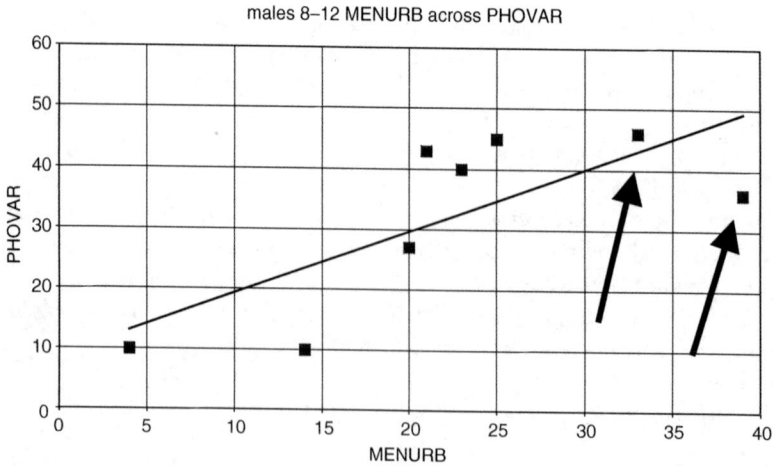

Figure 61   The two Kennethmont outliers: 8–12 male group

In the 14- to 17-year-old female group, there is one speaker, FM, who, along with only one other in the group, has a maximal score of 8/8 for SOCNET. Her dialect scores are interesting, in that she has the lowest PHOVAR and SSSCOR results, 5 (maximum 40) and 0.05 (maximum 1.0) respectively, of any in the group. Again, the expected norm enforcement effect of networks is not in evidence, but attention is drawn to her LEXREC score. It is higher than any other in the group, at 44/50. Her MENURB score is the second lowest in the group, which would seem to account for her low use of phonological dialect indicators, but the question of her exceptional lexical knowledge is not easily answered. Her other social scores are all average for the group. I could argue that networks are more effective at maintaining vernacular language at the lexical level than at the phonological and morphological levels, but this view is not supported by the rest of the data. SOCNET is not correlated with LEXREC overall or in any single group. Listening to the recording of the interview again does not reveal anything out of the ordinary, and so the case must remain unexplained.

In the 25- to 40-year-old female group, there is a speaker, SA, who has an exceptionally low SOCNET score of 2/8 (the mean for the group is almost 6/8, and in fact, 2/8 is the lowest score in the entire database). This is similar to the case of Hannah, the speaker from Belfast, discussed below in section 7.4, who scored 0/5 on Milroy's network scale. The difference here is that SA does not use language any differently from the rest of her peers. All of her other social and linguistic scores are normal for the group. These two examples show that the investigator cannot always find an explanation for individual outliers in the data, which strengthens the argument for large samples.

In the 14- to 17-year-old male group, there is one individual, CR, who displays different scores from the group in many categories. His dialect indices are lower than the group means: PHOVAR 10/40 (mean 22.4), SSSCOR 0 (mean 0.35, maximum 1.0) and LEXREC 18/50 (mean 30.4). His SOCNET score is lower than average at 4/8 (mean 6.25), and this seems to be some evidence to support networks, though his MENURB score is also lower than average at 10/40 (mean 12.4), while his SOCLAS score is higher than average at 7/8 (mean 5.875). It seems the whole sociological profile for CR differs from the rest of the individuals in the group, and so there may be interactions between the various social factors that influence his language use.

In the 25- to 40-year-old male group, there are two individuals with very similar dialect indices: AR and WM. Their scores are as follows:

	PHOVAR	maximum	SSSCOR	maximum	LEXREC	maximum
AR	55	56	0.90323	1.0	45	50
WM	49	56	0.92857	1.0	46	50

The interesting thing is that neither SOCNET nor SOCLAS are able to account for this similarity of language use between these two men. AR scores 4/8 for SOCNET, and WM a maximal score of 8/8. For SOCLAS, AR scores 6/8, and WM 2/8. Listening to the recordings again reveals that AR is a teacher at Huntly Academy, someone who is proud of local traditions, and who speaks the dialect fluently. WM is a saddler, also very proud of local traditions, and fluent in the dialect. The similarities in their dialect indices can only be explained by reference to MENURB. AR scores 30/40, and WM 37/40 (the mean is 27.4). The difference in their MENURB scores is not nearly as great as the differences in their SOCNET and SOCLAS scores.

In the 8- to 12-year-old male group, there is one individual, GW, whose scores are abnormal for the group. His indices are as follows:

index	MENURB	SOCNET	SOCLAS	ATTDIA
GW	4	4	4	25
mean	22.375	6	4.25	30.5

index cont.	NATPRI	PHOVAR	SSSCOR	LEXREC
GW cont.	27	10	0	11
mean cont.	33.5	32.125	0.465938	29.375

The entire sociological profile for GW would appear to predict a low degree of use of the dialect. His high degree of mental urbanisation, shown in his low MENURB score, along with his low ATTDIA and NATPRI scores all seem to interact to produce exceptionally low dialect scores. But it is the difference between his MENURB score and the mean MENURB score for the group which reveals the most. Here is a boy whose identification with the local group is extremely low, who in almost every answer shows a solidarity with the supra-local group, and who would move to the city at the first opportunity that presents itself. His spontaneous speech score reveals that he did not use any phonological or morphological features of the dialect at all, making him one of only four people in the entire database to achieve a 0 score for this variable.

The outliers in the data mostly serve to confirm what the large-scale correlations showed: apart from AGE, the most powerful predictor of dialect maintenance is the degree to which the individual identifies with the local group. Where MENURB could not account for lexical use in the case of FM, it did account for phonological features.

7.3 Geolinguistics

It has been tempting to apply a quantitative geolinguistic analysis to the Huntly data. However, as the model proposed by Chambers and Trudgill (1998) takes only population size and distance into consideration, it would benefit greatly from the inclusion of geomorphological factors. A community only 25 miles distant from an urban centre, but with a mountain range separating the two, might be less influenced by that centre than another community 50 miles away, but with only flat land separating the two, and a network of roads connecting them.

While the influence of Standard English emanating from London has been felt for centuries throughout Britain, and has been the basis for Scottish Standard English, it would be rather difficult to measure its current direct influence on rural Scots. The influence of the Scottish Standard English emanating from Edinburgh on Aberdeen city speech is probably considerable, as the urban features of a major cultural and economic centre tend to leap intervening rural areas and arrive in smaller urban centres, a process which has been discussed by, among others, Trudgill (1983). Aberdeen city speech is the nearest urban model for the Huntly farming community, and any features of language perceived by rural people as emanating from Aberdeen may be viewed more favourably than if they were coming straight from an identifiably English source like London. Even though the latter may be the original source of some of the features, they may have to go through a type of 'acculturation process' first. This softening-up process may allow them to be seen more as 'modern' and 'urban', than as 'English'. More important for this study is the question of what type of individual and social characteristics will be linked to the adoption of such features.

The results of the influence of Aberdeen city speech, along with other factors, such as education and the media, are to systematically erode the phonological and morpho-lexical features found in rural areas like Huntly. The distribution of non-standard features in Britain is often regional in rural areas, and mostly social in urban areas. This means that the supralocal form is to be found at the upper end of the social scale in most British cities. The same is true of Scots features found in

Aberdeen city speech. But the target is not fixed, and what we see evolving in, for example, Aberdeen, is more a levelled, mainstream urban Scottish English, rather than a simple adoption of Scottish Standard English. Morphological features like {-nae} as the negator in words like cannae, 'cannot' and lexical items like ken, 'know' are not part of Scottish Standard English, yet they survive. While this new levelled urban Scottish English does contain features of Scottish Standard English, it does not seem to have adopted, for example, London features, like [f] and [v] for /θ/ and /ð/.[3] The evolution of this levelled urban Scottish English is similar to the situation in London and the Home Counties, with RP and the evolving Estuary English.

As a result of the above-mentioned reservations about the geolinguistic model in its current state, the focus of this book has been an account of the main sociological influences upon dialect maintenance, and the quantitative geolinguistic model proposed by Chambers and Trudgill (1998) has not been applied to the Huntly data.

7.4 Social networks: a comparison of Huntly with the Belfast study

It would be natural to compare the results of the Huntly study with those of Lesley Milroy in Belfast. The Huntly study has 64 informants to the 46 of the Belfast study. A larger sample will make the results more reliable for statistical testing. As the groundwork for this type of research was laid down by the Belfast study, it has been a relatively simple matter to replicate the methodology used. At the same time, a number of other independent variables not used in the Belfast study were included, in order to test their possible influence, and to check if there was any interaction between the different independent variables.

The Belfast study has been referred to by sociolinguists for two decades now, and cited in most introductory sociolinguistics textbooks. However, it seems that relatively little close examination has been made of the data (a notable exception is Labov 2001, discussed below). Hardly any replication studies have been conducted, though many sociolinguistic studies have included a network analysis as part of the methodology employed (Lippi-Green 1989, Pedersen 1994). As Chambers (1995) points out:

> Beginning with Milroy (1980), sociolinguists have discussed the network measures of density and multiplexity (for example, Coates 1986: chapter 5, Wardhaugh 1992: chapter 5) although they have

not yet been applied directly in any sociolinguistic study (Chambers 1995: 71–72).

In sum then, Milroy concludes from her results that the main claim of the social network framework, that a dense, multiplex network will have a strong norm-enforcement effect on the individual, is supported. She does, however, point to certain constraints on the capacity of network structure to influence language use, saying that the relationship between the two is not absolute. She notes that its influence is most felt in communities where traditional sex/network equivalence patterns are preserved. When these patterns are disturbed for some reason, such as geographical mobility or high male unemployment, the relationship between network and language use is less close (Milroy 1980: 162). This compromises the general applicability of the model.

She also admits that the question of why some speakers are more closely integrated into local networks than others cannot easily be answered, and that this places limitations on how we should interpret correlations between language use and network structure. In other words, the line of causality is by no means pre-determined and necessary. She asks the question 'does a person choose to be more or less closely integrated into his community and to signal his choice when he speaks?' She cites Le Page as saying that

> The individual creates his system of verbal behaviour so as to resemble those common to the group or groups with which he wishes from time to time to be identified, or so as to be unlike those from which he wishes to be distinguished (Le Page 1968, cited in Milroy 1980: 182, my emphasis).

In other words, does a personal network score, such as those achieved during the Belfast study, reflect a psychological (attitudinal) fact, or does it simply reflect in a neutral way the individual's informal relationship structures? (Milroy 1980: 214). This has become the central question in the Huntly study. In fact Milroy does point to the effect of attitudinal factors:

> It is important to emphasise that the network strength scale is designed fundamentally as a tool for measuring differences in an individual's level of integration into the local community. It is not claimed that this scale is the only means of doing so; for example attitudinal factors are likely to be good indicators. However, the major

advantage of the scale adopted here is that the indicators are based on an explicit set of procedures for analysing social relationships (Milroy 1982: 144–145).

Such an explicit set of procedures has been designed for attitudinal factors and used in the Huntly study.

The update

In their 1992 paper, J. Milroy and L. Milroy develop the model, attempting to integrate it with the social class model, with Højrup's (1983) concept of Life Modes, and also to account for how an individual comes to be in a particular social network. They point to the limitations of the consensus-based social class model. Their model is conflict-based at two levels: the macro- and micro-levels.

This concept is shown in figure 62, which is taken from J. and L. Milroy (1992: 22).

Problems

There are, however, some problems with the notion that factors at the macro level produce different modes of production, which in turn produce network structures, which in turn produce certain forms of language use. The model is forced to take the speaker's mental orientation and freedom of choice into account, at least as far as Life Mode 2 goes. Notice that the flow chart splits here, indicating that a certain life mode will not simply produce a certain level of network integration, but that the individual has the power to choose what level of integration s/he wishes, though this point is not commented upon in the text. Surely this freedom of choice is also to be acknowledged when it comes to using language? In fact, there is a discussion in Milroy (1980), of two women in the same area, in the same age group, who show great variation in language use and integration into social networks.

Paula and Hannah, for example, differ greatly in their level of integration into the local networks. Paula has a large family of her own, visits frequently with neighbours, and belongs to an informal bingo-playing group. Her neighbours are also her work-mates. Hannah, on the other hand, has no children or kin in the area (she is the child of a Protestant/Catholic mixed marriage). She belongs to no local informally constituted group of the kind we have described in chapter three as a high-density cluster, and her work-mates are not from the

Clonard. [...] A glance at table 5.4 will remind the reader that although the social status of the two women was very similar, *their patterns of language use were quite different.* [...] It will also be recalled that Paula seemed to be much more closely integrated than Hannah, in terms of kin, work and friendship ties, into the local community. In fact, Paula scores two and Hannah scores zero on the network strength scale, reflecting the difference in the character of their everyday social ties (Milroy 1980: 134, 152, my emphasis).

This is a curious example. The Milroys (1992: 22) claim that macro socio-economic and political factors precipitate people of the same social

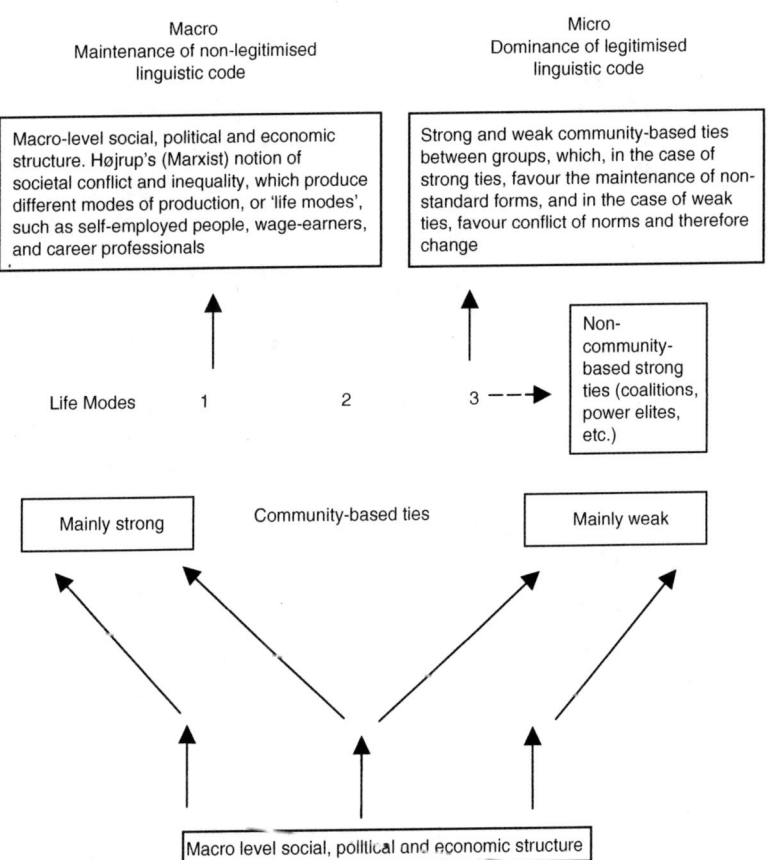

Figure 62 J. and L. Milroy's concept of language change

class into the same mode of production, say, wage-earning worker mode. This worker life mode then supposedly triggers dense, multiplex, area-bound networks.

> [...] the different types of network structure that we distinguished in the previous section can be seen to a considerable extent as springing from differences in the life-modes of different individuals.
>
> Just as different types of network structure emerge from the economic conditions associated with life-modes 1 and 2, so a certain type of personal network structure is likely to follow from life-mode 3.
>
> [...] this chain of dependence running from political and socio-economic structures through life-modes to network structure and ultimately to sociolinguistic structure [...].
>
> [...] these economically determined life-modes give rise not only to the social and cultural differences described by Højrup, but to different kinds of network structure (Milroy and Milroy 1992: 19–22, emphasis mine).

If these macro socio-economic and political factors are the actuators of modes of production, then they have surely placed these two women of the same social class into the same modes of production, as seen in figure 62. This worker life mode (Højrup's life mode 2) should then produce similar levels of network integration, and these two women should then have similar network and language scores. However, they do not. The inability of the model to account for the different network and language scores of these two women is clear. If attitudinal factors had been measured, perhaps more light would have been shed on their differing linguistic scores, although mental orientation to the local group was not measured in Milroy's study. Milroy concludes that people in her survey behaved linguistically as they did because of the normative influence of their peer group, but Romaine (1984: 37) asks what kind of explanation it is. Cameron (1997) writes that

> The social network is a theoretical construct which cannot 'make' any individual speaker do anything. Yet if we take away the idea of the network's ability to enforce linguistic norms, all we are left with is statistical correlations. Of these, Romaine comments: 'the observed correlations between language and group membership tell us nothing unless fitted into some more general theory' (1984: 37). What is

this 'general theory' to be? Clearly, it needs to engage with the whole issue of how individuals relate to groups and their norms – in Romaine's words, it must make reference to 'rationality, intentionality and the function of social agents and human actors' (1984: 26) (Cameron 1997: 61).

This concept of intentionality has become increasingly important in this book.

7.5 Other critiques of social networks

Labov (2001) points out that L. Milroy takes the balanced view of networks, that they should be considered along with other means of gathering information that will aid our understanding of language use. He objects to the view that networks can replace other measures of social structure, in particular the measurement of social class through occupation, education, or indices of consumption. In such a view, 'the study of social networks is presented as a higher form of social analysis than the study of social class and more suitable for socio-linguistic analysis' (Labov 2001: 326). In theory, a network-only approach may seem plausible. It is worth citing in full what Labov has to say on this:

(Recording all the speech of a community with a large number of speakers and modelling the speech community) through the mechanics of interaction alone, with no reference to education, income, occupation, ethnicity, status, prestige or stigma, or other attitudes . . . is attractive in many ways: it is conceptually econom-ical and it is based upon the act of speaking itself. The best network studies must fall short of this hypothetical goal. Most of them are devoted to one or two isolated groups of a dozen speakers or so. It is no easier to understand the sociolinguistic behaviour of such an isolated small group than it is to understand the speech of an isolated individual. The social significance of the speaker's use of linguistic variables, across different topics, channels, tasks, addresses and social contexts, is a derivative of variation in the wider com-munity (Bell 1984, Preston 1989). Unless a representative sample of that wider community is available, interpretations of the indi-vidual or the small group are largely a matter of guesswork (Labov 2001: 326).

He goes on to write that the linguistic significance of social network data is maximal when:

> Previous studies have identified the major linguistic variables of the wider community and traced their patterns of stylistic and social variation. Social class, age, gender and ethnicity will continue to explain the greatest part of the variance [...].
>
> All the members of the group share the same social history in terms of residence and dialect contact. When they do not, the effect of these differences in social history must be accounted for by wider studies of the type indicated in (1) (Labov 2001: 327).

Labov points to the fact that most network studies focus on small groups that continue to use a non-standard form of language, which is under threat from a surrounding regional standard, with the expectation that those individuals who have greater density and multiplexity will maintain the local dialect more. In order to find the leaders of language change, such studies look to those individuals who have more (weak tie) connections to other groups. But our perspectives on social network research, he writes, cannot but be changed by Eckert's (2001) book, reporting on the results of her Belten High data, which shows that patterns of clothing, spatial location, smoking, and cruising are linked to the leaders of sound change. This indicates that simply knowing several locals, or interacting with them on a regular basis, does not necessarily correlate with adherence to language norms. It is more a matter of understanding the details of how that person chooses to signal attitudes or orientations to such groups, for example, in clothing, smoking and language.

Labov's examination of the Belfast data

Labov (2001) applies regression analyses to the Belfast data given in the appendices in Milroy (1980). What he discovers is that network effects are strongest for the two male-dominated variables (th) and (a), the most overtly recognised stereotypes of working class Belfast speech. The rest do not show significant correlations. The two variables which show current change, (i) and (o), show no network effects. He then splits the data by gender, and re-applies the regression analyses. There are only four significant network coefficients, one in the male data, and three in the female data (Labov 2001: 331). The output appears in table 36 (adapted from Labov 2001: 330).

Table 36 Regression coefficients: 9 Belfast variables by network

gender	(th)	(a)	(e¹)	(e²)	(ʌ¹)	(ʌ²)	(ai)	(i)	(o)
male	no	no	3.26*	no	no	no	no	no	no
female	6.64*	0.23**	no	no	no	no	no	no	6.2**

* At the level p < 0.05.
** At the level p < 0.01.

This does not seem to be strong statistical evidence for a network effect. Labov notes that

> it is also somewhat unexpected that for the stereotypical, male-dominated variables (a) and (th), the network effect appears only among women, and not among men as we might expect (Labov 2001: 331).

When analysing the data separately for the three neighbourhoods, Labov finds that network scores are related to sound changes in only 2 of 9 possibilities for Ballymacarrett, 1 for Clonard, and 2 for Hammer. In addition, he notes that gender seems more important than network:

> Milroy's figure 6.1, designed to show that network influences (th) in Ballymacarrett but not in other neighbourhoods, corresponds here to a large gender effect of 37.4%, and no significant network effect (Labov 2001: 332).

Milroy points to a high degree of correlation between gender and network (1980: 159). The network scores are higher among men than among women. This fact has been related to the explanation of the diffusion of linguistic change (for example, Downes 1998: 35). Labov's table 10.4, reproduced here as Table 37, shows the means for the Belfast data.

The difference of 0.82 between the male and female scores falls far short of statistical significance: it is only about half of the standard deviations. Labov notes that:

Table 37 Mean network scores for Belfast, from Labov (2001: 332)

gender	mean	standard deviation
female	2.09	1.59
male	2.91	1.44

there is more correlation between network scores and linguistic variables for women than for men. Whether or not men have greater density and/or multiplexity in their social relations than women, this fact does not appear to be related to linguistic behaviour. Most importantly...women show the only correlation of network scores with change in apparent time. As we shall see below, the effect of social networks on linguistic variation is almost entirely a female phenomenon in Philadelphia (Labov 2001: 333).

Labov notes Milroy's statement that in the long run, detailed quantitative analysis demonstrates 'the very great complexity of various sources of influence on a speaker's language' and that the results of the analysis indicate merely that 'particular bits' of the language are particularly significant...to different subgroups of the population (Milroy 1980: 163–165, cited from Labov 2001: 333). Milroy admits that network patterns vary greatly across the sexes, age groups and areas in her study, and that network functions consistently only in Ballymacarrett, while in Hammer and Clonard, there is 'little significant correlation between language use and network structure (Milroy 1980: 159, cited from Labov 2001: 333).

Labov's Philadelphia data shows no significant network effect at all for men. The only significant correlations between network and sound change are to be found in the females in the data, but these correlations are in fact stronger than those for the females in the Belfast study (Labov 2001: 341). Labov has the following to say about the results:

> Social network factors do not replace the effect of age, social class, neighbourhood, or ethnicity. The social network effects are not the largest, but they add essential information to the description of the leaders of linguistic change. Furthermore, they suggest that the leading position of women in linguistic change reflects a style of interaction that is different from that used by men (Labov 2001: 344).

7.6   Networks in urban language change

By contrast to a situation like that of Huntly, in a community where the vernacular is a rapidly changing urban variety, such as the one found in Eckert's (1999) study in Belten High School, strong network ties would be required for a speaker to gain access to the constantly changing vernacular norms. This might be less true of inner-city Belfast in the 1970s, with its 'urban villages'. In Eckert's study, the focus is on teenagers as agents of change, because of that group's positive motivations for the use of non-standard and innovative forms. The direction of change is away from the standard in favour of the young, 'with it' urban variety, which is driven and determined by the innovating group: the teenagers. This is normal, and supported by the results obtained in other studies. In the case of the Doric, and other archaic rural dialects, the direction of change is away from the vernacular towards the (at least regional) standard. In order for speakers to have access to the constantly changing vernacular norms in an urban community like Belten High, they need to be well integrated into local social networks. By contrast, in the case of a community like the Huntly farmers, the vernacular is available, and has been for centuries, from the community's older folk, such as grandparents, and in everyday speech events between farming and fishing folk and in village shops, for example. It is passed on to children, and acquired by all, irrespective of how dense and multiplex their social networks may be. Those who are losing the vernacular are losing it in favour of the levelled urban variety found in Aberdeen, which, as mentioned, is similar to Scottish Standard English, with certain characteristic north-eastern phonetic and prosodic features and some non-standard grammatical features.[4] Of course, a few teenage slang terms are to be expected, but these do not normally last the passage into adulthood. This is shown in figure 63.

It is true that, in Milroy's urban Belfast data, the vernacular is mostly conservative. This is different from the situation in Belten High. In Belfast, the complex communities which make up the three working-class communities studied have migrated at different times from different parts of Belfast's rural hinterland (Milroy 1980: 78). The people in the Clonard are more conscious of having a rural family background than those in the Hammer, with Ballymacarrett people showing the lowest degree of communal memory of a rural background (p. 78). One Clonard man of 53 remembered being brought to Belfast from the countryside as a child (p. 78). It may be true that some of the linguistic conservatism noted is due to this rural influence. The effect of this communal memory of rural roots in the Clonard may be a certain sense of solidarity among the community, and, if so, they may signal this in their speech. The strong sense of 'us and them' is often preserved in such working-class communities, and shown by language loyalty. Milroy does in fact point to the influence of attitudinal factors on language maintenance.

To some extent, [network] multiplexity and density subsume other, less easily measurable variables. This can be demonstrated by referring to Elsie D, one of the older women in Ballymacarrett. Elsie D placed a low affective value on her relationships with her neighbours and appeared to reject 'local team' values. Devising a reliable measure of these attitudes would have been difficult and was in any case unnecessary, for the reason that the low level of multiplexity in her personal network ties formed what might be described as an 'objective correlative' to her subjective attitudes. [...] it is worth noting in this context that both network patterns, and *attitudinal factors suggest themselves as a basis for the measurement of degree of integration into the community* (Milroy 1980: 140, emphasis mine).

This suggests the greatest potential improvement to the network framework: the inclusion of attitudinal factors. In the Huntly study, those speakers with high MENURB scores have a highly positive mental orientation to the local group. This is clear from their answers to the questionnaire. This mental orientation is likely to cause such speakers to positively evaluate local behavioural (including linguistic) norms. This in turn is likely to yield a high percentage of use of these norms, as was seen in chapters 5 and 6.

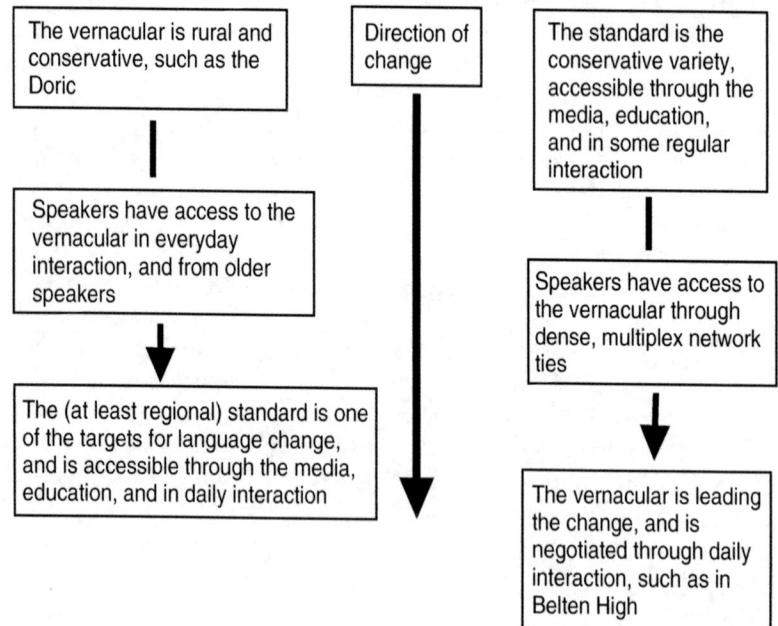

Figure 63 Possible links: social networks and access to vernacular norms

7.7 Expanding orientations beyond the local

Over time, certain rural individuals may become less resistant to the behavioural norms of the city, and even come to favour them over local norms, which may take on increased connotations of rural backwardness. In the Huntly study, it is those speakers who have a higher degree of mental urbanisation, or an attitude of openness to supra-local norms, who are at the forefront of change. Those with more positive orientations to the local rural group resist change. Perhaps those who have higher degrees of mental urbanisation have begun to broaden an earlier local positive mental orientation to include supra-local norms. Milroy cites Haugen as saying that 'the modern nation state extends some of the loyalties of the family and the neighbourhood or the clan to the whole state' (1966: 103, cited from Milroy 1980: 190). The implications of this are far-reaching. If these categories of identity become less important, it follows logically that certain social values associated with local linguistic forms, and which maintain them, may be transferred to less localised forms (p. 190). This is supported by the results of the Huntly study. The social variable MENURB has measured the orientation of the individual to the local rural area versus the city, and, by extension, solidarity with the local group, and its linguistic norms, on the one hand, and with the larger scale group of Aberdeen city and Aberdeenshire on the other. It is those speakers with the most positive attitude to the city who display the fewest vernacular features. Perhaps those rural people who have extended their loyalties to include the nearest city may begin to look to the linguistic features of its speakers as the norm. Those individuals in smaller cities who extend their loyalties to include the cultural centre or capital may do the same. As Milroy allows:

[...] complex attitudinal factors, in addition to more obvious ones such as upward mobility, are probably involved in the association between a loosened network structure and a movement towards a standardised norm (1980: 190).

The features of Aberdeen city speech are highly relevant, as it is the closest city, and the centre of wealth and culture in the north-east. Those individuals with high degrees of mental urbanisation will travel to the city more often to go to the theatre, shops, and to visit friends. They will not only be exposed to urban speech more, but also be more receptive to it.

This is the norm to which north-easterners look, and these are the features which are adopted.

7.8 Developing Pedersen's notion of composite life modes

The Huntly MENURB index is a development of Pedersen's (1994) notion of how a rural person can develop a complex, or composite life mode, which will affect the way they perceive themselves relative to the local rural community. In other words, Pedersen has indicated that Højrup's (1983) concept of Life Modes needs to be re-evaluated in the light of the changing circumstances of rural people.

She writes that, as a result of the blurring of the urban-rural distinction often found in the modern world, an individual's life mode can become composite: either rural or urban oriented, and this will have implications for their social (including linguistic) behaviour. I take this concept further, and ask what exactly she means by 'rural- or urban-oriented' life mode. Surely this is an attitudinal factor. If, as Life Mode Theory has it, one is 'placed' into a certain life mode by macro-level social and economic factors, but has opinions on (orientations to) these categories, which are pivotal to social behaviour patterns,[5] then the latter are surely more influential than the large-scale categories over which the individual has no choice. In the Huntly study, MENURB is a scalar index score of just how rural- or urban-oriented these individuals' composite life modes are. This has become the central issue in this book: to show that an individual's degree of mental urbanisation can be quantified and used as an analytical tool to compare with dialect use. Pedersen's (1994) concept has thus been developed for variationist studies, and the results have shown that in Huntly this attitudinal factor in fact correlates more strongly with dialect maintenance than any other sociological factor, except age.

We therefore propose a mental urbanisation index as follows:

1. A positive cultural orientation to the city, manifest in, for example, dress code.
2. Interest in television programmes dealing with city life and issues.
3. A desire to take up a career in the city, rather than working in the local area.
4. A desire to keep abreast of technological developments, e.g. owning a PC.
5. A desire to leave the local area and move to the city.

6. A feeling of being at ease when in the city.
7. A positive perception of city people.
8. A tendency to abandon traditional local dishes in favour of fast food and international dishes.
9. Favouring career and ambition over peace and quiet and a good family life.
10. Free time spent in the city, rather than exploring the local countryside.

This index should be used not instead of, but alongside, the more traditional indices, such as social class and social network, when conducting rural studies.

7.9 Wider implications

The Huntly MENURB index measures something which is at an abstract level 'urban' versus 'rural', but it could be developed to function in urban centres as well. There is ample evidence that urban vernaculars are surviving, and though dialect features are in rapid decline in most urban centres in Britain, there seems to be a tenacious resistance as far as accent features are concerned. Some would argue that certain non-standard features, unique to certain urban centres, are on the increase (Stoddart, Upton and Widdowson 1999: 78). If a questionnaire could be designed along the same lines as that used in Huntly, but modified to be locally relevant, posing questions along the lines of 'local' versus 'non-local', it could enhance our understanding of vernacular maintenance more generally. There is no reason why the concept should not apply in urban centres. This point will be followed up in chapter 8.

7.10 Local team values

Labov's (1963) Martha's Vineyard study showed that those islanders with stronger 'local team values'[6] used more local dialect features than others. In addition, those who had moved to the mainland for a time, and returned to the island, used local dialect features even more than those who had stayed. This is despite the fact that they had been involved in social networks on the mainland, where non-local norms were used. But, after returning to the island, despite all this presumed pressure from the networks on the mainland, they, as a result of wanting to demonstrate their positive attitudes to the local island group, and their integrative motivations, used strong local language features in their

Table 38 Centralisation in Martha's Vineyard (Labov 1963: 39)

Attitudes	(ay)	(aw)
Positive	63	62
Neutral	32	42
Negative	09	08

speech. They were 'island-oriented', or more precisely, 'locally-oriented'. Labov's data is shown in table 38.

Those people with the most positive attitudes towards the island and its traditions centralise the onsets of diphthongs frequently, regardless of their age, and those with negative attitudes about their home environment centralise them very infrequently.

Eckert (1988: 206) explains the differences in the social groups in Belten High in terms of their allegiance to the region. The Burnouts seek a 'direct connection' to the urban centre of the region and adopt the variants associated with it. The Jocks are less committed to the region as many of them anticipate leaving it in the immediate future. The result is that they are less motivated to adopt the regional markers, as was found on Martha's Vineyard. Chambers (1995: 250) writes that 'the underlying cause of sociolinguistic differences, largely beneath consciousness, is the human instinct to establish and maintain social identity'. Such a social identity will most certainly be revealed in the person's social behaviour, which includes language use.

Those speakers in the Huntly study who indicated this kind of orientation have consistently shown higher dialect scores than those who did not. One potential problem with this reading is that if, as discussed above, reported attitudes are to be viewed with caution, then surely MENURB score are also suspect. After all, the answers to the questions record only reported attitudes to a certain entity: the local rural community. While this is true, the focus of the questioning is not linguistic, but more about local solidarity, and as such, the respondents are unlikely to have made a mental connection with dialect use, as they would have with ATTDIA. The way the questions were phrased drew their attention away from reporting what they felt they ought to report in respect of national or dialectal loyalty, and allowed feelings about the local rural community to be accessed. The results speak for themselves. The high degree of correlation with dialect use, and the size of the sample virtually eliminate the chance of this happening by chance. This agrees with Labov's (1963), Lippi-Green's (1989), and Pedersen's (1994) findings, that show mental orientation to the local group to be a powerful predictor of language use, and that (at least in the case of the latter two studies), social networks were not.

7.11 Other attitudinal studies

In chapter 2 I discussed the relationship between attitudes and language use. Giles *et al.* ask the question: to what extent are people's language attitudes predictive of their linguistic behaviour (1987: 591)? They conclude that the results of research show a complex relationship between the two, but cite Jaccard (1981) as saying that

> The individual may be said to possess an attitude towards performing each of the behavioural alternatives available. The individual will decide to perform that alternative for which the most positive attitude is held. Thus, the prediction of behaviour is based on an intra-individual comparison of behavioural alternatives, and each person's attitude towards speaking a variety of language might have to be measured (for a variety of situations) in order to predict accurately (Jaccard 1981, cited from Giles et al. 1987: 592).

Macafee and McGarrity's (1999) study tested for links between attitudes to the local variety and actual language use. As the respondents in the study were all urban, the Huntly MENURB questionnaire would not have been appropriate. However, as the MENURB index measures degree of solidarity and identity with the local speech community (rural versus urban), perhaps a similar measure would have proved useful in the Aberdeen city study. People reported attitudes to language, but as was pointed out by the authors, they may have been referring to the idealised rural language. A modified questionnaire, such as one asking about degree of identity and solidarity with the local urban community versus the national community as a whole, may have yielded some stronger correlations between this mental orientation and language use. Ladegaard (2000: 238) correctly cautions against viewing correlations between attitudes and language as automatically implying causation, as other factors could be at work. However, the multiple regression models used in this study separate the influences of the different factors out, and so at least partially account for this problem, though no kind of correlation deals directly with causation.

7.12   Language change in north-east Scots: a local perspective

Hendry (1997) believes that the long-term drift from Scots to English, if allowed to continue unchecked, will result in the eventual demise of the language, and that large-scale educational indifference and public apathy do not aid the matter. This agrees with findings on language planning efforts elsewhere, such as in Ireland (Hindley 1990). There, people's attitudes are positive to the government's continued support of Gaelic, but, at a pragmatic level, people continue to send their children to English-medium schools, as a way of ensuring that they 'get on' in life. Corrigan (1992) writes that this brings consequences for low-status languages. 'Parents who believe that the language which they speak is "backward" are unwilling to lumber their offspring with a similar disadvantage' (1992: 146).

Hendry believes that children are the key to language survival, and has conducted research into the language use of children. His sample is taken from 10-year-olds across the north-east of Scotland. He believes that the most powerful threat to dialect and minority language survival is the technology revolution in media and communications. He cites Wilson (1993), who writes:

> The uniquely picturesque language of this area, which forms a vital part of our heritage, is in danger of extinction, due to pressures towards conformity with Standard English. Since the advent of modern forms of communication, especially radio and television, our distinctive modes of speech are rapidly disappearing from everyday life, and are being replaced to a large extent by the Received Pronunciation of modern English, with Scottish overtones (Wilson 1993: 111, cited from Hendry 1997: 32).

Hendry also writes about the problems involved in finding an orthography for north-east Scots, as it has always been predominantly an oral form of communication, and even fluent speakers would not attempt to express it in writing. He blames the fact that, until recently, the written form has not been encouraged in schools.

Hendry's data shows that the dialect scores are highest in the 'heartland' districts of Banff/Buchan and Gordon, and lowest in Aberdeen city and Kincardine/Deeside. He attributes this to the different settlement patterns of non-Scots-speaking in-migrants. The influx of people in the oil-related industries has been influenced by existing variations in the local infrastructure, such as availability of roads, local education, medical services, leisure, recreational, and shopping facilities. The heartland areas have not seen as many newcomers as, for example, Aberdeen city and Kincardine/Deeside. In addition to the effect of variation in infrastructure, remoteness from Aberdeen will result in an area being less likely to be settled by in-migrants. His data bears this out. From within the top-scoring 6 percent of the sample (forty-eight children), 77 percent came from rural schools. Similar differences where noted in the lowest-scoring 6 percent of the children (Hendry 1997: 85). The rural schools are less likely to have as many incomers than urban schools in and around Aberdeen. Gender does not seem to have an effect on dialect scores in his sample.

Corrigan (1992) writes:

> In those 'unstable' bilingual communities where one language is (or becomes) more powerful than another...the recessive language allows the more prestigious to intrude upon all its domains (1992: 145).

This is clearly a factor in the linguistic situation in north-east Scotland.

7.13 Modern sociolinguistics and the term 'vernacular'

The term 'vernacular' is not one used very often in sociolinguistics nowadays, the preferred terms being 'non-standard variety', or better 'local variety'. In the light of the Huntly study, and the focus on the maintenance of local versus non-local language forms, it will be useful to give an overview of some existing definitions of the term 'vernacular'. Macaulay (1997) criticises Milroy's (1980) use of the term to refer to a form of speech that is non-standard and of low prestige (pp. 10, 18, 119, 173, 176, 182, 184, cited from Macaulay 1997: 14). What she refers to though, is a few 'marked phonological features, which are found in the most casual speech of some working-class speakers in Belfast' (Macaulay 1997: 15). He also takes issue with her reporting of the level of use of this code. Milroy writes that people use their vernacular most of the time (1980: 12). However, later she writes that 'the base of the vernacular is certainly narrow in terms of the number of speakers at a high level' (p. 93), and that women on average 'use the vernacular variably at a much lower level than men (p. 159). Milroy makes it clear that the speakers in her sample were lower working class, and that she recorded good-quality data, in group sessions where the participants were well-acquainted with each other. As Macaulay asks, what these people were speaking, if not the vernacular (1997: 14)? Thus, when

Milroy refers to the use of 'vernacular norms', she refers to a speaker using these marked phonological features more frequently than others in the sample, as signals of working-class loyalty in Belfast. This is very different from, for example, Labov's reference to Black English Vernacular as a vernacular, which is characterised by a wide range of rules that differentiate it from other varieties of American English (p. 15).

Labov uses the term in the sense of 'the vernacular' as well as to refer to a 'speaker's vernacular', or unmonitored speech. Bell's (1997) concept of speaker style as audience design gives us a model which sees all speech as being situated within a social context, and may offer a way around the problem of whether speech is vernacular or not.

The vernacular and age

Macaulay points out that both Labov and Milroy relate the term 'vernacular' very closely to age. Milroy defines an urban vernacular as 'the kind of speech the majority of speakers of a city (usually low-status speakers) acquire in their adolescent years' (1980: 24). She also claims (though she has not systematically investigated this) that adolescents are 'more consistent vernacular speakers' than adults (1980: 191, cited from Macaulay 1997: 16). Labov claims that 'the most consistent vernacular is spoken by those between the ages of 9 and 18 (1973: 83), and defines the vernacular as 'that mode of speech that is acquired in pre-adolescent years' (1981: 3, cited from Macaulay 1997: 16). This rather specific use of the term does not agree with other uses, such as the classic one, in which Latin and Greek were contrasted with the vernaculars arising in Europe, and Crystal's one:

> A term used in sociolinguistics to refer to the indigenous language or dialect of a speech community, e.g. the vernacular of Liverpool, Berkshire, Jamaica, etc. (1980: 375, cited from Macaulay 1997: 12)

There may be conflicting forces at work in teenage speech, as most research shows them to use maximally non-standard speech, though there are cases where they use more standard speech than the oldest speakers. The latter result is mostly found in peripheral areas, such as rural parts and smaller urban centres with traditional varieties.

Alternatives

What Macaulay is advocating is a more cautious use of the term 'vernacular', and instead, for researchers to specify such terms as 'local variety', 'social variety', 'age-graded variety', and 'style' as the case may be. The idealised 'vernacular' is not monolithic by any means, and the search for such a form may lead to the undervaluing of other forms. As the aim of sociolinguistic investigation should be to describe the totality of speech use in a community, it may be safer to use the term 'vernacular' only in Haugen's sense of 'undeveloped language' as regards its functionality in a community (Macaulay 1997: 17). In this narrower sense, the Scots spoken in the Huntly area would most certainly be called a vernacular (Macaulay, personal communication, 2000), as it is undeveloped by comparison with Standard English.

The vernacular and the standard

Macaulay writes that the primary identifying feature of Scottish people is their speech, as most have no desire to speak 'English English' (Trudgill 1984).

Yet those higher up the educational and social scales are more likely to speak a form of English closer to English English than those lower down. Thus there is a tension between the 'prestige function', where prestige is identified with higher social class, and the 'unifying and separatist' functions, where they are identified with national pride and ethnic identity (Macaulay 1997: 27).

He writes that the use of the terms 'standard' and 'non-standard' in the study of social dialects is a carry-over from dialect geography (1997: 29). The obvious difference between social and regional dialects is that with the former there are no geographical barriers between them. Social differences arise because speakers, though potentially in contact with each other, are separated by a social order (p. 29). But regional differences, he believes, can also serve a social function, as in Scotland and the American South. Choices made between varieties are not made lightly by any speaker (Leach 1954: 49, cited from Macaulay 1997: 30). Macaulay goes along with Myers-Scotton, who writes that

[...] the guiding research question for studies of switching should not be so much, what social factors or interactional features determine code choice? But rather, what is the relation between linguistic choices and their social consequences, and how do speakers know this? (Myers-Scotton 1988: 180, cited from Macaulay 1997: 30).

Macaulay writes that it is crucial to avoid the standpoint that middle-class speech is a reference against which other speech should be measured, with the implication that speakers of non-standard varieties aim at the standard, but fail (p. 30). By most definitions, Schwyzertütsch is not a standard language, but it would be ludicrous to assume that its speakers simply fail to hit the 'target' standard language: German. As Macaulay says, there are simply two standards (p. 30), and, as in the Scots situation, each has its own attractions.

In this chapter, I discussed the outliers in the data, using ethnographic methods to explain, if possible, the reasons for individuals having vastly different scores from those of other of the same sex and age. I reviewed the geolinguistic model, compared the results of the Huntly study with those of the Belfast study, discussed critiques of the network framework, offered a more elaborate method for approaching the concept of mental orientation. I discussed the wider implications for sociolinguistic theory, and compared our notion of mental orientation with Labov's 'local team values', before discussing other attitudinal studies, a study on language use in Aberdeenshire, and a critique by Macaulay of Milroy's use of the term 'vernacular'. In the next chapter, I discuss the implications of my findings for future research.

Notes

1. See section 3.4.5.
2. As is suggested is the case in Cardiff by Mees and Collins' (1999) data.
3. Although Stuart-Smith (1999) shows this feature in Glasgow.
4. Robert Millar, personal communication. A lack of quantitative studies in Aberdeen city makes a direct comparison difficult.
5. Pedersen (1994) notes a strong tendency for those with rural-oriented rural life modes to use more dialect features, though does not systematically test this.
6. A term from Blom and Gumperz (1972).

8
Implications for Future Research

In this chapter, I acknowledge the great potential in the social network concept, providing the framework is developed to allow for a more accurate picture to be obtained of the structural and interactional details of the individual's network. I offer a sociolinguistic model of language change, which takes into account many more of the possible factors operating on the process. I also detail future plans for the Huntly data.

A study such as this will naturally have strengths and weaknesses. The potential problems of the quantitative method have been outlined above. It is hoped that the small-scale ethnographic studies in chapter 7 have gone some way towards overcoming the impression that all of the individuals studied have become mere numbers, contributing only in some small way to the overall patterns for their sex and age groups. The potential problems with the questions asked in the questionnaire have also been pointed out. The problem is common in such quantitative studies, though with some thought the Huntly questionnaire could be improved and adapted for other studies. The point is that any model that is to function well across a variety of sociolinguistic studies will have to be more complex and inclusive than a simple class- or network-based one. It may seem that the critique of some of the established models has been too severe. This is not the intention, though it has been possible to suggest improvements, to the extent that a model which includes a variety of possible extralinguistic factors, and attempts to account for resistance to language change, will be suggested below.

8.1 Networks: the potential

It should be made clear at this point that the alternative social preconditions to language change proposed in this study do not ignore the

227

potential influence a network may have on an individual. It is felt that, while people are free to make choices when it comes to social (including linguistic) behaviour, they are nevertheless constrained by what is *available* to choose from. A guest at a banquet can only select from what is on the tables. The question of who is the *agent* is important, though. That is not to say, however, that once such choices have been made, and individuals are involved in local social networks, they will be unaffected by local linguistic norms. The model needs to become more inclusive, and to allow for the many factors which operate on the process of vernacular maintenance.[1] Social networks must have some effect on social behaviour, and in certain contexts, perhaps urban centres, this influence will be more keenly felt than in others. However, it seems more likely that mental attitude, solidarity,[2] or orientation is the driving force behind choices made about levels of social network integration and language use. This can account for a high degree of correlation between network indices and language use, as well for low degrees of correlation, as found in the Huntly data, where mental urbanisation is found to be more important. In fact, Milroy repeatedly points to the importance of mental orientation:

> Both the low-status vernaculars and RP may be viewed as owing their relative stability to covert ideologies of solidarity and reciprocity (1980: 185).

Douglas-Cowie (1978) also refers to the effect of mental factors in her study of code switching in a Northern Irish village:

> It has also been possible to show that differences in the linguistic behaviour of individuals (which may often be obscured in larger scale studies dealing in grouped scores) may be accounted for by socio-psychological factors...such as the degree of an individual's social ambition (Douglas-Cowie 1978, cited from Trudgill 1978: 51).

8.2 Suggestions for a more realistic sociolinguistic model of change

A model which took account of such attitudinal factors would greatly enhance our understanding of the dynamics of vernacular maintenance. Such a model would need to recognise the agency of the individual speaker in the process. Andersen (1989) writes that there is an element of intentionality to language use, and that this intentionality is involved in both stability *and* change. In other words, dialect maintenance is partly explained by reference to the individual as acting with intent. A more effective model would need to include the concepts shown in figure 64. In section 2.7, I discussed Myers-Scotton's (1998) concept of the consequences of linguistic choices. The alternative to the existing notion of the link between social network and dialect maintenance presented above allows for just such choice. The link proposed in the social network framework has the network as the agent, exercising its influence on the person, who is effectively the patient. In addition to this, the question of how the person has come to belong to the network in the first place is not answered satisfactorily in, for example Milroy (1980).

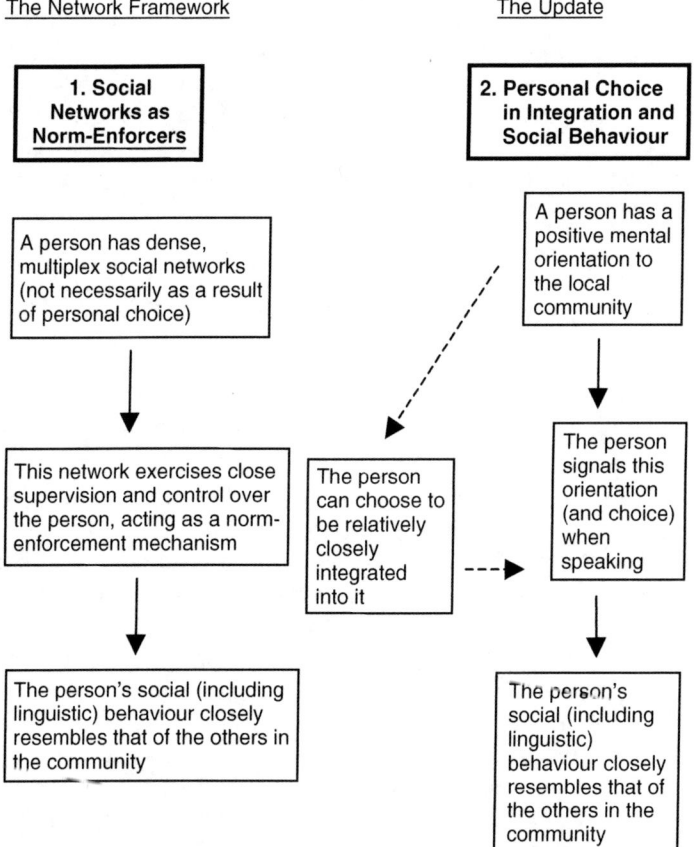

Figure 64 Suggestions for updating the social network framework

In network-based studies, the individual passively follows the norms and values prescribed by the network, and the end result is that he or she displays local behavioural norms.

On the other hand, given that personal choice is acknowledged in so many other linguistic studies (Omdal 1984, Giles et al. 1987, Macaulay 1991, Carter and Sealey 2000, Ladegaard 2000), we may want to now question the strength of this link. The right-hand side of the diagram above shows the same end result as the one on the left, but is not proposed as a *causal* link in the strong sense of the word. Rather it is seen as one of the possible social preconditions for language maintenance. The suggested update to the model can account for data such as Milroy's showing a high correlation between language use and social network scores (the dotted lines). At the same time it can account for a lack of correlation between these two variables, such as is found in Pedersen (1994) and in the Huntly study. The dotted line shows that a person's positive mental orientation *can* cause that person to choose a relatively high degree of integration into a local network, but that this is not automatic. Such an attitude is, however, likely to cause a high degree of behavioural integration, as is shown by Pedersen's data and that from the Huntly study. It is not suggested for a moment that linguistic norms found within a speech community or social network will not have an influence on a person's speech; merely that the speaker has the power to choose whether to copy these features. It is a question of adoption and agency.

Personal character traits, such as relative introversion, will affect personal choice in integration into local social networks, but will still allow the person to signal local solidarity with language use. This will produce low correlations between social network scores and language use on the one hand, and high correlations between attitudes to the local group and language use on the other. Of course, this viewpoint does not explain how those speakers who have a positive mental orientation to a local *urban* speech community and would like to signal this in their language use, but decide to have relatively low degrees of network integration, gain access to changing vernacular norms. In fact, it is much more powerful as an explanatory device for *rural* speech communities where the vernacular is a conservative, rather than innovative variety. In this type of speech community, the vernacular norms are available in the speech of older people and in everyday speech events between farming and fishing folk, and in village shops, for example. Access to them is not dependent upon high levels of integration into social networks. They have been in use for generations, and are therefore known by people in the community, and can be used in speech to signify a less or more positive mental orientation to the local community.

8.3 Conclusion

Urban and rural speech communities often differ from each other in marked ways, and our research methodologies must take this into account. The structure of local social networks, people's attitudes, the direction of language change, and social class structures may differ radically from rural to urban communities, so as to have dissimilar effects on dialect maintenance. While social network strength indices have been shown to correlate (if weakly) with dialect maintenance in some urban areas, such as Ballymacarrett in Belfast (Milroy 1980), the picture may be more complicated. The data from Austria (Lippi-Green 1989), Denmark (Pedersen 1994) and Huntly reveal that certain attitudinal factors are important to our understanding of dialect maintenance. In Huntly, the measure of a person's degree of mental urbanisation, reflected in the MENURB index, has indicated a high degree of correlation between such attitudes and dialect use. This factor alone has proved a reliable predictor of dialect maintenance in this rural community. Perhaps McIntosh's (1961) notion of 'resistant types', discussed in chapter 1, may be now be better understood, given that *maintaining* a non-standard variety of necessity requires *resisting* the incoming standard variety. Understanding the social 'mechanisms' involved in language change in rural communities may be more complex than simply applying models developed in urban studies.

The social network has often been seen as a monitor of social behaviour, exercising close supervision and control over a community's linguistic norms. People with dense, multiplex networks are seen as being almost pressured into conformity. The Huntly study has shown that, at least for this rural community, there is no correlation between network indices and dialect maintenance. An individual's free choice in matters such as degree of integration into local social networks and dialect use is a crucial factor. The data analysis has shown that such linguistic choices are highly correlated with the individual's degree of local solidarity. Though this is not seen as a *cause* of dialect maintenance, it is perhaps better seen as a precondition for change, or lack of change. Its presence or absence is likely to have a facilitating or retarding effect on change. This may call into question the validity of social networks as a *rigorous* analytical tool, not only in rural, but also urban areas. The ability of the network to function strongly as a 'norm-enforcement mechanism' seems far too mechanical, and denies the speaker a choice in using local language forms. The presence of network norms is perhaps a *stimulus*, but the *response* the individual makes will be mediated by other factors, such as attitudes.

In fact, the question of how a speaker comes to belong to a network is not addressed satisfactorily by the network framework. The implied causal link between network and language use proposed needs revision. More work will need to be done in urban areas to test the alternative modes of analysis identified here. While the community studied here is rural, the implications for general sociolinguistic theory are wide reaching. Pedersen's notion of *composite* life modes has been expanded, to the extent that the question of what in fact is meant by 'mental urbanisation' has been addressed. It is believed that the concept encompasses not only 'rural versus urban', but something more widely applicable: 'local versus non-local'. This is what Labov discovered in his 'local team values' on Martha's Vineyard, and it is something which needs to be investigated more rigorously.

Suggestions for a sociolinguistic model of dialect maintenance

A network-only analysis cannot uncover all the complex factors involved in dialect maintenance. Milroy's Belfast study certainly involved a lengthy period in the field, which brought with it immense benefits in terms of the degree of understanding of the local community that was achieved. But replication studies which simply arrive at a network index based upon individual's responses to questions about, for example, their degree of involvement in local community activities, may be over simplistic, as the lack of correlation between such indices and vernacular maintenance in Huntly suggests. A model which incorporates a more detailed account of the structural *and* interactional nature of the individual's network, as well as attitudinal factors, such as those identified here, may bring us closer to understanding the process of language change.

Such a model might, for example, develop a composite dialect maintenance index. This composite index might consist of indices for, e.g. social network, which would need to measure the structural and interactional features of an individual's network. This might be achieved by for example showing the speaker a sociogram, and then asking them to draw one for themselves, showing the distance between themselves and the network contact, whether the links were multiplex or not, and details of the direction of flow of goods and services. These factors could be incorporated into two separate network indices (see diagram below) along with the answers to the network questionnaire used by Milroy. Various attitudinal indices could be obtained that could be included in a composite dialect maintenance index. Such a methodology would need to consider all of the potential social factors involved in language change. Other predictive factors such as age and sex, for example, would need to be included in the composite index. Adolescents are expected to lead change, whether away from, or towards the standard, and a negative weighting could be given to individuals in this age group. Different weightings could be applied to rural and urban individuals. Below is a suggested framework for such a composite index. In order to consider the potential influence of each of these factors simultaneously, a multiple regression analysis, as detailed in chapter 6, would need to be used. This yields an r-squared value (as a percentage), which shows to what extent the variance in the dependent variable is predicted by the individual scores in the independent variable. Once the influences of the various independent variables have been tested by the multiple regression analysis, any major differences found between one study and the next will need to be explained. This will involve ethnographic and qualitative insights, and need to compare historical, social, political, demographic and other factors across communities. The implications of a more complex predictive model such as this are very promising for our understanding of the sociolinguistic factors involved in the process of dialect maintenance.

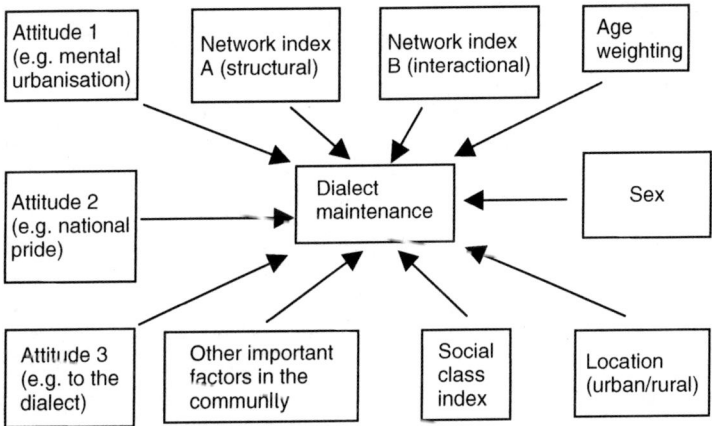

Figure 65 Suggested framework for composite dialect maintenance index

As for the Scots language spoken in the north-east, there is no doubt that it is in decline. It is hoped that the recordings obtained during this study will be of use to future researchers. The recordings will be digitised, re-mastered, tagged and copied onto CD-ROMs.[3] As a tagged, searchable corpus, the data will have much to offer in the way of research potential. Searches could be made for, say, particular morpho-syntactic features in the corpus, as well as patterns of correlation between them and other linguistic or extra-linguistic features. Different angles can be taken on approaching the actual recordings. The corpus contains around 50 hours of recording, and even instrumental phonetic studies could be done using the data. Patterns of interaction between the social variables and the 12 *individual* linguistic variables could be investigated, as was done in chapter 4 for AGE. This would have the effect of testing whether any of the linguistic variables is more influenced than the others by such factors as social networks or mental urbanisation. These and other ideas will be the motivating force behind future small-scale projects based upon the Huntly corpus.

Notes

1. In many academic arguments, sides are taken, and a 'no compromise' line is followed. Some researchers seem to feel that a phenomenon X must be explained either by phenomenon Y or Z, and the possibility that both can have a (lesser or greater) effect on X is often not considered.
2. Corrigan (1992) also points to the importance of strong loyalties in language acquisition and use.
3. This will not only have the effect of making them clearer, as the re-mastering process removes any hiss and crackle, but also of preserving them in a forward-looking format. Cassettes are negatively affected by magnetic fields, and prone to stretching. They cannot be searched easily and quickly, as they have to be scanned 'blind', by rewinding or fast-forward winding. The CD-ROM is impervious to magnetic fields like computer monitors, and can be indexed for easy searches. Though it must be protected from direct sunlight, this is not normally a problem for archived materials.

Appendices

Appendix 1: Questionnaire: National Pride.

4 str. agree	3 agree	2 neutral	1 disagree	0 str. disagree

1. I am proud to be Scottish.
2. I get on better with local people than with people from England and abroad who come to live here.
3. I prefer regional Scottish newspapers.
4. I am happy that the vote for an independent parliament was successful.
5. I feel that we are a separate nation and different from other folk who make up the rest of the UK.
6. I enjoy cultural events such as ceilidhs, poetry and dancing where traditional food is served.
7. I am proud of ancient heroes such as William Wallace and more recently, those politicians who have done much for the fight for recognition as an independent nation.
8. I often listen to traditional Scots music and modern Scots singers such as Caper Caillie, Runrig, The Proclaimers, etc.
9. I am proud of our Scots traditions, such as kilts, bagpipes and haggis.
10. I think our country is very beautiful; something to look after and be proud of.

Appendix 2: Questionnaire: Attitude to the Dialect.

1. Our language is not just a sub-standard form of English, but has its own proud history and literature.
2. Formal education and the media are killing the Doric.
3. There should be more programmes on radio and TV using the Doric.
4. I participate in Doric activities such as singing, poetry, story-telling and language classes.
5. Schools should encourage knowledge and use of the Doric.
6. The Doric is old-fashioned.
7. One should always speak Standard English to children.
8. I only speak the Doric to friends and family members.
9. I only use the Doric in jokes.
10. The north-east folk should conserve Doric words and phrases.

Bibliography

Adams, J. (1799). *The Pronunciation of the English Language Vindicated from Imputed Anomaly and Caprice*. Edinburgh. *English Linguistics 1500–1800, 72*. In R. C. Alston (ed.) (1968). Menston: Scholar Press.

Agheyisi, R. and Fishman, J. (1970). 'Language attitude studies: A brief survey of methodological approaches.' *Anthropological Linguistics* 12:5, 137–57.

Aitchison, J. (2001). *Language Change. Progress or Decay?* Cambridge. CUP.

Aitken, A. (1979). 'Scottish Speech: A historical view, with special reference to the Standard English of Scotland'. In A. Aitken and T. McArthur (eds.) *Languages of Scotland*. Edinburgh: Chambers.

Aitken, A. (1979b). 'Studies on Scots and Scottish Standard English today'. In A. Aitken and T. McArthur (eds.) *Languages of Scotland*. Edinburgh: Chambers.

Aitken, A. (1981a). The good old Scots tongue: Does Scots have an identity? In E. Haugen, J. McClure and D. Thomson (eds.). *Minority Languages Today*. Edinburgh: Edinburgh University Press.

Aitken, A. and Stevenson, A. (1990) (eds.). *A Dictionary of the Older Scots Tongue*. Aberdeen: Aberdeen University Press.

Andersen, H. (1989). 'Understanding linguistic innovations'. In L. Breivik and E. Håkon Jahr (eds.). *Language Change. Contributions to the Study of its Causes*. Berlin: Mouton de Gruyter.

Barnes, J. (1954). 'Class and Committee in a Norwegian Island Parish', *Human Relations, 7*.

Beal, J. (1997). 'Syntax and Morphology'. In C. Jones (ed.) *The Edinburgh History of the Scots Language*. Edinburgh: Edinburgh University Press.

Bell, A. (1997). 'Language Style as Audience Design'. In N. Coupland and A. Jaworski (eds.). *Sociolinguistics: A Reader and Coursebook*. London: Macmillan Press Ltd.

Berkowitz, S. (1982) *An Introduction to Structural Analysis: The Network Approach to Social Research*. Toronto: Butterworth & Co.

Blom, J. and Gumperz, J. (1972). 'Social meaning in linguistic structures: Code-switching in Norway'. In J. Gumperz and D. Hymes (eds.) *Directions in Sociolinguistics. The Ethnography of Communication*. New York: Holt Rinehart and Winston pp. 407–434.

Bloomfield, L. (1933). *Language*. Chicago: University of Chicago Press.

Boas, F. (1911). *Handbook of American Indian Languages*, part 1, Washington.

Boissevain, J. (1974). *Friends of Friends: Networks, Manipulators and Coalitions*. Oxford: Basil Blackwell.

Boissevain, J. (1987). 'Social Networks'. In *Sociolinguistics* 1. New York: de Gruyter.

Breckler, S. (1984). 'Empirical validation of affect, behaviour, and cognition as distinct components of attitude'. *Journal of Personality and Social Psychology* 46: 1191–1205.

Britain, D. (1991). *A Geolinguistic Analysis of Speech Variables in the Fens*. Colchester: University of Essex (Unpublished PhD Thesis).

Buchan, J. et al. (1924). *The Scottish Tongue*. London: Cassell & Co.

Butters, R. (1997). 'Dialectology and Sociolinguistic Theory'. In A. R. Thomas (ed.) *Issues and Methods in Dialectology*. Bangor: University of Bangor Press, pp. 1–13.

Cameron, D. (1997). 'Demythologising Sociolinguistics'. In N. Coupland and A. Jaworski (eds.). *Sociolinguistics. A Reader and Coursebook*. London: MacMillan Press Ltd.

Carter, B. and Sealey, A. (2000). 'Language, structure and agency: what can realist theory offer to sociolinguistics?' *Journal of Sociolinguistics* 4(1), 3–20.

Chambers, J. and Trudgill, P. (1980). *Dialectology*. Cambridge: CUP.

Chambers, J. (1995). *Sociolinguistic Theory: Linguistic Variation and its Social Significance*. Cambridge, Massachusetts: Blackwell.

Chambers, J. (1996). 'Mapping Social Dimensions'. *Abstracts from the Papers of Methods IX: Ninth International Conference on Methods in Dialectology*. Department of Linguistics, University of Wales Bangor.

Chambers J. and Trudgill, P. (1998). *Dialectology*. (2nd edn.). Cambridge: CUP.

Cheshire, J. (1982). *Variation in an English Dialect*. Cambridge: CUP.

Cheshire, J., Gillett, A., Kerswill, P. and Williams A. (1999). 'The role of adolescents in dialect levelling'. Final report submitted to the Economic and social Research Council, June 1999 (ESRC ref. R000236180).

Chirrey, D. (1999). 'Edinburgh: descriptive material'. In P. Foulkes and G. Docherty (eds.). *Urban Voices. Accent Studies in the British Isles*. London: Arnold.

Cochran, M., Larner, M., Riley, D., Gunnarson, L., and Henderson, C. (eds.) (1990). *Extending Families: The Social Networks of Parents and their Children*. Cambridge: CUP.

Cohen, A. (1964). *Attitude Change and Social Influence*. New York: Basic Books.

Cohen, A. (ed.) (1982). *Belonging*. Manchester: Manchester University Press.

Coseriu, E. (1962). *Teoria del Lenguaje y Linguistica General*. Madrid: Editorial Gredos.

Coupland, N. and Jaworski, A. (eds.) (1997). *Sociolinguistics. A Reader and Coursebook*. London: MacMillan Press Ltd.

Douglas-Cowie, E. (1978). 'Linguistic code-switching in a Northern Irish village: social interaction and social ambition'. In P. Trudgill (ed.) (1978). *Sociolinguistic Patterns in British English*. London: Arnold.

Downes, W. (1998). *Language and Society*, (2nd edn.). Cambridge: Cambridge University Press.

Eckert, P. (2000). *Linguistic Variation as Social Practice*. Oxford: Blackwell.

Eckert, P. (1988). 'Adolescent social structure and the spread of linguistic Change.' *Language in Society* 17, 183–207.

Edwards, J. (1982). 'Language attitudes and their implications among English Speakers'. In E. Ryan and H. Giles (eds.) 1982. *Attitudes towards language variation. Social and applied contexts*. London: Edward Arnold, pp. 20–33.

Fasold, R. (1984). *The Sociolinguistics of Society*. Oxford: Blackwell.

Fennell, B. (2001). *A History of English: A Sociolinguistic Approach*. Blackwell: Oxford.

Festinger, L. (1962). *A Theory of Cognitive Dissonance*. London: Tavistock Publications.

Figueroa, E. (1994). *Sociolinguistic Metatheory*. Oxford: Elsevier Science Ltd.

Fisher, J. and Bornstein, D. (1984). *In Forme of Speche is Chaunge: Readings in the History of the English Language*. London: University Press of America.

Foulkes, P. and Docherty, G. (eds.) (1999). *Urban Voices. Accent Studies in the British Isles*. London: Arnold.

Frankenburg, R. (1969). *Communities in Britain*. Harmondsworth: Penguin.

Gal, S. (1979). *Language Shift: Social Determinants of Linguistic Change in Bilingual Austria*. New York: Academic Press. Gerritsen, M. (1988). 'Sociolinguistic developments as a diffusion process'. In U. Ammon, N. Dittmar, and K. Mattheier (eds.) *Sociolinguistics: an International Handbook of the Science of Language and Society*. Berlin: de Gruyter, pp. 1574–1591.

Giles, H., Taylor, D. and Bourhis, R. (1973). 'Towards a theory of interpersonal accommodation through speech: Some Canadian data.' *Language in Society* 2, 177–192.

Giles, H., Hewstone, M., Ryan, E., and Johnson, P. (1987). 'Research on language attitudes'. In U. Ammon, N. Dittmar, and K. Mattheier (eds.) *Sociolinguistics: an International Handbook of the Science of Language and Society*. Berlin: de Gruyter, pp. 585–597.

Granovetter, M. (1974). *Getting a Job*. Cambridge, Massachusetts: Harvard University Press.

Grant, W., and Murison, D. (eds.). *Scottish National Dictionary* (vol. 8) (1971). Edinburgh: Neill & Co. Ltd.

Greenwood, J. (1994). *Realism, Identity and Emotion: Reclaiming Social Psychology*. London: Sage.

Gumperz, J. (1971). *Language in social groups*. Essays edited by Anwar S. Dil. Stanford: Stanford University Press.

Hägerstrand, T. (1967b). *Innovation Diffusion as a Spatial Process*. Chicago: University of Chicago Press.

Hatch, E. and Lazaraton, A. (1991). *The Research Manual: Design and Statistics for Applied Linguistics*. Newbury House.

Hendry, I. (1997). 'Doric – an investigation into its use amongst primary school children in the north east of Scotland'. Thesis submitted for M.Litt, University of Aberdeen.

Hernández-Campoy, J. (1996). *Models of Analysis in the Diffusion of Sociolinguistic Innovations*. Murcia. Unpublished Paper.

Hindley, R. (1990). *The Death of the Irish Language*. London: Routledge.

Hinskens, F. (1996). *Dialect Levelling in Limburg. Structural and Sociolinguistic Aspects*. Linguistische Arbeiten. Tübingen: Max Niemeyer.

Højrup, T. (1983). 'The concept of life-mode'. *Ethnologica Scandinavica* 1983: 15–50.

Hymes, D. (1997). 'The Scope of Sociolinguistics'. In N. Coupland and A. Jaworski (eds.) (1997). *Sociolinguistics. A Reader and Coursebook*. London: MacMillan Press Ltd.

Jaccard, J. (1981). 'Attitudes and behaviour: implications of attitudes toward behavioural alternatives'. *Journal of Experimental Social Psychology* 17, 286–307.

Jamieson, J. (ed.) (1861). *Etymological Dictionary of the Scottish Language* (2nd edn.). Edinburgh: Tait.

Johnson, N. (1995). 'The Renaissance of Nationalism'. In R. J. Johnston, P. J. Taylor, and M. J. Watts (eds.). *Geographies of Global Change*. Oxford: Blackwell, pp. 97–110.

Johnston, P. (1997). 'Older Scots Phonology and its Regional Variation', in C. Jones (ed.) (1997). *The Edinburgh History of the Scots Language*. Edinburgh: Edinburgh University Press.

Johnston, P. (1983). 'Irregular style variation patterns in Edinburgh speech'. *Scottish Language* 2: 1–19.

Jones, C. (ed.) (1991). *A Treatise on the Provincial Dialect of Scotland, by Sylvester Douglas*. Edinburgh: Edinburgh University Press.

Jones, C. (1997). 'Phonology'. In *The Edinburgh History of the Scots Language*. Edinburgh: Edinburgh University Press.

Keller, R. (1994). *On Language Change. The Invisible Hand in Language*. London: Routledge.

Kerswill, P. (1994). *Dialects Converging. Rural Speech in Urban Norway*. Oxford: Clarendon.

Kerswill, P. and Williams, A. (1994). *The Role of Adolescents in Dialect Levelling*. Unpublished Research Proposal to the ESRC.

Kerswill, P. (1996). 'Children, adolescents and language change'. *Language Variation and Change* 8, 177–202.

Kerswill, P. and Williams, A. (1997). 'Creating a new town koiné: children and language change in Milton Keynes'. *University of Reading Working Papers in Linguistics* 3, 205–258.

Kerswill, P. and Williams, A. (2000). 'Creating a new town koiné: children and Language change in Milton Keynes'. *Language in Society* 29(1), 65–115.

Kerswill, P. and Williams, A. (2001a) '"Salience" as an explanatory factor in language change: Evidence from dialect levelling in urban England'. In M. C. Jones and E. Esch (eds.) *Contact-induced language change. An examination of internal, external and non-linguistic factors*. Mouton de Gruyter.

Kurath, H. (1972). *Studies in Area Linguistics*. Indiana: Indiana University Press.

Kynoch, D. (1994). *Teach Yourself Doric*. Aberdeen: Scottish Cultural Press.

Labov, W. (1966). *The Social Stratification of English in New York City*. Washington: Centre for Applied Linguistics.

Labov, W. (1973b). *Sociolinguistic Patterns*. Philadelphia: University of Pennsylvania Press.

Labov, W. (1980). 'The social origins of sound change'. In W. Labov (ed.), *Locating Language in Time and Space*. New York: Academic Press, 251–264.

Labov, W. (1986). 'De facto segregation of black and white vernaculars'. In D. Sankoff (ed.) *Diversity and Diachrony*. Amsterdam/Philadelphia: Benjamins, pp. 1–24.

Labov, W. (1997). 'Linguistics and Sociolinguistics'. In N. Coupland and A. Jaworski (eds.) (1997). *Sociolinguistics. A Reader and Coursebook*. London: MacMillan Press Ltd.

Labov, W. (2001). *Principles of Linguistic Change. Volume 2: Social factors*. Oxford: Blackwell.

Ladegaard, H. (2000). 'Language attitudes and sociolinguistic behaviour: Exploring attitude-behaviour relations in language'. *Journal of Sociolinguistics* 4/2, 214–233.

Lane, L. A. (1997). 'A report on field methods for ethnodialectology: a case Study of Thyborøn, Denmark'. In A. R. Thomas (ed.) *Issues and Methods in Dialectology*. Bangor: University of Bangor Press, pp. 144–158.

Lass, R. (1980). *On Explaining Language Change*. Cambridge: CUP.

Lass, R. (1987). *The Shape of English. Structure and History*. London: J. M. Dent.

Lave, J. and Wenger, E. (1991). *Situated Learning: Legitimate Peripheral Participation*. Cambridge: CUP.

Leach, E. (1954). *Political Systems of Highland Burma*. Cambridge, Massachusetts: Harvard University Press.

Lenneberg, E. (ed.). (1967). *Biological Foundations of Language*. New York: Wiley.

Le Page, R. (1978). 'Projection, focusing and diffusion, or steps towards a Socio-linguistic theory of language'. *York Papers in Linguistics* 9, University of York.

Le Page, R. and Tabouret-Keller, A. (1985). *Acts of Identity*. Cambridge: CUP.

Lippi-Green, L. (1989). 'Social network integration and language change in progress in a rural alpine village'. *Language in Society* 18.

Löw, D. (1997). 'The Doric in Pitmedden: Language attitudes in a Scottish Village'. Unpublished Master's Thesis. Heidelberg: Ruprecht-Karls-Universität.

Lüdtke, H. (1994). 'Invisible-hand processes and the universal laws of language change'. In R. Keller. *On Language Change. The Invisible Hand in Language*. London: Routledge.

Macafee, C. (1994). *Traditional Dialect in the Modern World: A Glasgow Case Study*. Frankfurt: Peter Lang.

Macafee, C. (1997). 'Ongoing change in modern Scots' In C. Jones (ed.). *The Edinburgh History of the Scots Language*. Edinburgh: Edinburgh University Press.

Macafee, C. (1997). 'Older Scots Lexis'. In C. Jones (ed.). *The Edinburgh History of the Scots Language*. Edinburgh: Edinburgh University Press.

Macafee, C. and McGarrity, B. (1999). 'Scots Language Attitudes and Language Maintenance'. Leeds Studies in English. Dialectal Variation in English: Proceedings of the Harold Orton Centenary Conference 1998, pp. 165–179.

Macafee, C. (ed.) (in progress) *The Maintenance of Scots: New Research on Lowland Scots and Related Languages*. (provisional title)

Macafee, C. (1983). *Varieties of English Around the World: Glasgow*. Amsterdam: Benjamins.

Macaulay, R. and Trevelyan, G. (1973). *Language, Education and Employment In Glasgow*. Final report to the SSRC.

Macaulay, R. (1991). *Locating Dialect in Discourse*. Oxford: OUP.

Macaulay, R. (1997) *Standards and Variation in Urban Speech. Examples from Lowland Scots*. Benjamins: Amsterdam.

MacQueen, J. (1967). *Robert Henryson: A Study of the Major Narrative Poems*. Oxford: Clarendon Press.

Maehlum, B. (1987). 'Kodeveksling i Hemnesberget: Myte eller virkelighet?' *Norsk lingvistik tidsskrift* 1, 29–44.

Mather, J. and Speitel, H. (eds.) (1975). *The Linguistic Atlas of Scotland*. London: Croom Helm.

Marshall, J. (2000). 'Testing social network theory in a rural setting'. In University of Reading, Department of Linguistic Science Working Papers, vol. 4, pp. 123–174.

Marshall, J. (2001). ' The sociolinguistic significance of the glottal stop in north-east Scots', in University of Reading, Department of Linguistic Science Working Papers, vol. 5.

McClure, J. (1979). 'Scots: Its range of uses'. In A. Aitken and T. McArthur (eds.) *Languages of Scotland*. Edinburgh: Chambers.

McClure, J. (ed.) (1983). *Scotland and the Lowland Tongue*. Aberdeen: Aberdeen University Press.

McDavid, R. (1948). 'Post-vocalic /r/ in South Carolina: A Social Analysis'. *American Speech* 23: 194–203.

McIntosh, A. (1961). *Introduction to a Survey of Scottish Dialects*. Edinburgh: Thomas Nelson and Sons.

McMahon, A. (1994). *Understanding Language Change*. Cambridge: CUP.

Mees, I. and Collins, B. (1999). Cardiff: A real-time study of glottalisation. In P. Foulkes and G. Docherty (eds.). *Urban Voices. Accent Studies in the British Isles.* London: Arnold.

Mewett, P. (1982). 'Associational categories and the social location of relationships in a Lewis crofting community'. In A. Cohen (1964). *Attitude Change and Social Influence.* New York: Basic Books, pp. 101–30.

Milroy, L. (1980). *Language and Social Networks.* Oxford: Blackwell.

Milroy, J. and Milroy, L. (1985). 'Linguistic change social network and speaker innovation'. *Journal of Linguistics* 21, 339–384.

Milroy, L. and Milroy, J. (1992). 'Social network and social class: Towards an integrated sociolinguistic model'. *Language in Society* 21, 1–26.

Milroy, L. and Milroy, J. (1997). 'Network Structure and Linguistic Change'. In N. Coupland and A. Jaworski (eds.). *Sociolinguistics. A Reader and Coursebook.* London: MacMillan Press Ltd.

Milroy, J. (2001). 'Language ideologies and the consequences of standardization'. *Journal of Sociolinguistics* vol. 5, no. 4, 530–555.

Mitchell, J. (1969). 'The concept and use of social networks'. In J. C. Mitchell, (ed.) *Social Networks in Urban Situations.* Manchester: Manchester University Press, pp. 1–50.

Mitchell, J. (1986). 'Network Procedures'. *The Quality of Urban Life.* D. Frick (ed.). Berlin: de Gruyter.

Morer, T. (1715). *A Short Account of Scotland.* London.

Murison, D. (1979). 'The Historical Background'. In A. Aitken and T. McArthur (eds.). *Languages of Scotland.* Edinburgh: Chambers.

Myers-Scotton, C. (1998). *Codes and Consequences. Choosing Linguistic Varieties.* Oxford: OUP.

Myers-Scotton, C. (1988). 'Code switching as indexical of social negotiations'. In M. Heller (ed.) (1988). *Codeswitching. Anthropological and Sociolinguistic Perspectives.* Berlin: Mouton de Gruyter.

Neubert, A. (1976). 'What is sociolinguistics? Three postulates for Sociolinguistic research'. *Archivum Linguisticum* 7, 152–160.

Oxford English Dictionary. (1989). (2nd edn.). Various volumes. Oxford: Clarendon Press.

Omdal, H. (1994). 'From the Valley to the City: Language Modification and Language Attitudes'. *Sociolinguistics and Language Contact* 7, 116–148.

Pedersen, I. (1994). 'Linguistic Variation and Composite Life Modes'. In B. Nordberg (ed.) *The Sociolinguistics of Urbanisation: The Case of the Nordic Countries.* Berlin: de Gruyter.

Reid, E. (1978). 'Social and stylistic variation in the speech of children: some Evidence from Edinburgh'. In P. Trudgill (ed.). *Sociolinguistic Patterns in British English.* London: Arnold.

Rickford, J. (1987). 'The haves and have nots: Sociolinguistic surveys and the assessment of speaker competence'. *Language in Society* 16, 149–177.

Rogers, E. (1987). 'Progress, problems, and prospects for network research: investigating relationships in the age of electronic communication technologies'. Social Networks 9(4), 285–310.

Romaine, S. (1978). 'Postvocalic /r/ in Scottish English: Sound change in progress?' In P. Trudgill (ed.). *Sociolinguistic Patterns in British English.* London: Arnold.

Romaine, S. (1982a). *Socio-Historical Linguistics: Its Status and Methodology.* Cambridge: CUP.

Romaine, S. (1984). 'The Status of Sociological Models and Categories in Explaining Linguistic Variation', *Linguistische Berichte*, 90, 25–38.

Romaine, S. (1989). 'The role of children in linguistic change'. In L. Breivik and E. Jahr (eds.). *Language Change: Contributions to the Study of its Causes.* Berlin: Mouton de Gruyter, pp. 199–225.

Røyneland, U. (2000). 'Methodological problems and possible solutions in a study of dialect levelling'. Paper presented at ICLaVE, Barcelona, July 2000.

Ryan, E. and Giles, H. (eds.) 1982. *Attitudes Towards Language Variation. Social And Applied Contexts.* London: Edward Arnold.

Scott, J. (1991). *Social Network Analysis: A Handbook.* London: Sage.

Scottish Office Education Department (1991). Curriculum and Assessment in Scotland, National Guidelines: *English Language 5–14.* Edinburgh: Scottish Office Education Department, 67–68.

Sealey, A. and Carter, B. (2001). 'Social categories and sociolinguistics: applying a realist approach'. International Journal of the Sociology of Language, 152.

Simpson, J. and Weiner, E. (1989). *The Oxford English Dictionary.* Oxford: Clarendon Press.

Smith, J. (2000). 'Synchrony and diachrony in the evolution of English: Evidence from the far reaches of Scotland'. Unpublished D.Phil. dissertation, University of York.

Soja, E. (1989). *Post-modern Geographies: The Reassertion of Space in Critical Social Theory.* London: Verso.

Steinsholt, A. (1962). *Målbryting i Hedrum.* Oslo: Universitetsforlaget.

Stewart, G. (1877). *Shetland Fireside Tales.* Cited from *Oxford English Dictionary* (2nd edn.) vol. XII (1989). Oxford: Clarendon Press, p. 788.

Stoddart, J., Upton, C. and Widdowson, J. (1999). 'Sheffield dialect in the 1990s: revisiting the concept of NORMS'. In P. Foulkes and G. Docherty (eds.). *Urban Voices: Accent Studies in the British Isles.* London: Arnold.

Stokowski, P. (1994). *Leisure in Society.* London: Mansell.

Stuart-Smith, J. (1999). 'Glottals past and present: a study of t-glottalling in Glaswegian'. In C. Upton and K. Wales (eds.). *Leeds Studies in English.* Leeds: University of Leeds.

Stuart-Smith J. (1999). 'Glasgow: accent and voice quality'. In P. Foulkes and G. Docherty (eds.). *Urban Voices. Accent Studies in the British Isles.* London: Arnold.

Taylor, M. (1974). 'The great southern Scots conspiracy: Patterns in the development of Northern English'. In J. Andersen and C. Jones (eds.). *Historical Linguistics.* Amsterdam: North-Holland, pp. 403–406.

Thelander, M. (1982). 'A qualitative approach to the quantitative data of Speech variation.' in S. Romaine (ed.), *Sociolinguistic Variation in Speech Communities.* London: Edward Arnold, pp. 65–83.

Trudgill, P. (1978). *Sociolinguistic Patterns in British English.* London: Arnold.

Trudgill, P. (1983). *On Dialect.* Oxford: Blackwell.

Trudgill, P. (1986). *Dialects in Contact.* Oxford: Blackwell.

Watt, D. and Milroy, L. (1999). 'Patterns of variation and change in three Newcastle vowels: is this dialect levelling?' In P. Foulkes and G. Docherty (eds.). *Urban Voices. Accent Studies in the British Isles.* London: Arnold. pp. 25–46.

Weinreich, U., Labov, W. and Herzog, M. (1968). 'Empirical foundations for a theory of language change'. In W. Lehmann and Y. Makiel (eds.). *Directions for Historical Linguistics: A Symposium*. Austin: University of Texas Press, pp. 95–188.

Wells, J. (1982). *Accents of English 2. The British Isles*. Cambridge: CUP.

Wicker, A. (1969). 'Attitudes versus actions: The relationship of verbal and Overt behavioural responses to attitude objects'. *Journal of Social Issues* 25: 41–78.

Williams, A. and Kerswill, P. (1999). 'Dialect levelling: change and continuity in Milton Keynes, Reading and Hull'. In P. Foulkes and G. Docherty (eds.). *Urban Voices. Accent Studies in the British Isles*. London: Arnold. pp. 141–162.

Williams, F. (1974). 'The identification of linguistic attitudes'. *International Journal of the Sociology of Language* 3, 21–32.

Wilson, J. (1923). *The Dialect of Robert Burns as Spoken in Central Ayrshire*. Oxford: OUP.

Wilson, W. (1993). *Speak o' the North East*. Aberdeen: NES Publications.

Wölck, W. (1965). *Phonematische analyse der sprache von Buchan*. Heidelberg: Carl Winter.

Wolfson, N. (1976). 'Speech Events and Natural Speech: Some Implications for Sociolinguistic Methodology'. *Language in Society* 7, 215–239.

Index